THE EVERYTHING®
LOW-GLYCEMIC COOKBOOK

Dear Reader,

You may have recently been told by your doctor or a nutritionist that you need to follow a low-glycemic diet. Perhaps you are someone who already follows a gluten-free diet, but now have been challenged with a diagnosis of being prediabetic (also called metabolic syndrome). You may even already have type 1 or type 2 diabetes. No matter your situation, if you meet any of those criteria, this book will be a big help to you.

For me, this book is very personal. Not only have I been gluten-free (due to gluten sensitivity) since 2007, but I'm also prediabetic. This basically means that I have to be very careful about the specific types of carbohydrates I eat. If I eat too many sugary foods or foods that have a high-glycemic index (such as gluten-free macaroni and cheese, cupcakes, or mashed potatoes), I'll have a "sugar" crash or a "carb" crash within about an hour. My body will be completely overwhelmed with the sugars from these foods, and I'll want to sleep for several hours to allow my body to "normalize" again.

It's not only unhealthy for my body; it's not a good way to live. I don't know about you, but I really enjoy life much more when I eat the right foods (in correct portions) and my body feels healthy and balanced.

This book was written for anyone who has similar health struggles or who simply wants to learn how to cook wholesome gluten-free, low-glycemic recipes. I'm not a nutritionist or a doctor, but I've sought help from registered dietician Cheryl Harris, MPH, RD (*www.gfgoodness.com*) who has given me great advice on creating meals and menus based around low-glycemic foods that make my body and my mind feel great. I hope you will enjoy incorporating a variety of both gluten-free and low-glycemic recipes from this book in your everyday meal planning. Happy Eating!

Carrie S. Forbes

Welcome to the EVERYTHING® Series!

These handy, accessible books give you all you need to tackle a difficult project, gain a new hobby, comprehend a fascinating topic, prepare for an exam, or even brush up on something you learned back in school but have since forgotten.

You can choose to read an Everything® book from cover to cover or just pick out the information you want from our four useful boxes: e-questions, e-facts, e-alerts, and e-ssentials.

We give you everything you need to know on the subject, but throw in a lot of fun stuff along the way, too.

We now have more than 400 Everything® books in print, spanning such wide-ranging categories as weddings, pregnancy, cooking, music instruction, foreign language, crafts, pets, New Age, and so much more. When you're done reading them all, you can finally say you know Everything®!

QUESTION

Answers to
common questions

FACT

Important snippets
of information

ALERT

Urgent
warnings

ESSENTIAL

Quick
handy tips

PUBLISHER Karen Cooper

MANAGING EDITOR, EVERYTHING® SERIES Lisa Laing

COPY CHIEF Casey Ebert

ASSISTANT PRODUCTION EDITOR Alex Guarco

ACQUISITIONS EDITOR Lisa Laing

SENIOR DEVELOPMENT EDITOR Eileen Mullan

EVERYTHING® SERIES COVER DESIGNER Erin Alexander

Visit the entire Everything® series at *www.everything.com*

THE EVERYTHING® LOW-GLYCEMIC COOKBOOK

Carrie S. Forbes

Avon, Massachusetts

To Michael: Because I've always, always been sure of you. To LeeEllen: For listening to all my renditions of "Puff the Magic Dragon" and never turning down an opportunity to watch Law & Order. *I love you both!*

An Everything® Series Book.
Everything® and everything.com® are registered trademarks of F+W Media, Inc.

Published by Adams Media, a division of F+W Media, Inc.
57 Littlefield Street, Avon, MA 02322 U.S.A.
www.adamsmedia.com

Contains material adapted and abridged from *The Everything® Gluten-Free Baking Cookbook* by Carrie S. Forbes, copyright © 2013 by F+W Media, Inc., ISBN 10: 1-4405-6486-8, ISBN 13: 978-1-4405-6486-4; *The Everything® Gluten-Free Slow Cooker Cookbook* by Carrie S. Forbes, copyright © 2012 by F+W Media, Inc., ISBN 10: 1-4405-3366-0, ISBN 13: 978-1-4405-3366-2; *The Everything® Glycemic Index Cookbook, 2nd Edition* by Lee-Ann Smith Weintraub, MPH, RD, copyright © 2010, 2006 by F+W Media, Inc., ISBN 10: 1-4405-0584-5, ISBN 13: 978-1-4405-0584-3; and *The Everything® Paleolithic Diet Book* by Jodie Cohen and Gilaad Cohen, copyright © 2011 by F+W Media, Inc., ISBN 10: 1-4405-12046-X, ISBN 13: 978-1-4405-1206-3.

ISBN 10: 1-4405-7086-8
ISBN 13: 978-1-4405-7086-5
eISBN 10: 1-4405-7129-5
eISBN 13: 978-1-4405-7129-9

Printed in the United States of America.

10 9 8 7 6 5 4 3 2 1

Library of Congress Cataloging-in-Publication Data

Forbes, Carrie S., author.
 The everything low-glycemic cookbook / Carrie S. Forbes.
  pages cm. -- (An everything series book)
 Includes index.
 ISBN-13: 978-1-4405-7086-5 (pb)
 ISBN-10: 1-4405-7086-8 (pb)
 ISBN-13: 978-1-4405-7129-9 (ebook)
 ISBN-10: 1-4405-7129-5 (ebook)

1. Low-carbohydrate diet--Recipes. 2. Glycemic index --Popular works. 3. Reducing diets--Recipes. I. Title.
 RM237.73.F67 2013
 641.5'6383--dc23

2013034179

Always follow safety and commonsense cooking protocol while using kitchen utensils, operating ovens and stoves, and handling uncooked food. If children are assisting in the preparation of any recipe, they should always be supervised by an adult.

Cover photos © Jennifer L. Yandle.

This book is available at quantity discounts for bulk purchases.For information, please call 1-800-289-0963.

Contents

Acknowledgments

Many thanks to the readers of GingerLemonGirl.com. Without you this cookbook would never have become a reality. I hope these recipes will help you to have a healthy and delicious low-glycemic, gluten-free life!

Also a HUGE thanks to Cheryl Harris, MPH, RD, CWC, CLC, of HarrisWhole Health.com and *www.gfgoodness.com*. You are the best nutritionist and wellness coach on the planet. Thank you for helping me better understand a low-glycemic diet and how to make it happen in my everyday life. Thanks also for your amazing expertise on this project and for helping me to truly love my life these past three years. I would not be the person I am today without your wise counsel and guidance.

Thanks also to Lisa Laing, my editor at Adams Media, for believing in this project and desiring to see it come to life!

And to anyone who struggles with not only following a gluten-free diet, but a low-glycemic one as well . . . this book was meant just for you!

Introduction

Over the years, an endless number of fad diets have come and gone. The Grapefruit Diet, the HCG Diet, the Cabbage Soup Diet, the Hollywood Diet, the Atkins Diet, the 17 Day diet, the Zone Diet, the South Beach Diet, the Blood Type Diet, and the list goes on and on. Nearly all of these diets can be effective if they are followed strictly, but the problem is sticking to them. Most people can follow these diets well for a week or two, but they will "fall off the wagon" because of the rigid food restrictions, and consequently feel bad about it.

That's why the low-glycemic diet is so great. It is not so much a "diet" as a more balanced way of eating. As long as you don't have any food allergies or dietary restrictions due to circumstances like celiac disease, you can basically eat whatever you want. You simply learn how to limit when you can have foods considered "high-glycemic" and for the majority of your meals and snacks to eat more foods that are lower on the glycemic index and therefore are digested more slowly in the body. However, even with the food restrictions of celiac disease or wheat allergies, eating low glycemic isn't nearly as restrictive as most fad diets.

The concept of a low-glycemic diet has been around since the mid-1960s and was originally created for patients with diabetes. At the time, some doctors believed a diet that was focused on a well-rounded food plan, paying close attention to the type of carbohydrates being consumed, would help patients have better control over their blood sugar levels. Carbohydrates are categorized as either simple or complex. Simple carbohydrates are foods such as table sugar (sucrose), milk sugar (lactose), or fruit sugar (fructose). Complex carbohydrates, which are molecularly more elaborate and harder to digest, include vegetables, whole grains, and beans. In 1981, researchers David Jenkins and Thomas Wolever of the University of Toronto Department of Nutritional Sciences created and established the Glycemic Index and published a study that suggested that using this system would be a much more accurate way of classifying carbohydrates for diabetes patients.

Since the glycemic index was developed, dozens of "low-carb" diets have emerged. Many of the diets are based on similar science and theory as the Low-Glycemic diet, such as the Sugar Busters Diet, the Zone Diet, the Protein Power Diet, and even the South Beach Diet.

In 1997 Walter Willett, an epidemiologist and nutritionist, did further research and helped to create "glycemic load," an even more accurate way to measure or rate carbohydrates in comparison to the glycemic index. Glycemic load takes into consideration the amount of food eaten, where the glycemic index does not. For example, popcorn has an overall glycemic index of 72, which is considered high, yet a serving of two cups only has 10 net carbs (overall carbohydrates minus the fiber content) and a glycemic load of 7, which is considered quite low. So when you are creating meals and planning menus, keep in mind the glycemic load of individual servings and not just the glycemic index of foods. Each recipe in this book will tell you where the dish ranks on the glycemic index to help you make great choices.

The recipes in this book are also gluten-free. This may not appeal to everyone who needs to follow a low-glycemic diet, but most of the recipes are naturally gluten-free, meaning you don't have to buy special ingredients to make them. The majority of recipes in this book call for healthful whole ingredients such as vegetables, meats, chicken, and eggs, and some include dairy such as shredded cheese, milk, or a milk substitute (such as almond milk—a great choice for those who are intolerant to dairy proteins). All of these ingredients are naturally gluten-free, making them safe for a wider variety of people. So you may be eating many gluten-free foods already without even realizing they are gluten-free. That is the goal of this book—to provide healthy, delicious low-glycemic recipes that everyone can enjoy.

CHAPTER 1

The Glycemic Index

The glycemic index (GI) is an effective tool for managing weight and controlling blood sugar levels. In the following sections you will learn how to successfully use this tool in daily meal planning. Knowing how to select low GI foods is the first step. This cookbook provides delicious recipes to help you achieve your health and wellness goals. This book also focuses on recipes that are gluten-free for those who need a low-glycemic diet, have celiac disease, a wheat or gluten intolerance, or just wish to follow a paleo-type diet. A paleo-type diet is a diet that basically imitates the nutritional choices of our hunter-gatherer ancesters. The Paleo diet consists of eating whole foods including animal proteins, fresh vegetables and fruits, high-quality fat sources (such as coconut oil, olive oil, and avocados), and nuts and seeds.

What Is the Glycemic Index?

The glycemic index is a simple and valuable tool that can be used to help choose the right carbohydrate foods to keep blood sugar levels stable. It is a numerical index that ranks foods based on their glycemic response in the body. Lower GI foods are more slowly digested and absorbed and, therefore, produce gentler fluctuations in blood sugar and insulin levels. Higher glycemic index foods cause a quicker rise in blood sugar and insulin. Knowing how to choose the right carbohydrate foods, plan balanced meals, and select the right portion sizes are the keys to weight control, disease prevention, and overall good health.

FACT

Eating controlled portion sizes is a basic part of any healthful eating plan, and a low-glycemic diet is no exception. Remember, when you're using the glycemic index, it is best followed when you eat reasonable serving sizes at meals and as snacks. These amounts are listed in the Glycemic Index Value Table at the end of the chapter.

The glycemic index levels of foods are determined by tests performed in clinical settings. The scientists feed human test subjects a determined portion of the test food and then draw and test samples of their blood at specific intervals. The test subjects' blood sugar response to a carbohydrate food is compared to the blood sugar response to an equal portion of pure glucose. Glucose, which has a GI level of 100, is the reference food for GI testing. For example, if the subjects are given orange juice, and it raises their blood sugar level only 50 percent as much as pure glucose, orange juice is given a glycemic index level of 50. Based on its GI level, a food can be assigned to one of three GI categories:

- Low GI: 55 or less
- Moderate GI: 56–69
- High GI: 70 or more

It's healthful to eat a wide variety of low-glycemic foods while minimizing high-glycemic foods. Each recipe's nutritional statistics include its glycemic index level to help you plan your day's meals.

Who Can Benefit from the Glycemic Index?

A diet that follows the glycemic index (even when following a gluten-free diet plan) can benefit everyone. This is not a restrictive diet that eliminates major food groups or pushes expensive supplements. Using the GI is a simple way to start eating better now. People with diabetes, metabolic syndrome, and weight-management issues have a lot to gain from implementing the principles of the glycemic index in their lifestyle. However, a GI diet is not just for those with special health needs; it is a healthful and balanced way of eating for anyone who wants to take care of his or her body, feel good, and live longer.

QUESTION

May I use the glycemic index if I am a vegetarian?
Absolutely! A GI diet is vegetarian friendly because it allows a variety of plant-based protein foods such as beans, nuts, and tofu.

How the Glycemic Index Works

When you eat carbohydrate foods, your pancreas releases insulin into your bloodstream to carry sugar to your cells, which is used for energy. Intake of high GI foods and general overeating causes elevated circulating insulin levels in the blood. Insulin works to lower blood sugar levels by turning excess sugar into stored fat. When insulin levels are high, the body is not able to burn stored body fat. Even with increased physical activity and exercise, it can be difficult to lose weight when insulin levels are consistently elevated. Elevated blood insulin is also associated with increased appetite, sugar cravings, high blood triglycerides, high blood pressure, heart disease, and diabetes.

Carbohydrate foods include grains, fruits, starchy vegetables, nuts, and legumes. However, not all carbohydrates are nutritionally equal, and they can differ greatly on the glycemic index. Also, common sense cannot always accurately predict the GI level of certain foods. For example, although honey is quite sweet, it actually has a lower GI level than white bread. Research shows that different types of carbohydrates have significantly different effects on blood sugar levels and appetite. Although equal portions of jasmine rice and brown rice have a similar number of calories, their GI levels are nothing alike. Brown rice, a lower GI food, will have less of an impact on insulin secretion while satisfying hunger.

ALERT

The dessert recipes in this book include sweet ingredients but avoid high-glycemic sugars and sweeteners. Alternatives such as honey, coconut palm sugar, and fresh fruit are incorporated to satisfy the sweet tooth.

Benefits of the Glycemic Index

The primary goal of a diet that follows the glycemic index is to minimize and prevent insulin-related health problems such as diabetes, heart disease, and obesity. This goal is accomplished by avoiding foods that have the largest impact on blood sugar. By keeping blood sugar levels stable, insulin levels remain constant. As a result of its role in reducing insulin fluctuations, a low GI diet is often recommended for individuals who are at risk for developing diabetes.

Eating foods that cause a large, fast glycemic response may lead to an initial quick surge in energy, followed shortly by a decrease in blood sugar, which results in lethargy, hunger, mood swings, and fat storage. Replacing high GI foods with low GI foods helps sustain energy levels throughout the day. A low GI diet that prevents these ups and downs in blood sugar and insulin helps achieve appetite control and mood stability while preventing weight gain.

A low-glycemic diet has been clinically proven to help those with type 1, type 2, or gestational diabetes. It can also help people who are overweight, have excess abdominal fat, or have been diagnosed with prediabetes or high triglyceride levels and low levels of HDL (or good) cholesterol.

Limitations of the Glycemic Index

Testing the glycemic index of foods is both expensive and time-consuming because it requires the participation of human subjects. Each year thousands of new food products flood the grocery store shelves; most are not tested because GI testing is not mandatory. If you don't know the GI of a particular food, the Nutrition Facts food label may provide some clues. Foods that are higher in protein, fat, and dietary fiber and lower in carbohydrates often have a lower GI.

Although the GI levels of foods are tested individually, the foods are often eaten with other foods. The GI level of a meal depends on the GI levels of all the foods consumed together. Food preparation technique and food processing also impact the GI level of the meal. The recipes in this cookbook are based on combining low GI ingredients to create foods and meals that are GI friendly.

Carbohydrate Metabolism

To better understand why low-glycemic index eating is healthful, it is important to be knowledgeable about carbohydrate metabolism. Let's start by defining some important terms.

Helpful Definitions

Insulin, a natural hormone made by cells in the pancreas, is responsible for controlling the level of sugar in the blood. When carbohydrates (sugar) are absorbed in the intestines and enter the bloodstream, blood sugar levels rise. In response to rising blood sugar levels, insulin is secreted, which enables sugar to enter the cells to be used for energy.

Cortisol, a hormone released by the adrenal glands, works to stabilize blood sugar levels by rising as blood sugar levels fall. High cortisol levels are associated with the storage of body fat around the belly.

Metabolic syndrome is characterized by a group of risk factors for diabetes and heart disease, which include excessive fat around the abdomen, high blood pressure, abnormal lipid levels (high cholesterol), and insulin resistance.

Insulin resistance is a condition in which the body makes insulin but is unable to use it properly. As a result, the body needs more insulin to help sugar enter the cells. Individuals with insulin resistance have elevated levels of both insulin and sugar in the blood, which increases the risk of developing diabetes and heart disease.

Leptin is a key hormone in energy metabolism. Studies show that low levels of leptin are associated with the accumulation of body fat and diabetes. Low levels tell the brain to eat more, and high levels signal satiety or fullness. Individuals with low levels are prone to overeating and gaining weight. Losing weight can help regulate leptin levels.

QUESTION

How is metabolic syndrome diagnosed?
Metabolic syndrome is present if three or more of the following risk factors are identified: high serum triglycerides (≥150 mg/dL), reduced HDL "good" cholesterol (men < 40 mg/dL, women < 50 mg/dL), elevated waist circumference, high blood pressure, and high blood sugar.

Glycemic Index Versus the Low-Carb Diet and the Paleo Diet

The body requires three types of major nutrients to work efficiently: carbohydrates, fats, and proteins. Carbohydrates are a major source of energy in the diet, one that the brain prefers as fuel.

Do not confuse a low–glycemic index diet with a low-carbohydrate diet. Low-carb diets restrict many sources of carbohydrates such as breads, potatoes, sweets, fruits, and vegetables in order to put the body in a state of ketosis. In ketosis, the body uses stored fat for energy, and rapid weight loss may occur. However, not only is the potential for health risks a concern with such a diet, the long-term sustainability of a high-fat, high-protein diet is also highly unlikely. Many people who follow low-carb diets initially lose weight only to regain it once they return to their old eating habits.

A low GI diet focuses on choosing healthy, low-glycemic foods to promote weight loss and wellness. Fruits, vegetables, beans, nuts, and whole grains, lean proteins and heart-healthy fats comprise the meals. Following a low GI diet allows a large variety of readily available nutritious foods; it is more a way of life than a diet.

A Paleo diet is based on consuming foods such as meats, nuts, seeds, fruits, and vegetables that were available during the Paleolithic period. Since legumes (beans), dairy (in strict versions of the diet), and grains are not part of this diet, the Paleo diet is naturally gluten-free and dairy-free. Many of the recipes in this book can easily be made "Paleo." In fact, more than 150 of the recipes—main dishes, side dishes, vegetarian dishes, breakfast dishes, and even desserts—are already Paleo friendly. For example, over 75 percent of the recipes in Chapters 8, 9, and 10 meet this qualification.

ALERT

Because some low-carb diets are extremely restrictive, there are inherent potential health concerns. Restricting fruits and vegetables that contain vitamins, minerals, antioxidants, phytochemicals, and fiber results in inadequate dietary levels of these essential nutrients. Low-carb diets are high in protein and fat, including saturated fat, which may increase the risk of heart disease.

Low GI Carbs Are Good for the Brain

Although the muscles can use either fat or carbohydrates for energy, the brain relies primarily on carbohydrates. Mental performance increases with the consumption of healthful carbohydrate-rich foods. Studies have shown that after eating a low- glycemic and low-carbohydrate meal, test subjects display improved intellectual performance in areas such as short-term memory, mathematics, and reasoning. This is true not only for the average person, but also for college students, elderly individuals, and even patients with Alzheimer's disease. Such studies have shown that the improvement in memory and intellectual performance is greater with low GI meals as compared to meals containing high GI carbohydrates.

Food and Appetite

The types of foods you eat often dictate how much food you eat. This is because some foods are better at suppressing appetite and controlling hunger. It is also important to consider the quality of food in managing weight. Foods that contain a lot of calories and fat in a standard serving are referred to as being "energy-dense." For example, a large chocolate-chip cookie can have as many as 500 calories, the same number of calories as six fresh peaches. It is easier to consume excess calories from the one cookie than from the six peaches, since you generally aren't going to consume that many peaches in one sitting. When eating mostly low energy-dense foods, your appetite will become suppressed by eating fewer calories and less fat.

How does energy density relate to the glycemic index? The principle of energy density explains why choosing simply a low-fat or low-carb diet for weight control is not always the best answer. Often, low-fat foods are supplemented with sugar to make them taste better, and they end up having just as many calories as the alternatives. At the same time, some low-carb diets are high in fat, and fat is extremely energy-dense. A diet using the glycemic index allows for reasonable amounts of carbohydrates, fat, and protein and places more emphasis on the type of fat than on the total amount. The GI diet includes many servings of fruits, vegetables, and lower GI carbohydrates—an approach that focuses on the quality of the foods.

Low GI and Gluten-Free

Gluten is the term used for several types of proteins found in wheat, barley, and rye. The proteins gliadin and glutelin found in these grains form a substance called gluten. Gluten is a "storage protein," which means that it holds the key ingredients for the grains to continue thriving. These grains are used in many baked goods because gluten provides excellent elasticity, structure, and texture. Gluten causes pizza to have a chewy, stretchy texture. It gives French bread its soft white center and chewy crust and makes cinnamon rolls stretchy, soft, and light. Gluten helps give structure to bread dough when rising, so that the bread becomes tall and stays tall after baking and cooling. Gluten is found primarily in traditional breads, pasta, cakes, muffins, crackers, and pizza, all foods that are typically high on the glycemic index.

Avoiding gluten can be difficult for several reasons. The biggest reason is that it's not often listed on the package because it's simply a protein found in a number of foods and food products. In addition to wheat, the following foods, mostly derivatives of wheat, also contain gluten:

- Barley
- Bulgar
- Couscous
- Durum flour
- Farina
- Graham flour
- Kamut
- Rye
- Semolina
- Spelt
- Triticale (a cross between rye and wheat)

Many of the whole grains listed here can be a healthful addition to a low-glycemic diet if you do not need to avoid gluten. However, these gluten-containing grains still contain carbohydrates and still should be eaten in moderation.

Celiac Disease

Celiac disease (also known as celiac sprue or gluten-sensitive enteropathy) is an auto-immune and digestive disorder that occurs in about one in 100 people in the United States. For people with this disorder, gluten can cause serious damage to their intestines if it is ingested. If you have celiac disease or gluten intolerance, gluten damages the "villi" in your intestines. Since the villi (fingerlike projections that contain most of the enzymes needed for digestion) are damaged for those with celiac disease, their bodies have enormous difficulty ingesting the healthy nutrients their bodies need such as fat, calcium, iron, and folate (a water-soluble B vitamin). Some of the symptoms of celiac disease and gluten intolerance include:

- Digestive problems such as bloating, vomiting, excess gas and/or pain, severe and/or chronic diarrhea, irritable bowel, weight loss, or weight gain
- Constant and/or severe headaches or migraines
- Low levels of iron (anemia)
- Skin rashes (also known as dermatitis herpetiformis)
- Bone or joint pain
- Depression and/or anxiety
- Seizures
- Infertility
- Unexplained fatigue
- Failure to thrive, or the inability to have normal physical and intellectual growth (often seen in children with celiac disease)

Most people have a healthy immune system that prevents the body from being harmed by gluten, but for those with celiac disease, the only effective treatment is avoiding foods with gluten altogether.

To be tested for celiac disease and/or gluten sensitivity, visit your family doctor or a gastroenterologist, who will do a blood test to check for high levels of certain types of antibodies. If your blood test comes back with positive results for celiac disease, your doctor may then choose to do a biopsy of your small intestine to check for damage to the villi. A diagnosis is usually given using a combination of these diagnostic tests. Gluten sensitivity (as opposed to celiac disease) is sometimes diagnosed if a patient tests negatively for the disorder, yet his or her body reacts with symptoms that are similar to celiac disease. The most effective treatment for either condition is to avoid all foods with gluten by following a gluten-free diet.

Glycemic Index, Fiber, and the Gluten-Free Diet

Fiber plays an important role in overall wellness and healthy weight control. There are many benefits to choosing high-fiber foods and eating enough fiber. Studies have shown that the quality of carbohydrates is important in preventing diabetes and controlling appetite. Since high-fiber foods help to improve satiety after meals, eating sufficient amounts of fiber is necessary for weight control. Traditionally, societies that have more plant-based dietary fiber in their cuisine experience less chronic illness.

Many gluten-free processed foods contain highly refined gluten-free flours and starches that do not contain a lot of fiber or nutrients. These foods are also often very high in refined sugars and unhealthy fats. For these reasons, it's very important to include healthful, naturally gluten-free, unprocessed foods in your diet to make sure you are getting adequate amounts of dietary fiber.

Do you know how much dietary fiber is recommended daily? The recommended daily amount of dietary fiber is 25 grams for women and 38 grams for men. Americans fall short of these goals with an average intake of only 15 grams of fiber per day. Many low GI foods such as whole grains (such as brown rice, quinoa, and teff), fresh fruits, and vegetables are excellent sources of fiber.

Principles for Meal Planning

Being well prepared by keeping low GI foods stocked in the pantry will have you on your way to eating a low GI diet. Plan a weekly menu using the recipes in this book. Go shopping at the market ahead of time to gather the ingredients needed for the recipes.

Certain ingredients and staple items appear in many of the recipes. It is a good idea to keep these items in stock so you will have a low-GI kitchen. Some of these ingredients include honey, coconut palm sugar, almond flour, brown rice flour, arrowroot starch, olive oil, balsamic vinegar, red wine vinegar, whole-grain gluten-free pasta, brown rice, nuts, canned and dry beans, Italian seasoning, garlic, flaxseeds, gluten-free soy sauce, and Dijon mustard.

LOW GI FOODS

- All nonstarch vegetables, such as lettuce, broccoli, spinach, onion, and green beans
- Most fruits, including stone fruits, apples, berries, cherries, and citrus fruits
- Nuts, beans, seeds, and legumes (Note: Legumes are not allowed on a Paleo diet)
- Plain, unsweetened yogurt and cheese (choose low-fat or nonfat when possible)

- Minimally processed whole grains, such as steel-cut oats, brown rice, whole-grain (or multigrain) gluten-free breads, whole-grain gluten-free pastas such as brown rice, quinoa, or corn pastas. (Note: Grains are not allowed on a Paleo Diet.)

HIGH GI FOODS

- Refined flours, starches, and grains
- Processed breakfast cereals
- Sweetened beverages such as soda and juice
- Dried fruits and dates
- Starchy vegetables such as white potatoes and corn
- Refined sugar and sweeteners

Be careful when choosing a food if you are unsure of its glycemic index level. It is best to look foods up before assuming that their GI level is low. For example, grapes have a low GI value, but raisins have a moderate GI value because they have a high concentration of fruit sugar. Take serving size into account as well. For example, a serving size of grapes is 1 cup but only ¼ cup for raisins.

Glycemic Index Value Table

▼ **GLYCEMIC INDEX VALUES OF COMMON FOODS**

Food and Serving Size	Glycemic Index Value
Fruits	
Apple, 1 medium	38
Apple juice, 1 cup	40
Apricots, fresh, 3 medium	57
Apricots, canned, 3 halves	64
Avocado, ¼ cup	<20
Banana, unripe	30
Banana, under-ripe	51
Banana, over-ripe	82

Blueberries, 1 cup	40
Cantaloupe, ¼ small	65
Cherries, 10 large	22
Grapes, green, 1 cup	46
Grapefruit, ½ medium	25
Grapefruit juice, 1 cup	48
Kiwi, 1 medium, peeled	52
Mango, 1 small	55
Orange, 1 medium	44
Orange juice, ¾ cup	50
Papaya, ½ medium	58
Peach, 1 medium	42
Peach, canned, ½ cup	30
Pear, 1 medium	38
Pear, canned, ½ cup	44
Pineapple, 2 slices	66
Plum, 1 medium	39
Raspberries, 1 cup	40
Strawberries, 1 cup	40
Watermelon, 1 cup	72
Vegetables	
Acorn squash, ½ cup	75
Bean sprouts, 1 cup	<20
Beets, canned, ½ cup	64
Bell peppers, 1 cup	<20
Broccoli, 1 cup	<20
Brussels sprouts, 1 cup	<20
Butternut squash, ½ cup	75
Cabbage, 1 cup, raw	<20
Carrot, 1 cup, raw	49
Carrot juice, 1 cup	43
Cauliflower, 1 cup	<20
Celery, 1 cup	<20
Corn, ½ cup	55
Green beans, 1 cup	54
Green peas, 1 cup	48
Parsnips, ½ cup	97
Potatoes, French fried, 4 ounces	75
Potatoes, instant mashed, 4 ounces	88

Potatoes, mashed, ½ cup	74
Potatoes, red-skinned, baked, 4 ounces	93
Potatoes, russet, baked	85
Spaghetti squash, ½ cup	<20
Spinach, 1 cup, raw	<20
Sweet potato, baked, 3 oz.	46
Sweet potatoes, boiled, ½ cup	54
Tomato sauce, ½ cup	37
Zucchini, 1 cup	<20
Grains	
Bagel, 1 small, plain	72
Barley, pearled, boiled, ½ cup	25
Banana bread, 1 slice	47
Bread, gluten-free (store-bought, multigrain), 1 slice	79
Bread, gluten-free (store-bought, white), 1 slice	80
Brown rice, cooked, ⅓ cup	48
Brown rice flour, 1 cup	81
Buckwheat, ⅓ cup	25
Buckwheat, puffed, ¾ ounce	65
Corn chips, plain, salted, 1 ounce	42
Corn tortilla, 1 tortilla	70
Cornmeal, ⅓ cup	68
Couscous, cooked, ½ cup	65
Dark rye bread, 1 slice	76
French baguette, 1 ounce	95
Hamburger bun, 1 item	61
Instant rice, cooked, ½ cup	65
Melba toast, 6 pieces	70
Millet, boiled, 2½ ounces	71
Oatmeal, instant, 6 ounces	82
Oats, steel-cut, 6 ounces	52
Oats, rolled, 6 ounces	58
Pasta, gluten-free, corn, 1¾ ounces	78
Pasta, gluten-free rice noodles, 2¾ ounces	61
Pasta, gluten-free mung bean noodles, 1¾ ounces	33
Pasta, gluten-free rice vermicelli, 2 ounces	58

Pasta, spaghetti, cooked, 1 cup	41
Pasta, spaghetti, whole wheat, 1 cup	37
Pasta, whole wheat, ½ cup	37
Polenta (cornmeal), boiled, 6¾ ounces	68
Pumpernickel bread, 1 slice	51
Quinoa, boiled, 1 ounce	53
Raisin bread, whole-grain, 1 slice	44
Rye bread, 1 slice	51
Rice cakes, puffed, plain, ¾ ounce	82
Rice crackers, plain, ⅓ ounce	91
Rice, basmati (white), 2 ounces	58
Rice, instant, white, 2 ounces	87
Rice, precooked, brown, 5 ounces	48
Rice, precooked, long-grain, 5 ounces	48
Rice, sweet (glutinous), 2 ounces	98
Wheat tortilla, 6"	30
White bread, 1 slice	70
Whole wheat bread, 1 slice	69
Wild rice, boiled, 2⅓ ounces	57
Dairy and Dairy Alternatives	
Almond milk (unsweetened), 1 cup	27
Coconut milk (canned), ½ cup	<1
Cheese, Cheddar, 1 ounce	<1
Cheese, cottage, 1 ounce	<1
Cheese, mozzarella, 1 ounce	<1
Cheese, Parmesan, 1 ounce	<1
Milk, whole, 1 cup	27
Milk, 1%, 1 cup	23
Milk, fat-free, 1 cup	32
Soy milk, original, 1 cup	44
Soy yogurt, fruit, 2% fat, 1 cup	36
Yogurt, low-fat, berry	28
Yogurt, nonfat, berry	38
Yogurt, nonfat, plain	14
Beans and Nuts	
Almond flour (unblanched), 100 gm (or about 1 cup)	<1
Baked beans, ½ cup	48
Black beans, boiled, ¾ cup	30

Black-eyed peas, canned, ½ cup	42
Broad beans, ½ cup	79
Cashews, 1 ounce	22
Chickpeas, canned, drained, ½ cup	43
Kidney beans, canned, drained, ½ cup	52
Lentils, boiled, ½ cup	30
Lima beans, ½ cup	32
Mung beans, ½ cup	31
Peanuts, 1 ounce	15
Pecans, raw, 1 ounce	10
Pinto beans, canned, ½ cup	45
Soybeans, boiled, ½ cup	18
Miscellaneous	
Agave nectar, 1 tablespoon	11
Arrowroot starch/flour, 1 cup	76
Coconut flour, 2 tablespoons	3
Coconut palm sugar, 1 tablespoon	35
Chocolate, dark, 1 ounce	41
Honey, 1 tablespoon	58
Maple-flavored syrup, 1 tablespoon	68
Maple syrup, pure, 1 tablespoon	54
Sugar, white, 1 tablespoon	68
Sushi, salmon	48

CHAPTER 2

Appetizers and Condiments

Chipotle Mayonnaise

This dressing will add a nice flavor to most meat, poultry, or fish dishes.

INGREDIENTS | SERVES 8

2 large eggs

2 tablespoons lemon juice

1 teaspoon mustard powder

2 tablespoons minced chipotle peppers

1½ cups grapeseed oil

1. Place the eggs, lemon juice, mustard powder, and chipotle peppers into a food processor and pulse until blended.

2. Slowly drizzle the grapeseed oil into the egg mixture, and continue to pulse until completely blended.

Per serving: Calories: 379 | Fat: 42 g | Protein: 1.5 g | Sodium: 16 mg | Fiber: 0 g | Carbohydrate: 0 g | Sugar: 0 g | GI: Zero

Parmesan Artichoke Dip

For a more savory dip, reduce the amount of mayonnaise to 2 cups and stir in 2 cups of room-temperature sour cream immediately before serving. For fewer servings, cut the recipe in half and reduce the cooking time.

INGREDIENTS | SERVES 24

2 (13½-ounce) jars marinated artichoke hearts

4 cups mayonnaise

2 (8-ounce) packages cream cheese, cubed

12 ounces (3 cups) freshly grated Parmesan cheese

4 cloves garlic, peeled and minced

1 teaspoon dried dill

½ teaspoon freshly ground black pepper

Instead of . . .

Instead of using artichokes, you can use fresh or frozen spinach (drained of all liquids). For a heartier dip, add 1 pound of fresh lump crabmeat and ½ teaspoon of Old Bay Seasoning.

1. Drain and chop the artichoke hearts. Add to a 2.5-quart slow cooker along with the mayonnaise, cream cheese, Parmesan cheese, garlic, dill, and pepper. Stir to combine. Cover and cook on low for 1 hour; uncover and stir well.

2. Re-cover and cook on low for an additional 1–1½ hours or until the cheese is melted completely and the dip is heated through. To serve, reduce the heat setting of the slow cooker to warm. Serve with gluten-free tortillas, rice crackers, or gluten-free toast points.

Per serving: Calories: 344 | Fat: 35 g | Protein: 6 g | Sodium: 456 mg | Fiber: 0 g | Carbohydrates: 2 g | Sugar: 0.5 g | GI: Very low

Swedish Meatballs with Gravy

No one will ever guess these uniquely spiced meatballs simmering in a savory gravy are gluten-free. To make them dairy-free, simply substitute almond milk for the milk and coconut oil for the butter.

INGREDIENTS | SERVES 4

1 slice gluten-free bread
4 tablespoons whole milk, divided
¼ cup finely diced onion
2 tablespoons butter, divided
1 pound ground beef
1 egg
¼ teaspoon ground black pepper
¼ teaspoon ground allspice
¼ teaspoon ground nutmeg
2 tablespoons brown rice flour
1 cup gluten-free beef broth

1. In a small bowl, crumble up the bread and add 2 tablespoons milk to soften it. Set aside. In a small skillet over medium-high heat, soften the onions in 1 tablespoon of butter for about 3–5 minutes until softened and translucent.

2. In a large bowl, mix together the softened bread, onions cooked in butter, ground beef, egg, pepper, allspice, and nutmeg. Mix together thoroughly and roll tablespoons of the meat mixture into small meatballs.

3. Brown meatballs over medium-high heat (in small batches) in a nonstick skillet and then transfer them to a greased 4-quart slow cooker.

4. In the same skillet used to brown the meatballs, whisk the remaining tablespoon of butter and the brown rice flour over medium-high heat. Whisk for 1–2 minutes to toast the flour. Slowly pour in the beef broth, whisking constantly. Cook for 3–5 additional minutes until you have a thickened gravy. Whisk in the remaining 2 tablespoons of milk.

5. Pour the gravy over the meatballs in the slow cooker. Cover and cook on high for 3–4 hours or on low for 6–8 hours.

Per serving, about 5 meatballs per serving: Calories: 326 | Fat: 19 g | Protein: 26.5 g | Sodium: 347 mg | Fiber: 0.5 g | Carbohydrates: 10.5 g | Sugar: 1.5 g | GI: Low

Turkey Lettuce Wraps

Turkey is a low-fat protein source that kids are sure to love. Although these wraps are a bit more complex to put together, you can make a larger batch of the filling and serve it over salad at a later meal.

INGREDIENTS | SERVES 4

3 tablespoons walnut oil

3 shallots, chopped

1 piece lemongrass, thinly sliced

1 serrano pepper, thinly sliced

½ teaspoon freshly ground black pepper

1½ pounds ground turkey

⅓ cup fresh lime juice

2 tablespoons sesame oil

4 tablespoons coconut oil

½ cup Thai basil leaves, thinly sliced

8 large butter lettuce leaves

1. In a large skillet, heat the walnut oil over medium heat.

2. Add the shallots, lemongrass, serrano pepper, and black pepper. Cook until the shallots soften, about 4 minutes.

3. Add the ground turkey and stir frequently until cooked through, approximately 8–10 minutes.

4. Add the lime juice, sesame oil, and coconut oil and cook for 1 minute.

5. Turn the heat off and mix in the basil leaves.

6. Wrap the mixture in the lettuce leaves and serve.

Per serving, 2 stuffed lettuce leaves: Calories: 381 | Fat: 29 g | Protein: 40 g | Sodium: 1 mg | Fiber: 1 g | Carbohydrate: 1 g | Sugar: 0 g | GI: Very low

Chicken Nuggets

These chicken nuggets are fantastic for kids and adults.
Mix them in a green salad or serve with sweet potato fries.

INGREDIENTS | SERVES 4

2 boneless, skinless chicken breasts, cut into bite-size pieces
½ cup olive oil
4 cloves garlic, minced
¼ teaspoon ground black pepper
½ cup almond flour

1. Place chicken in a shallow dish.

2. In a small bowl, mix the olive oil, garlic, and pepper.

3. Pour over the chicken and marinate for 30 minutes in the refrigerator.

4. Preheat the oven to 475°F.

5. Place the almond flour in a shallow bowl.

6. Remove the chicken from the marinade and dredge in almond flour to coat.

7. Bake in a baking dish for 10 minutes or until brown.

Per serving: Calories: 369 | Fat: 28 g | Protein: 20 g | Sodium: 2 mg | Fiber: 2 g | Carbohydrate: 12 g | Sugar: 2 g | GI: Very low

Hot Chicken Buffalo Bites

Love buffalo wings? Then you will love these chicken bites even more; they are made with juicy chicken breasts so you won't have to worry about bones. They are easy to make and much less messy!

INGREDIENTS | SERVES 6

3 large chicken breasts, cut into 2" strips
2 tablespoons brown rice flour
¼ cup melted butter
3 cloves garlic, peeled and minced
⅓ cup Frank's RedHot sauce
¼ cup gluten-free ranch dressing

Fresh Garlic Versus Garlic Powder

In a pinch, use 1½ teaspoons garlic powder in this recipe. The garlic flavor won't be quite as pungent and rich as when you use fresh garlic, but it will still be easy and enjoyable.

1. Place chicken pieces into a greased 2.5-quart slow cooker.

2. In a medium saucepan over medium-high heat, whisk the brown rice flour and melted butter for 2–3 minutes to toast the flour.

3. Slowly whisk in the garlic and Frank's RedHot sauce. Pour the sauce over the chicken in the slow cooker.

4. Cover and cook on high for 3 hours or on low for 6 hours. Serve with ranch dressing as a dip. If using a larger slow cooker, make sure to reduce cooking time by about half.

Per serving: Calories: 227 | Fat: 15 g | Protein: 18 g | Sodium: 511.5 mg | Fiber: 0 g | Carbohydrates: 4 g | Sugar: 0.5 g | GI: Very low

Mango Pork Morsels

In this recipe, the mango provides natural sweetness and a tropical flair. Plate and pierce each morsel with a toothpick.

INGREDIENTS | SERVES 10

1½ pounds lean pork loin, cubed

2 mangoes, cubed (see sidebar)

3 cloves garlic, minced

1 jalapeño, seeded and minced

1 tablespoon salsa

¼ teaspoon salt

¼ teaspoon freshly ground black pepper

2 teaspoons ground chipotle

1 teaspoon New Mexico chili powder

½ teaspoon oregano

2 tablespoons orange juice

2 tablespoons lime juice

1. Quickly brown the pork in a nonstick skillet over medium heat. Add the browned pork and cubed mango to a 4-quart slow cooker.

2. In a small bowl, whisk together the garlic, jalapeño, salsa, salt, pepper, chipotle, chili powder, oregano, and the orange and lime juices. Pour over the mango and pork. Stir.

3. Cook on low for 6 hours; remove the cover and cook on high for 30 minutes. Stir before serving.

Per serving: Calories: 32 | Fat: 0 g | Protein: 0.5 g | Sodium: 73 mg | Fiber: 1 g | Carbohydrates: 8 g | Sugar: 6.5 g | GI: Very low

How to Cut Up a Mango

Slice the mango vertically on either side of the large flat pit. Then, using the tip of a knife, cut vertical lines into the flesh without piercing the skin. Make horizontal lines in the flesh to form cubes. Use a spoon to scoop out the cubes. Repeat for the other side.

Pineapple Teriyaki Drumsticks

Serve this crowd-pleasing favorite as a hearty appetizer. Pair leftovers with steamed rice for a great lunch.

INGREDIENTS | SERVES 12

12 chicken drumsticks

8 ounces canned pineapple slices in juice

¼ cup gluten-free teriyaki sauce or gluten-free soy sauce

1 teaspoon ground ginger

¼ cup gluten-free hoisin sauce

1. Preheat the oven to broil on high.

2. Arrange the drumsticks in a single layer on a broiling pan. Broil for 10 minutes on high, flipping the drumsticks once halfway through the cooking time.

3. Add the juice from the pineapple into a 4- to 6-quart slow cooker. Add the teriyaki sauce, ginger, and hoisin sauce. Stir to combine.

4. Cut the pineapple rings in half. Add them to the slow cooker.

5. Add the drumsticks to the slow cooker and stir to combine. Cover and cook on low for 4–6 hours or on high for 2–3 hours.

Per serving: Calories: 146 | Fat: 6.5 g | Protein: 15 g | Sodium: 377 mg | Fiber: 0.5 g | Carbohydrates: 6 g | Sugar: 5 g | GI: Very low

Stuffed Mushroom Caps

These appetizers are a bit more exciting than traditional bread-crumb recipes. They are stuffed with protein and fats to ensure more macronutrients in each bite.

INGREDIENTS | SERVES 10

20 button mushrooms
2 tablespoons walnut oil or olive oil
½ pound chopped ground turkey
4 cloves garlic, minced
½ cup finely chopped walnuts
½ teaspoon ground black pepper

1. Preheat the oven to 350°F.

2. Remove stems and hollow out the mushroom caps. Dice the stems and place them in a medium bowl.

3. Heat the walnut oil in a medium frying pan, and cook the ground turkey and garlic for 5–8 minutes, or until the turkey is no longer pink.

4. Add the mushrooms, walnuts, and pepper to the ground turkey, and cook until the mushrooms are soft, about 8 minutes.

5. Stuff the turkey mixture into the mushroom caps and place on a cookie sheet.

6. Bake 20 minutes or until golden brown on top.

Per serving: Calories: 88 | Fat: 7 g | Protein: 7 g | Sodium: 2 mg | Fiber: 1 g | Carbohydrate: 2 g | Sugar: 1 g | GI: Very low

Balsamic Almonds

These sweet-and-sour almonds are a great addition to a cheese platter or appetizer plate.

INGREDIENTS | SERVES 15

2 cups whole almonds
½ cup dark brown sugar
½ cup balsamic vinegar
½ teaspoon kosher salt

Healthful Almonds

Botanically speaking, almonds are a seed, not a nut. They are an excellent source of vitamin E and have high levels of monounsaturated fat, one of the two "good" fats responsible for lowering LDL cholesterol.

1. Place all the ingredients into a 4-quart slow cooker. Cook uncovered on high for 4 hours, stirring every 15 minutes or until all the liquid has evaporated. The almonds will have a syrupy coating.

2. Line two cookie sheets with parchment paper. Pour the almonds in a single layer on the baking sheets to cool completely. Store in an airtight container in the pantry for up to 2 weeks.

Per serving: Calories: 108 | Fat: 6 g | Protein: 3 g | Sodium: 83 mg | Fiber: 1.5 g | Carbohydrates: 11 g | Sugar: 9 g | GI: Low

Scallops Wrapped in Bacon

This common party appetizer has been revamped for Paleo with nitrate-free bacon. You are sure to like these much better than the old unhealthy version.

INGREDIENTS | SERVES 10

2 tablespoons olive oil
20 large scallops
2 tablespoons minced garlic
20 slices uncured, nitrate-free bacon

1. Heat the olive oil in a large frying pan over medium-high heat. Sauté the scallops in the oil with the garlic until the scallops are lightly browned. Remove scallops and garlic and set aside to cool.

2. Cook the bacon slightly on each side in the same frying pan and use it to wrap the scallops. Do not overcook the bacon or it will not wrap around the scallops.

3. Secure each appetizer with a toothpick and serve warm.

Per serving: Calories: 159 | Fat: 15 g | Protein: 13 g | Sodium: 291 mg | Fiber: 0 g | Carbohydrate: 0 g | Sugar: 0 g | GI: Zero

Cinnamon-and-Sugar Pecans

Not only a tasty snack, these sweet chopped pecans are also delicious sprinkled over Sunday Morning French Toast (see recipe in Chapter 3).

INGREDIENTS | SERVES 12

3 cups pecan halves

3 tablespoons butter, melted

2 teaspoons vanilla

½ cup sugar

1 teaspoon cinnamon

½ teaspoon salt

1. Add all ingredients to a 4-quart slow cooker. Stir to coat the nuts evenly. Cover and cook on low for 4–5 hours or on high for 2 hours, stirring occasionally.

2. Uncover and continue to cook on low for another hour, stirring occasionally, to dry the nuts. Next, spread the nuts evenly on a baking sheet lined with parchment paper or aluminum foil until they are completely cooled. Store them in an airtight container in the pantry for up to 2 weeks.

Per serving: Calories: 249 | Fat: 22.5 g | Protein: 2.5 g | Sodium: 98 mg | Fiber: 3 g | Carbohydrates: 12.5 g | Sugar: 9.5 g | GI: Very low

Roasted Spicy Pumpkin Seeds

This spicy seed recipe is sure to be a favorite snack for the family. They are quick to prepare and easy to grab for on-the-go snacks.

INGREDIENTS | SERVES 6

3 cups raw pumpkin seeds

½ cup olive oil

½ teaspoon garlic powder

Ground black pepper, to taste

Pumpkin Seed Benefits

Pumpkin seeds have great health benefits. They contain L-tryptophan, a compound found to naturally fight depression, and pumpkin seeds are high in zinc, a mineral that protects against osteoporosis.

1. Preheat the oven to 300°F.

2. In a medium bowl, mix the pumpkin seeds, olive oil, garlic powder, and black pepper until the pumpkin seeds are evenly coated.

3. Spread them in an even layer on a cookie sheet.

4. Bake for 1 hour and 15 minutes, stirring every 10–15 minutes until the seeds are toasted.

Per serving: Calories: 532 | Fat: 50 g | Protein: 17 g | Sodium: 13 mg | Fiber: 3 g | Carbohydrate: 12 g | Sugar: 1 g | GI: Very low

Walnut-Parsley Pesto

Walnuts add a significant blast of omega-3 fatty acids to this delicious pesto.

INGREDIENTS | SERVES 4

½ cup walnuts
8 cloves garlic
1 bunch parsley, roughly chopped
¼ cup olive oil
Freshly cracked black pepper, to taste

Pesto for All

Pesto is a generic term for anything made by pounding. Most people are familiar with traditional pesto, which is made with basil and pine nuts, but many prefer this variation with parsley and walnuts.

1. Chop the walnuts in a food processor or blender. Add the garlic and process to form a paste. Add the parsley; pulse into the walnut mixture.

2. While the blender is running, drizzle in the oil until the mixture is smooth. Add pepper to taste.

Per serving: Calories: 229 | Fat: 23 g | Protein: 3 g | Sodium: 6 mg | Fiber: 1 g | Carbohydrate: 4 g | Sugar: 0 g | GI: Very low

Red Pepper Coulis

Coulis can be made using any fruit or vegetable. For variety, experiment by adding herbs and spices.

INGREDIENTS | SERVES 8

6 medium red bell peppers
1 tablespoon olive oil
Freshly cracked black pepper, to taste

1. Preheat oven to 375°F.

2. Toss the red peppers with the oil in a medium bowl. Place the peppers on a racked sheet pan and put in the oven for 15–20 minutes, until the skins begin to blister and the red peppers wilt.

3. Remove them from the oven and immediately place the red peppers in a glass or ceramic container with a top. Let the peppers sit for approximately 5 minutes, and then peel off the skin. Stem, seed, and dice the peppers.

4. Place the peppers in a blender and purée until smooth. Season with black pepper.

Per serving: Calories: 39 | Fat: 1.5 g | Protein: 0.5 g | Sodium: 1.5 mg | Fiber: 1.5 g | Carbohydrate: 6 g | Sugar: 1 g | GI: Very low

Italian Dressing

Try doubling this recipe and storing the dressing in a glass jar. It will keep for several days and is much better than store-bought.

INGREDIENTS | MAKES 1 CUP

⅓ cup balsamic vinegar

½ teaspoon dry mustard

1 teaspoon lemon juice

2 cloves garlic, chopped

1 teaspoon dried oregano, or 1 tablespoon fresh oregano leaves

Salt and pepper, to taste

½ cup extra-virgin olive oil

Put all the ingredients except the olive oil into a blender and blend until smooth. Whisk in the oil slowly in a thin stream. Bottle it and give it a good shake before serving.

Per serving (2 tablespoons): Calories: 63 | Fat: 7 g | Protein: 0 g | Sodium: 200 mg | Fiber: 0 g | Carbohydrates: 0 g | Sugar: 0 g | GI: Zero

Balsamic Vinaigrette and Marinade

Because balsamic vinegar is very sweet, it needs a slightly sour counterpoint. In this recipe, it's lemon juice. It also needs a bit of zip, like pepper or mustard. Use this vinaigrette as a dressing or a marinade.

INGREDIENTS | MAKES 1 CUP

2 cloves garlic, minced

2 shallots, minced

⅓ cup balsamic vinegar

Juice of ½ lemon

Salt and pepper, to taste

½ teaspoon Dijon-style mustard

½ cup olive oil

Place all the ingredients except the olive oil in a blender. With the blender running on a medium setting, slowly pour the oil into the jar. Blend until very smooth. Cover and store in the refrigerator for up to 7 days.

Per serving (2 tablespoons): Calories: 76 | Fat: 7 g | Protein: 0 g | Sodium: 150 mg | Fiber: 0 g | Carbohydrates: 2 g | Sugar: 2 g | GI: Zero

The Condiment of Kings

Mustard is one of the oldest condiments, having been used for more than 3,000 years. The first mustards were made from crushed black or brown mustard seeds mixed with vinegar. In 1856, the creator of Dijon mustard, Jean Naigeon, changed the recipe into what it is today—crushed mustard seeds mixed with sour juice made from unripe grapes.

French Dressing

This is a great dressing on a crisp green salad. You can also use it as a marinade for beef, chicken, or pork.

INGREDIENTS | MAKES 1 CUP

⅓ cup red wine vinegar

½ teaspoon Worcestershire sauce

1 clove garlic, chopped

2 tablespoons chopped fresh parsley

1 teaspoon dried thyme

1 teaspoon dried rosemary

Pinch sugar

⅔ cup extra-virgin olive oil

Mix all the ingredients except the olive oil in the blender. Slowly add the oil in a thin stream so that the ingredients will emulsify.

Per serving (2 tablespoons): Calories: 77 | Fat: 9 g | Protein: 0 g | Sodium: 50 mg | Fiber: 0 g | Carbohydrates: 1 g | Sugar: 1 g | GI: Zero

Lemon-Dill Dressing

This traditional dressing is best used on fish.

INGREDIENTS | SERVES 2

2 tablespoons olive oil

Juice of 1 lemon

1 teaspoon fresh dill

½ teaspoon ground black pepper

Combine all the ingredients, mix well, and serve on salad.

Per serving: Calories: 120 | Fat: 14 g | Protein: 0 g | Sodium: 0.5 g | Fiber: 0 g | Carbohydrate: 0 g | Sugar: 0 g | GI: Zero

Oils

Many salad dressing recipes call for olive oil, but feel free to experiment with various oils. Each oil has a different flavor and, more important, a different fat profile. Flaxseed oil is higher in omega-3 fatty acid than others. Walnut oil has a lower omega-6 to omega-3 ratio compared with others. Udo's oil is a nice blend of oils with various omega-3s, -6s, and -9s. These oils have a nice flavor and have the best to offer in a fat profile.

Creamy-Crunchy Avocado Dip with Red Onions and Macadamia Nuts

This is one of the best dips you can make. Try it with bagel chips, pita toast, or even good corn chips.

INGREDIENTS | SERVES 2

1 large ripe avocado, peeled, pit removed

Juice of ½ fresh lime

2 tablespoons minced red onion

2 tablespoons chopped macadamia nuts

1 teaspoon Tabasco or other hot red pepper sauce

Salt, to taste

Using a small bowl, mash the avocado and mix in the rest of the ingredients. Serve chilled.

Per serving: Calories: 229 | Fat: 22 g | Protein: 3 g | Sodium: 150 mg | Fiber: 0 g | Carbohydrates: 10 g | Sugar: 1 g | GI: Very low

Macadamia Nuts

Macadamia nuts are native to Australia. In the early 1880s, they were introduced to Hawaii, where much of today's macadamia nuts are grown. These nuts are a great source of monounsaturated fats, making them a heart-healthy food.

Homemade Hummus

Garlic lovers can add more garlic to this popular Middle Eastern dip. You can buy hummus at the store, but this recipe is easy to make and much cheaper.

INGREDIENTS | SERVES 12

1 (15-ounce) can chickpeas, drained

2 cloves garlic, chopped, or more to taste

½ small white onion, peeled and chopped

1 teaspoon Tabasco or other hot sauce

½ cup fresh flat-leaf parsley or cilantro, tightly packed

Salt and pepper, to taste

½ cup olive oil

Bagel chips or warm pita bread

Blend all the ingredients in the food processor or blender. Do not purée; the hummus should have a coarse consistency. Serve with bagel chips or warm pita bread.

Per serving: Calories: 128 | Fat: 9 g | Protein: 2 g | Sodium: 150 mg | Fiber: 4 g | Carbohydrates: 9 g | Sugar: 2 g | GI: Low

All-Natural Olive Oil Spray

To make your own olive oil spray, buy a clean spray bottle at a hardware store and fill it with olive oil. If you use a spray bottle that you have at home, make sure it has never contained anything that could leave a harmful residue. Use this spray as an alternative to nonstick sprays that don't taste like olive oil.

Grilled Peach Chutney

Grilled fruit is wonderful with meats, poultry, or fish. Grilled peach chutney is sublime!

INGREDIENTS | MAKES 2 CUPS

6 medium-size freestone peaches, halved and pitted

½ medium red onion, peeled and minced

2 jalapeños, cored, seeded, and minced

Juice of 1 lime

½ teaspoon ground cloves

½ teaspoon ground allspice

½ teaspoon ground coriander seeds

½ cup light brown sugar, or to taste

¼ cup white wine vinegar

1 teaspoon salt, or to taste

Freshly ground black pepper, to taste

Red pepper flakes, to taste

¼ bunch fresh cilantro, chopped

1. Grill the peaches, cut-side down, over a low flame until they are soft but not falling apart, about 5 minutes.

2. Cool them and then slip off the skins. Using a knife, cut the peaches into chunks and place them in a bowl. This method retains the juice and some texture.

3. Mix the rest of the ingredients into the bowl with the peaches. Cool, cover, and refrigerate until ready to serve. Warm just before serving.

Per serving (2 tablespoons): Calories: 45 | Fat: 0 g | Protein: 0 g | Sodium: 143 mg | Fiber: 1 g | Carbohydrates: 12 g | Sugar: 3 g | GI: Very low

Mint Chimichurri Sauce

Instead of the traditional mint jelly, use this mint chimichurri sauce to make a lamb recipe extra-special.

INGREDIENTS | MAKES 2 CUPS

2 cups fresh parsley

2 cups fresh cilantro

1 cup fresh mint

¾ cup olive oil

3 tablespoons red wine vinegar

Juice of 1 lemon

3 cloves garlic, minced

1 large shallot, quartered

1 teaspoon salt

1 small jalapeño, seeded and chopped

1. Wash the herbs, remove the stems, and chop the leaves.

2. In a blender, put the olive oil, vinegar, lemon juice, garlic, shallots, salt, and jalapeño. Blend the ingredients. Add the parsley, cilantro, and mint to the blender in batches and blend until the sauce is smooth.

Per serving (2 tablespoons): Calories: 98 | Fat: 10 g | Protein: 0 g | Sodium: 98 mg | Fiber: 1 g | Carbohydrates: 2 g | Sugar: 1 g | GI: Very low

Spicy Cilantro Dip

*Keep edamame, or soybeans, in the freezer so you can whip up this tasty dip
for unexpected guests.*

INGREDIENTS | SERVES 6

2 cups edamame

1 cup low-fat sour cream

3 tablespoons red wine vinegar

¼ cup lime juice

1 tablespoon olive oil

1 jalapeño, diced

1 bunch fresh cilantro leaves, chopped

1 medium red bell pepper, seeded and chopped

2 shallots, diced

¼ teaspoon salt

¼ teaspoon ground black pepper

1. Shell the edamame.

2. Combine the sour cream, vinegar, lime juice, and olive oil, and purée the mixture in a blender or food processor until smooth.

3. Add the edamame, jalapeño, cilantro, red bell pepper, shallots, salt, and pepper to the sour cream mixture and blend to a chunky texture.

4. Serve the dip chilled.

Per serving: Calories: 135 | Fat: 9 g | Protein: 6 g | Protein: 10 g | Sodium: 143 mg | Carbohydrates: 9 g | Sugar: 2 g | GI: Very low

Timesaving Tip

Edamame, or soybeans, are rich in iron, fiber, omega-3 fatty acids, and many other nutrients. Buy edamame that has already been removed from the shell to save time during preparation. You can often find shelled edamame in the freezer section at the supermarket.

Hollandaise Sauce

If you make hollandaise sauce in the blender or food processor, your sauce will not curdle.

INGREDIENTS | MAKES ¾ CUP

4 ounces sweet unsalted butter

1 whole egg

1 egg yolk

¼ teaspoon dry mustard

Juice of ½ lemon

⅛ teaspoon cayenne pepper

Salt, to taste

1. Melt the butter in a saucepan over very low heat. While the butter is melting, blend all the other ingredients, except the salt, in the blender or food processor.

2. With the blender running on medium speed, slowly add the butter, a little at a time. Return the sauce to a low heat and whisk until thickened. Add the salt and serve immediately.

Per Serving (1 ounce): Calories: 161 | Fat: 17 g | Protein: 2 g | Sodium: 60 mg | Fiber: 0 g | Carbohydrates: 0 g | Sugar: 0 g | GI: Zero

Béarnaise Sauce and Sauce Maltaise

If you substitute white wine vinegar for lemon juice and add chives in this recipe, you will have béarnaise sauce, a classic for steaks. If you substitute orange juice (preferably from a blood orange) for lemon juice, you'll have Sauce Maltaise, which is delicious with vegetables.

Fresh Tomato Sauce for Steak or Chicken

This is a versatile sauce—use it on any meat or poultry.

INGREDIENTS | SERVES 2

3 large fresh tomatoes

1 quart boiling water

2 cloves garlic, chopped

Salt and pepper, to taste

1 teaspoon Worcestershire sauce

2 tablespoons chopped parsley

Blanch the tomatoes in boiling water, drain them, slip off the skins, and chop the tomatoes. In a small bowl, mix the chopped tomatoes with the rest of the ingredients. Serve warm.

Per serving: Calories: 44 | Fat: 0 g | Protein: 2 g | Sodium: 123 mg | Fiber: 1 g | Carbohydrates: 10 g | Sugar: 1 g | GI: Very low

Rocking Salsa

This salsa is sure to be a winner at any party. Serve with gluten-free baked pita chips for a great appetizer.

INGREDIENTS | SERVES 2

½ cup chopped fresh cilantro
1½ cups chopped tomatoes
¼ cup sun-dried tomatoes
½ cup olive oil
2 teaspoons fresh-squeezed lime juice
1 teaspoon minced ginger
1½ teaspoons minced garlic
1 teaspoon minced jalapeño

Combine all the ingredients in a food processor and pulse quickly to blend. Be careful not to overdo it or you'll completely liquefy this salsa. It should have a slightly chunky texture.

Per serving: Calories: 132 | Fat: 14 g | Protein: 1 g | Sodium: 4 mg | Fiber: 1 g | Carbohydrate: 3 g | Sugar: 2 g | GI: Very low

Mango Salsa

This salsa is excellent with shrimp, crab legs, or fruit. Avoid using frozen mango since it tends to be mushy when thawed.

INGREDIENTS | MAKES 1 CUP

1 mango, peeled and diced
¼ cup minced sweet onion
2 teaspoons cider vinegar
2 jalapeños, cored, seeded, and minced
Juice of ½ lime
2 tablespoons finely chopped cilantro or parsley
Salt, to taste

Pulse all ingredients in the food processor or blender. Turn the mixture into a bowl, chill, and serve.

Per serving (1 ounce): Calories: 209 | Fat: 0 g | Protein: 2 g | Sodium: 108 mg | Fiber: 2 g | Carbohydrates: 54 g | Sugar: 8 g | GI: Low

Mango Facts

Did you know mangoes are the most popular fruit in the world? They are grown in tropical climates and therefore are available year-round. In many countries, unripe and ripe mangoes are eaten. The unripe mango is often pickled, seasoned, or made into a sauce and served with a savory meal. Sweet, ripe mangos can be made into juice, smoothies, and fruit salads.

Sesame Mayonnaise

This dressing is great on beef, turkey, or chicken burgers.

INGREDIENTS | SERVES 8

2 large eggs

2 tablespoons lemon juice

1 teaspoon mustard powder

2 tablespoons tahini paste

1½ cups grapeseed oil

1. Combine eggs, lemon juice, mustard powder, and tahini paste in a food processor, and pulse until blended.

2. Slowly drizzle the grapeseed oil into the egg mixture and continue to pulse until completely blended.

Per serving: Calories: 402 | Fat: 44 g | Protein: 2 g | Sodium: 20 mg | Fiber: 0.5 g | Carbohydrate: 1 g | Sugar: 0 g | GI: Zero

CHAPTER 3

Eggs and Dairy

Tomato and Feta Frittata

This frittata can be made for a quick and easy breakfast or a relaxed weekend brunch.

INGREDIENTS | SERVES 1

3 eggs
2 tablespoons crumbled feta cheese
½ cup chopped tomatoes
Salt and pepper, to taste

Breakfast, Lunch, or Dinner

Eggs provide a very healthy, satisfying breakfast that will help you stay full and satiated until your next meal. They are perfect for breakfast, lunch, or dinner and they are a more frugal option. Frittatas are a GI friendly, lighter option for a delicious and easy egg dish.

1. Pour the egg into a medium bowl.

2. Whisk the eggs, feta, and tomatoes.

3. Cook the egg mixture over medium heat in a small skillet coated with cooking spray for 4 minutes or until the eggs are firm. Do not stir.

4. Flip and cook the other side for 2 more minutes. Season with salt and pepper to taste.

Per serving: Calories: 126 | Fat: 11 g | Protein: 15 g | Sodium: 2,300 mg | Fiber: 2 g | Carbohydrates: 6 g | Sugar: 1 g | GI: Very low

Sunday Morning French Toast

If you would like to add more fiber to this easy gluten-free breakfast, simply add 1–2 tablespoons of ground flax seeds to the whisked eggs.

INGREDIENTS | SERVES 1

1 tablespoon salted butter
2 eggs
1 tablespoon vanilla extract
1 tablespoon cinnamon
2 slices gluten-free or grain-free bread

1. Heat a large griddle and brush with butter.

2. Crack the eggs into a shallow bowl and beat well with vanilla extract and cinnamon.

3. Cut the bread in half diagonally. Dip triangles of whole-wheat bread in the egg mixture, turning once to coat well.

4. Place the bread slices in the pan and cook for 2 minutes on each side, until crisp and golden brown.

Per serving: Calories: 453 | Fat: 19 g | Protein: 20 g | Sodium: 539 mg | Fiber: 4 g | Carbohydrates: 39 g | Sugar: 4 g | GI: Low

Sausage and Spicy Eggs

This is a very pretty dish that is not only a delicious breakfast but is also good for lunch or a late supper. Be careful not to use too much salt; most sausage has quite a lot of salt in it, so taste first.

INGREDIENTS | SERVES 4

1 pound Italian sweet sausage

¼ cup water

1 tablespoon olive oil

2 medium red bell peppers, roasted and chopped

1 jalapeño, seeded and minced

8 eggs

¾ cup 2% milk

2 tablespoons fresh parsley for garnish

Protein Variations

Feel free to use one pound of turkey sausage, regular breakfast sausage, ground beef, or even crumbled bacon instead of the Italian sausage for this recipe.

1. Cut the sausage into ¼" coins. Place them in a heavy frying pan with the water and olive oil. Bring to a boil; then turn down the heat to simmer.

2. When the sausages are brown, remove them and place on a paper towel. Add the sweet red peppers and the jalapeño to the pan, and sauté them over medium heat for 5 minutes.

3. While the peppers are sautéing, beat the eggs and milk together vigorously. Add the mixture to the pan and gently fold it over until it is puffed and moist.

4. Mix in the reserved sausage, garnish with parsley, and serve hot.

Per serving: Calories: 383 | Fat: 23 g | Protein: 35 g | Sodium: 89 mg | Fiber: 2 g | Carbohydrates: 8 g | Sugar: 2 g | GI: Low

Spinach and Gorgonzola Egg-White Omelet

This omelet is perfect when you don't want an overly filling breakfast. This recipe calls for egg whites only, which is helpful for people who don't like egg yolks. However, if you prefer to use the whole egg, simply use 4 large whole eggs instead of 8 whites.

INGREDIENTS | SERVES 2

1 (10-ounce) box, frozen chopped spinach, defrosted and drained of liquid

8 egg whites, well beaten

⅛ teaspoon ground nutmeg

1 teaspoon finely grated lemon zest

½ cup crumbled Gorgonzola cheese

Salt and pepper, to taste

The Versatile Omelet

The fantastic thing about an omelet is that you can stuff it with all kinds of ingredients. Various veggies, fruits, and cheeses, alone or in combination, make exciting omelets. Try mixing Cheddar cheese sauce and broccoli or Brie and raspberries for your next omelet and enjoy the flavors!

1. Prepare a medium nonstick pan with butter-flavored cooking spray. Make sure the spinach is thoroughly defrosted and drained.

2. Place the pan over medium-high heat. Pour in the beaten egg whites and sprinkle them with the nutmeg, lemon zest, and cheese. Spoon 1 cup of the spinach soufflé down the middle of the omelet. Reserve the rest for another use.

3. When the omelet starts to set, fold the outsides over the center. Cook until it reaches your desired level of firmness.

Per serving: Calories: 298 | Fat: 13 g | Protein: 32.5 g | Sodium: 604.5 mg | Fiber: 2 g | Carbohydrates: 18.5 g | Sugar: 2 g | GI: Low

Herbed Omelet with Vegetables

This omelet is a simple and healthy way to add an extra serving of vegetables to your day.

INGREDIENTS | SERVES 2

2 cups sliced white mushrooms

3 tablespoons 2% milk, divided

2 tablespoons sour cream

Salt and pepper, to taste

2 tablespoons chopped green onions

1 tablespoon chopped chives

¼ teaspoon dried tarragon

4 eggs

Use Coconut Milk Instead

If you prefer to make a dairy-free omelet, use full-fat coconut milk in place of the milk and sour cream listed. It will make the omelet creamy and delicious, and doesn't taste like coconuts.

1. Heat a large skillet on medium-high and coat it with cooking spray. Add the mushrooms and sauté until they are soft and the liquid evaporates, about 3–4 minutes.

2. In a medium bowl, mix together 1 tablespoon of milk, sour cream, salt, and pepper. Whisk well and set aside.

3. In another medium bowl, mix the remaining 2 tablespoons of milk, green onion, chives, tarragon, and eggs; stir well.

4. Pour the egg mixture into a greased pan over medium-high heat; spread it evenly over the pan. Once the center is cooked, cover the egg with the mushrooms. Loosen the omelet with a spatula and fold it over.

5. Place the omelet on a plate to serve and top with the sour cream mixture.

Per serving: Calories: 164 | Fat: 9 g | Sodium: 1,008 mg | Fiber: 0 g | Protein: 17 g | Carbohydrates: 5 g | Sugar: 1 g | GI: Very low

Mini Quiche

These are a tasty treat for breakfast and can be made in bulk.

INGREDIENTS | SERVES 8

6 large eggs
6 slices bacon
½ cup chopped broccoli
½ cup sliced mushrooms
½ cup diced onions
½ cup diced red bell pepper

1. Preheat the oven to 325°F. Line a muffin tin with 8 foil cups and spritz with nonstick cooking spray or brush with olive oil.

2. Whisk the eggs in a medium bowl and set them aside.

3. Cook the bacon in a small frying pan over medium heat until crisp, drain on paper towels, and chop into ½" pieces.

4. Spray a medium sauté pan with cooking spray. Sauté the remaining ingredients for 5 minutes.

5. Pour the eggs into foil cups, filling each two-thirds of the way.

6. Add the bacon and vegetables to each cup.

7. Bake 25 minutes or until golden brown.

Per serving: Calories: 118 | Fat: 8.5 g | Protein: 8 g | Sodium: 198 mg | Fiber: 0.5 g | Carbohydrate: 2 g | Sugar: 1 g | GI: Very low

Bacon and Vegetable Omelet

Bacon and eggs are a breakfast tradition. They are even more delicious served with fresh vegetables.

INGREDIENTS | SERVES 2

6 slices bacon, diced
1 yellow summer squash, chopped
1 cup sliced mushrooms
1 zucchini, chopped
¼ cup chopped fresh basil leaves
2 tablespoons olive oil
8 large eggs, beaten

1. In a large sauté pan over medium heat, cook the bacon until crispy. Add the vegetables and basil to the pan and sauté until tender, approximately 5–8 minutes.

2. Heat the olive oil in a second large sauté pan over medium heat.

3. Add the eggs and cook for 3 minutes on each side.

4. Place the vegetable-bacon mixture on one half of the eggs and fold over the other half to enclose the filling. Serve.

Per serving: Calories: 670 | Fat: 52 g | Protein: 39 g | Sodium: 849 mg | Fiber: 2 g | Carbohydrate: 11 g | Sugar: 1 g | GI: Very low

Poached Eggs

Poached eggs are very quick to make, but you must watch them or they will overcook. Time them exactly to get a perfect poached egg every time.

INGREDIENTS | SERVES 1

Water
1 teaspoon apple cider vinegar
2 large eggs

Vinegar on Paleo

Strict Paleolithic dieters do not use vinegar because it was not available during the Paleolithic period. If you are less strict, you can use it in salad dressings and in cooking. If you do use it, limit the intake to no more than twice weekly to promote good pH levels in your body.

1. Bring the water to a boil in a medium saucepan. Reduce the heat to medium-low so that the water is simmering.

2. Add the vinegar to the water.

3. Crack and carefully slide the eggs into the water.

4. Cook for exactly 3 minutes, remove with a slotted spoon, and serve.

Per serving: Calories: 150 | Fat: 10 g | Protein: 12 g | Sodium: 126 mg | Fiber: 0 g | Carbohydrate: 2 g | Sugar: 0 g | GI: Zero

Paleo Breakfast Bowl

This breakfast is a bit more exciting than an ordinary breakfast. Nitrate-free, uncured bacon is a real treat.

INGREDIENTS | SERVES 1

2 tablespoons olive oil
½ cup diced bacon
1 cup diced asparagus
2 large eggs

1. Heat the olive oil in a medium skillet over medium-high heat.

2. Cook the bacon and asparagus in the skillet until the asparagus is not quite tender, about 8–10 minutes. Remove to a small bowl.

3. In the same skillet, cook the eggs over easy (do not flip) about 5 minutes. Be sure that the yolks are runny.

4. Place the cooked eggs on top of the bacon mixture.

5. Mix and serve.

Per serving: Calories: 559 | Fat: 49 g | Protein: 23 g | Sodium: 534 mg | Fiber: 3 g | Carbohydrate: 7.5 g | Sugar: 0 g | GI: Very low

Deviled Eggs

This is a quick recipe that can be whipped up in no time. Kids and adults will love these, and they can be easily served at parties or family gatherings.

INGREDIENTS | SERVES 10

10 large eggs, hard-boiled
2 green onions, finely chopped
2 cloves garlic, finely chopped
1 stalk celery, finely chopped
1 teaspoon mustard powder
1 teaspoon ground black pepper
Sweet paprika, to taste

1. Peel the eggs, cut them in half lengthwise, and separate yolks from whites.

2. In a medium bowl, combine egg yolks, onions, garlic, celery, mustard powder, and black pepper. Mix well to form a paste.

3. Stuff the egg whites with the yolk mixture.

4. Sprinkle paprika over the eggs and serve.

Per serving (2 halves): Calories: 103 | Fat: 8 g | Protein: 7 g | Sodium: 97 mg | Fiber: 0 g | Carbohydrate: 1 g | Sugar: 0 g | GI: Zero

Egg Muffins

These are great to make in advance and take with you. They are also quite tasty with sliced avocado.

INGREDIENTS | SERVES 18

2 tablespoons olive oil
12 large eggs
2 medium zucchini
1 bell pepper, seeded and chopped
1 green onion (optional)
3 cups fresh spinach
1 cup cooked ham

1. Preheat the oven to 350°F.

2. Grease two muffin pans with olive oil.

3. In a large bowl, whisk the eggs well.

4. In a food processor, process the zucchini, pepper, and green onion until finely chopped but not smooth.

5. Add the chopped vegetables to the eggs.

6. Finely chop the spinach in the food processor and add to the egg mixture.

7. Stir in the ham and mix well.

8. Fill the muffin pans halfway with the egg mixture.

9. Bake for 20–25 minutes or until the eggs are set in the middle.

Per serving: Calories: 75 | Fat: 5 g | Protein: 5 g | Sodium: 108 mg | Fiber: 0.5 g | Carbohydrate: 2 g | Sugar: 1 g | GI: Very low

Spinach, Egg, and Bacon Breakfast Salad

Salad isn't just for lunch and dinner anymore. When you are following a low GI plan, salads are round-the-clock meals.

INGREDIENTS | SERVES 1

3 cups baby spinach leaves

4 large eggs, hard-boiled, peeled, and quartered

2 slices bacon, cooked and chopped

½ cup sliced cucumber

½ avocado, diced

½ apple, sliced

Juice of ½ lemon

1. Arrange the spinach leaves on a plate and top with eggs and bacon.

2. Add cucumber, avocado, and apple slices to the top of the salad.

3. Squeeze fresh lemon juice over the salad. Serve immediately.

Per serving: Calories: 694 | Fat: 44 g | Protein: 40 g | Sodium: 1,013 mg | Fiber: 10 g | Carbohydrate: 31 g | Sugar: 5 g | GI: Low

Salmon Omelet

This omelet is full of omega-3 fatty acids. It is well seasoned and will surely become a breakfast staple.

INGREDIENTS | SERVES 2

2 tablespoons olive oil

¼ cup chopped green onions

1 cup trimmed and chopped asparagus

1 tablespoon chopped fresh dill

6 ounces salmon

6 large eggs, beaten

1. In a large skillet over medium heat, combine the olive oil, green onions, asparagus, and fresh dill. Sauté until the asparagus is soft, 5–10 minutes, and set aside.

2. In the same skillet, sauté the salmon until flaky, about 10 minutes depending on the thickness of the steak. Set aside.

3. Wipe out the skillet and cook the eggs on both sides until lightly browned, about 5 minutes each side.

4. Place the salmon mixture on half of the egg, fold over, and serve.

Per serving: Calories: 490 | Fat: 33 g | Protein: 40 g | Sodium: 332 mg | Fiber: 4 g | Carbohydrate: 9 g | Sugar: 1 g | GI: Very low

Green Chilies and Egg Soufflé

Excluding the egg yolks from this soufflé helps reduce saturated fat for a lighter, healthier breakfast.

INGREDIENTS | SERVES 2

1 cup egg whites
Salt and pepper, to taste, divided
4 tablespoons unsalted butter
½ cup chopped red bell pepper
3 tablespoons diced green chilies
¼ cup shredded Monterey jack cheese
½ cup low-fat cottage cheese

Heat It Up!

For a spicier soufflé, add diced jalapeños or Thai chilies. If you want to keep the heat under control, remove and discard the inner membranes and seeds before chopping up the pepper. You may substitute green, yellow, or orange bell peppers for the red.

1. Preheat the oven to 400°F.

2. In a medium bowl, whip the egg whites to soft peaks, adding salt and pepper to taste.

3. In a heavy 9" oven-safe pan, melt the butter on high.

4. Add the bell peppers and chilies, season lightly with salt and pepper, and cook until tender.

5. Immediately fold the cheese and cottage cheese into the egg whites and spread the mixture evenly over the peppers and chilies. Place the pan in the oven and bake the soufflé for about 8 minutes until golden on top.

Per serving: Calories: 367 | Fat: 28 g | Protein: 24 g | Sodium: 1,011 mg | Fiber: 2 g | Carbohydrates: 6 g | Sugar: 1 g | GI: Very low

Eggs Florentine

Freshly ground black pepper goes well in this dish. You can use up to a teaspoon in the recipe. If you prefer to season lightly to accommodate individual tastes, be sure to have a pepper grinder at the table for those who want to add more.

INGREDIENTS | SERVES 4

9 ounces (2 cups) grated Cheddar cheese, divided

1 (10-ounce) package frozen spinach, thawed

1 (8-ounce) can sliced mushrooms, drained

1 small onion, peeled and diced

6 large eggs

1 cup heavy cream

½ teaspoon Italian seasoning

½ teaspoon garlic powder

½ teaspoon freshly ground black pepper

Make It Dairy-Free

To make egg casseroles dairy-free, replace the cream with full-fat coconut milk. There are many dairy-free alternatives available for Cheddar cheese; one, in particular, sold by Daiya Foods, is available shredded and melts beautifully in dishes like this.

1. Grease a 4-quart slow cooker with nonstick spray. Spread 1 cup of the grated cheese over the bottom of the slow cooker.

2. Drain the spinach, squeezing out any excess moisture, and add it in a layer on top of the cheese. Next, add the drained mushrooms in a layer and then top them with the onion.

3. In a small bowl, beat the eggs, cream, Italian seasoning, garlic powder, and pepper. Pour the mixture over the layers in the slow cooker. Top with the remaining cup of cheese.

4. Cover and cook on high for 2 hours or until the eggs are set.

Per serving: Calories: 605.5 | Fat: 51 g | Protein: 30 g | Sodium: 712 mg | Fiber: 3 g | Carbohydrates: 10 g | Sugar: 3 g | GI: Low

Ham and Cheese Slow-Cooker Omelet

Eggs, one of the most affordable proteins available, are naturally gluten-free. If you make a large family-size omelet like this on Sunday evening, you'll have ready-made breakfasts for the rest of the week.

INGREDIENTS | SERVES 5

10 eggs

½ teaspoon ground mustard

½ teaspoon salt

½ teaspoon paprika

½ teaspoon ground black pepper

½ teaspoon dill weed

1½ cups diced ham

1½ cups shredded Cheddar cheese

½ cup chopped green onions

How to Store Fresh Green Onions

Green onions, also referred to as spring onions or scallions, have small white bulbs and long green stalks. Both parts of the onion can be eaten. However, they will go bad if left in the refrigerator. The best way to preserve them is to buy two or three bunches, slice them all up, and place them in the freezer in a zip-top bag from which the air has been removed. They will stay fresh and can be used right from the freezer.

1. Whisk the eggs in a large bowl. Add in the mustard, salt, paprika, ground pepper, and dill weed. Stir in the diced ham.

2. Pour the egg mixture into a greased 2.5-quart slow cooker.

3. Sprinkle the cheese and green onions over the top of the egg mixture.

4. Cover and cook on high for 1½–2 hours or on low for 2½–3 hours.

Per serving: Calories: 352 | Fat: 25 g | Protein: 29 g | Sodium: 1,130.5 mg | Fiber: 0.5 g | Carbohydrates: 3 g | Sugar: 1.5 g | GI: Very low

Breakfast Quinoa with Fruit

Take a break from oatmeal and try this fruity quinoa instead!

INGREDIENTS | SERVES 4

1 cup quinoa

2 cups water

½ cup dried mixed berries

1 pear, thinly sliced and peeled if desired

½ cup dark brown sugar

½ teaspoon ground ginger

¼ teaspoon cinnamon

⅛ teaspoon cloves

⅛ teaspoon nutmeg

Place all the ingredients into a 4-quart slow cooker. Stir. Cook for 2½ hours on high, or around 4 hours on low, or until the quinoa has absorbed most of the liquid and is light and fluffy.

Per serving: Calories: 297 | Fat: 3 g | Protein: 6.5 g | Sodium: 14 mg | Fiber: 5 g | Carbohydrates: 64 g | Sugar: 32.5 g | GI: Low

What Is Quinoa?

Pronounced "keen-wah," quinoa is grown as a grain, although it's actually a seed. It's become very popular in recent years, being touted as a health food. The grain itself has been used for thousands of years in South America. It's a perfect addition to the gluten-free diet because of its high nutritional content.

Baked Oatmeal

A regional dish from Lancaster, Pennsylvania, this simple baked oatmeal is sweet and hearty. Serve it cut in squares and drizzled with maple syrup for breakfast, or for a unique dessert, serve it warm with ice cream.

INGREDIENTS | SERVES 6

3 cups gluten-free rolled oats

2 teaspoons baking powder

1 teaspoon salt

2 eggs, gently whisked

¼ cup butter, melted

¾ cup brown sugar

1½ cups milk

Room for Interpretation

As is, this simple oatmeal cake tastes like warm salty butter and brown sugar, yet you can make endless flavor variations with this dish. By adding any combination of raisins, chocolate chips, sliced almonds, pecans, chopped walnuts, diced apples, dried cherries, dried cranberries, several tablespoons of cocoa, vanilla, cinnamon, or freshly grated nutmeg, you can create your unique favorite adaptation.

1. In a large bowl, mix the oats, baking powder, and salt.

2. Make a well in the center of the dry ingredients, and add the eggs, melted butter, brown sugar, and milk. Mix thoroughly.

3. Lightly grease a 4-quart slow cooker. Pour the oatmeal batter into the slow cooker.

4. Cover the slow cooker and vent the lid with a wooden spoon handle or a chopstick. Cook on high for 3½–4 hours or on low for 6–7 hours. Make sure to keep an eye on the dish in the last hour of cooking to be sure it doesn't burn.

5. The baked oatmeal is finished when the edges are golden brown and a toothpick inserted in the middle comes out clean. This oatmeal is almost like a cake or brownie in texture; if you want creamier oatmeal, add an additional cup of milk to the batter before cooking.

Per serving: Calories: 387 | Fat: 14 g | Protein: 9.5 g | Sodium: 616 mg | Fiber: 4 g | Carbohydrates: 58 g | Sugar: 30.5 g | GI: Low

Irish Oatmeal and Poached Fruit

This breakfast will keep the kids fueled for hours! It has the perfect combination of slow-release starch and get 'em going fruit. The nuts will stave off hunger, too!

INGREDIENTS | SERVES 4

1 fresh peach, chopped
½ cup raisins
1 tart apple, cored and chopped
½ cup water
3 tablespoons honey
½ teaspoon salt
2 cups Irish or Scottish oatmeal
1½ cups nonfat milk
1½ cups low-fat yogurt
1 cup toasted walnuts

1. In a large saucepan, mix the peach, raisins, and apple with the water, honey, and salt. Bring to a boil and remove the pan from the heat.

2. Mix the oatmeal and milk with the low-fat yogurt. Cook according to package directions.

3. Mix in the fruit and cook for another 2–3 minutes. Serve hot, sprinkled with walnuts.

Per serving: Calories: 600 | Fat: 36 g | Protein: 32 g | Sodium: 203 mg | Fiber: 3 g | Carbohydrates: 61 g | Sugar: 10 g | GI: Moderate

Instant Oatmeal

Avoid instant oatmeal for breakfast, for cookies, and for making snacks. The oats in instant oatmeal are cut very thinly, and particle size is important. The larger the particles, the lower the food is on the GI.

Yogurt and Fruit Parfait

This fast and easy breakfast is packed full of calcium, fiber, and antioxidants.

INGREDIENTS | SERVES 1

1 cup nonfat yogurt
¼ cup blueberries
¼ cup sliced strawberries
4 tablespoons sliced almonds

Greek Yogurt

Try using Greek yogurt, preferably nonfat or low-fat, for a thicker, richer, and slightly tart parfait. Greek yogurt tastes great with sweet berries. For a simple snack, try adding a teaspoon of honey to plain Greek yogurt. What a treat!

1. Add ½ cup yogurt to a tall glass.

2. Layer half the berries and 2 tablespoons of almond slices on top of the yogurt.

3. Place the remaining yogurt on top of the layer of berries and almonds.

4. Add the remaining berries and 2 tablespoons of almonds to the top of the second yogurt layer.

Per serving: Calories: 303 | Fat: 12 g | Protein: 19 g | Protein: 8 g | Sodium: 60 mg | Carbohydrates: 32 g | Sugar: 3 g | GI: Moderate

Blueberry Antioxidant Smoothie

Blueberries contain one of the highest antioxidant levels found in fruit. This smoothie is refreshing as it fights free-radical oxidation in your body.

INGREDIENTS | SERVES 1

1 cup frozen blueberries
½ avocado
1 cup vanilla-flavored almond milk
⅛ teaspoon ground nutmeg
4–6 ice cubes

Combine all the ingredients in a blender and purée until smooth.

Per serving: Calories: 329 | Fat: 17 g | Protein: 13 g | Sodium: 141 mg | Fiber: 11 g | Carbohydrate: 39 g | Sugar: 5 g | GI: Low

Candy Bar Smoothie

This chocolate-and-coconut smoothie is a real treat when you are craving something sweet.

INGREDIENTS | SERVES 2

1 cup coconut milk

½ cup cacao nibs

3 tablespoons raw honey

½ teaspoon cinnamon

¼ teaspoon nutmeg

4–6 ice cubes

Combine all the ingredients in a blender and purée until smooth.

Per serving: Calories: 395 | Fat: 28 g | Protein: 2.5 g | Sodium: 16 mg | Fiber: 0 g | Carbohydrates: 39.5 g | Sugar: 7.5 g | GI: Moderate

Peach and Raspberry Smoothie

The mixture of raspberries and peaches is the basis of classic peach Melba—a wonderful dessert. This smoothie is rich and always sure to please.

INGREDIENTS | SERVES 2

2 fresh peaches, peeled, pitted, and quartered

1 cup fresh raspberries

1½ cups plain low-fat yogurt

2 tablespoons sugar or honey

1 teaspoon pure vanilla extract

6 ice cubes

2 raw, pasteurized eggs

Place all the ingredients in the blender and purée until well blended.

Per serving: Calories: 315 | Fat: 9 g | Protein: 88 g | Sodium: 45 mg | Fiber: 4 g | Carbohydrates: 34 g | Sugar: 4 g | GI: Low

Quick Breakfast

An easy, quick breakfast, smoothies are a tasty and nutrient-rich morning pick-me-up. They also make a healthful and satisfying lunch for active and busy lifestyles. For extra protein, add a scoop of plain protein powder to the recipe.

CHAPTER 4

Bread and Muffins

Apple Oatmeal Breakfast Bars

These easy oatmeal bars filled with fresh fruit can also be served as a less-sugary dessert.

INGREDIENTS | SERVES 9

¾ cup brown rice flour

¾ cup arrowroot starch

1 teaspoon baking powder

¼ teaspoon salt

1½ cups gluten-free rolled oats

⅓ cup brown sugar, packed

¾ cup Spectrum Organic Shortening or butter

2–3 small apples, any variety, seeds removed, coarsely chopped or grated

2 teaspoons ground cinnamon

½ teaspoon ground nutmeg

¼ cup sugar

1 tablespoon honey

Breakfast Bar Variations

If you're not a fan of apples, use peaches, pears, blueberries, or other berries in place of the apples. You could also substitute 1 cup of pumpkin purée, butternut squash purée, or even cooked and mashed sweet potatoes as well.

1. Preheat oven to 350°F. Grease an 8" × 8" baking dish with nonstick cooking spray or olive oil, or line with parchment paper.

2. In a large bowl, whisk the brown rice flour, arrowroot starch, baking powder, salt, rolled oats, and brown sugar. Using a pastry blender or a knife and fork, cut in the shortening or butter until it resembles small peas throughout the mixture. Mix with a fork until you have a crumbly dough. Press half of the mixture into the bottom of the baking dish.

3. In a small saucepan, mix the chopped apples, cinnamon, nutmeg, sugar, and honey. Cook on medium heat for 8–10 minutes, stirring every few minutes until the sugar is completely dissolved and the apples are soft. Pour the apple mixture over the dough in the baking dish.

4. Sprinkle the remaining crumbly dough mixture evenly over the apples.

5. Bake for 30–40 minutes until the tops of the bars are golden brown. Allow the bars to cool completely before cutting.

6. Store any remaining bars in an airtight container in the refrigerator for 2–3 days.

Per serving: Calories: 356 | Fat: 16 g | Protein: 3 g | Sodium: 125 mg | Fiber: 3 g | Carbohydrates: 50 g | Sugar: 20 g | GI: Low

Fluffy Buttermilk Biscuits

These fluffy, light biscuits are perfect when topped with jam and a slice of cheese.
Or dip them in your favorite soup!

INGREDIENTS | SERVES 9

1 cup brown rice flour, plus more for rolling out the dough

½ cup arrowroot starch

4 teaspoons xanthan gum

2 teaspoons baking powder

1 teaspoon baking soda

½ teaspoon salt

1 teaspoon sugar

½ cup cold butter or Spectrum Organic Shortening, cut into chunks

2 large eggs

⅓ cup buttermilk

Milk (optional)

Coarse salt (optional)

Make Savory Biscuits

To make these biscuits savory, add ½ teaspoon of garlic powder or Italian seasoning (or even both) to the dry ingredients. Or try a tablespoon of chopped fresh chives.

1. Preheat the oven to 425°F. Line a baking sheet with parchment paper, and sprinkle with some brown rice flour. Set aside.

2. In the bowl of a food processor, combine the dry ingredients and pulse to combine.

3. Add the butter and pulse until the butter is the size of a lentil or a pea. (Work quickly, because you want the butter to stay cold.)

4. Add the eggs and buttermilk, and run the food processor until the dough comes together in a ball.

5. Turn dough out onto baking sheet, and flour your hands with more brown rice flour. Working quickly, pat the dough into a square, approximately 10" × 10" × ¾" thick. Using a sharp knife, cut the dough into biscuits.

6. Gently rearrange the biscuits so they are not touching and have room to expand while baking. Gently brush the tops of the biscuits with milk, and sprinkle with coarse salt, if desired.

7. Bake for 14–16 minutes, or until golden-brown. Allow to cool for 5 minutes on a rack before serving. You can store any remaining biscuits in an airtight container on the counter for 2–3 days.

Per serving: Calories: 206 | Fat: 12 g | Protein: 3 g | Sodium: 420 mg | Fiber: 2 g | Carbohydrates: 22 g | Sugar: 1 g | GI: Low

Grain-Free, Egg-Free Pancakes

A common challenge with grain-free or low-glycemic, gluten-free baking is figuring out how to make recipes without eggs. These pancakes use chia seeds as the binding ingredient instead.

INGREDIENTS | SERVES 4

2 tablespoons chia seeds

6 tablespoons warm water

1½ cups blanched almond flour

1 tablespoon arrowroot starch or tapioca starch

½ teaspoon sea salt

½ teaspoon baking soda

½ teaspoon ground cinnamon

¼ cup unsweetened applesauce or plain pumpkin purée

½ cup almond milk

1½ teaspoons vanilla extract

Pure maple syrup or honey

2 tablespoons butter or Spectrum Organic Shortening

1. In a small bowl, whisk the chia seeds and warm water. Set aside to gel.

2. In a larger bowl, whisk the almond flour, arrowroot starch, sea salt, baking soda, and cinnamon. Make a well in the center of the dry ingredients, and pour in the chia seed mixture, applesauce, almond milk, and vanilla. Whisk all ingredients into a thick batter.

3. Heat coconut oil, butter, or nonstick cooking spray on an electric griddle or heavy skillet over medium-high until sizzling. Drop 1½ tablespoons of batter per pancake onto the grill or skillet, and cook for 3–4 minutes on one side until the bottom has browned. Then flip and cook for an additional 1–2 minutes until the underside has browned. Serve hot with butter and pure maple syrup or honey.

Per serving: Calories: 292 | Fat: 22 g | Protein: 11 g | Sodium: 468 mg | Fiber: 6 g | Carbohydrates: 16 g | Sugar: 4 g | GI: Very low

Fluffy Coconut Flour Pancakes

Coconut flour is extremely dry and acts almost like a sponge in baking. You need a lot of liquid to make these pancakes moist and delicious.

INGREDIENTS | SERVES 3

½ cup coconut flour

1 teaspoon baking soda

½ teaspoon sea salt

4 large eggs, room temperature

1 cup almond milk or coconut milk

1 tablespoon vanilla extract

1 tablespoon honey

2 tablespoons butter or Spectrum Organic Shortening

Keeping Pancakes Fluffy

Making grain-free pancakes can be a challenge if you aren't familiar with how to use the flours and how they work in recipes. The best way to keep these pancakes soft and fluffy is to make them relatively small, no more than 2"–3" in diameter. If they are larger than that, they take too long to cook through and will become dry, instead of light and fluffy.

1. In a large bowl, whisk coconut flour, baking soda, and sea salt. Make a well in the center of the dry ingredients, and pour in the eggs, almond milk, vanilla, and honey. Whisk all the ingredients into a thick batter.

2. Heat a little coconut oil, butter, or nonstick cooking spray on an electric griddle or heavy skillet over medium-high until sizzling. Drop 1½ tablespoons of batter per pancake onto the grill or skillet, and cook for 3–4 minutes on one side until the bottom has browned. Then flip and cook for an additional 1–2 minutes until the underside has browned.

3. Serve hot with butter or coconut oil and pure maple syrup, honey, or fresh strawberry jam.

Per serving: Calories: 207 | Fat: 10 g | Protein: 14 g | Sodium: 947 mg | Fiber: 12 g | Carbohydrates: 25 g | Sugar: 10 g | GI: Low

Easy Pancake Recipe

This pancake recipe is quick and easy and can be multiplied to make enough for an entire family. Once cooked, sprinkle the pancake with cinnamon or a small amount of agave nectar for an old-fashioned pancake taste.

INGREDIENTS | SERVES 1

1 banana
1 large egg
1 teaspoon nut butter of choice
2 teaspoons coconut oil

Bananas as Thickeners

Bananas can be a good replacement for flour. Bananas act as thickening agents in recipes that would normally be too fluid.

1. In a small bowl, mash the banana with a fork.

2. Beat the egg and add it to the banana.

3. Add the nut butter and mix well.

4. Lightly coat a large frying pan or griddle with oil and pour the entire pancake mixture onto preheated pan.

5. Cook until lightly brown on each side, about 2 minutes per side.

Per serving: Calories: 389 | Fat: 17 g | Protein: 9.5 g | Sodium: 66 mg | Fiber: 7 g | Carbohydrate: 54 g | Sugar: 5 g | GI: Low

Strawberry-Banana Pancakes

These pancakes are a great alternative to just having an egg with meat, which tends to be the go-to Paleolithic-diet breakfast choice.

INGREDIENTS | SERVES 1

3 egg whites, lightly beaten
1 banana, sliced
3–4 strawberries, sliced
1 tablespoon almond butter
½ teaspoon cinnamon

1. Preheat a small frying pan coated with nonstick cooking spray.

2. Combine egg whites, banana, strawberries, and almond butter in a medium bowl and mix well.

3. Pour into the pan, cover, and cook, about 2–3 minutes.

4. Flip the pancake to brown the other side.

5. Serve warm sprinkled with cinnamon.

Per serving: Calories: 279 | Fat: 10 g | Protein: 19 g | Sodium: 195 mg | Fiber: 5 g | Carbohydrate: 34 g | Sugar: 7 g | GI: Low

Lemon-Poppy Seed Muffins

These muffins are flavored with lemon gelatin dessert. However, if you're not a fan of gelatin, you can replace it with 1 tablespoon of fresh lemon zest and 2 teaspoons of lemon extract.

INGREDIENTS | SERVES 12

Muffins

2 cups blanched almond flour

½ cup arrowroot starch or tapioca starch

½ teaspoon sea salt

½ teaspoon baking soda

¾ cup coconut palm sugar or sugar

½ teaspoon freshly grated nutmeg

2 tablespoons poppy seeds

3 tablespoons lemon gelatin (about half of a 3-ounce package)

1 teaspoon lemon extract

3 large eggs

½ cup almond milk

Lemon Glaze (optional)

3 tablespoons fresh lemon juice

1 tablespoon fresh lemon zest

Scrapings from 1 vanilla bean pod

4 tablespoons honey

2 tablespoons melted coconut oil

Coconut Palm Sugar

Most recipes in this book that call for sugar can be made with coconut palm sugar instead. Palm sugar has a lower glycemic index than white table sugar, which means it doesn't digest in the body as quickly as cane sugar and therefore doesn't create a large spike of insulin in the body while it's being digested.

1. Preheat the oven to 350°F. Line a 12-cup muffin pan with paper liners.

2. In a large mixing bowl, whisk the flour, arrowroot starch, salt, baking soda, coconut palm sugar, grated nutmeg, poppy seeds, and gelatin.

3. In a smaller bowl, whisk the lemon extract, eggs, and almond milk. Pour the wet ingredients into the dry ingredients, and whisk until thoroughly combined. Pour the batter into the muffin pan.

4. Bake for 18–20 minutes until golden brown or until a toothpick inserted in the middle of a cupcake comes out clean.

5. Allow to cool in the pan for 10 minutes then transfer to a wire rack until completely cool.

6. If desired, make a lemon glaze by whisking the ingredients in a small bowl and then drizzling the glaze over the cooled muffins.

Per serving: Calories: 215 | Fat: 11 g | Protein: 7 g | Sodium: 177 mg | Fiber: 2 g | Carbohydrates: 23 g | Sugar: 14 g | GI: Low

Cinnamon Bun Muffins

Do you miss the big, sweet swirl of a cinnamon bun? These muffins have all the amazing flavor, but with less sugar, fat, and refined flours than a traditional cinnamon bun.

INGREDIENTS | SERVES 12

Muffins

1 cup blanched almond flour
2 tablespoons coconut flour
¼ teaspoon baking soda
¼ teaspoon sea salt
½ cup coconut palm sugar
¼ teaspoon ground cinnamon
½ cup unsweetened applesauce
3 large eggs
1 tablespoon vanilla extract

Cinnamon Swirl

¼ cup coconut palm sugar
1 tablespoon ground cinnamon
2 tablespoons melted butter or coconut oil

1. Preheat the oven to 350°F. Line a muffin pan with 12 paper liners and grease with butter, coconut oil, or nonstick cooking spray.

2. In a large bowl, whisk the almond flour, coconut flour, baking soda, salt, coconut palm sugar, and cinnamon. In a smaller bowl, whisk the applesauce, eggs, and vanilla. Mix the wet ingredients into the dry ingredients until you have a thick, smooth batter. Fill each paper liner two-thirds with batter.

3. In another small bowl, whisk the cinnamon swirl ingredients. Spoon 1½ teaspoons of mixture over each muffin. Use a toothpick or a knife to swirl the cinnamon and sugar gently over the top of the batter.

4. Bake for 25–30 minutes until the tops of the muffins are golden brown and a toothpick inserted in the middles comes out mostly clean with just a small amount of crumbs.

5. Cool for 10–15 minutes before serving.

Per serving: Calories: 147 | Fat: 8 g | Protein: 4 g | Sodium: 93 mg | Fiber: 2 g | Carbohydrates: 17 g | Sugar: 14 g | GI: Low

Blueberry Almond Scones

These slightly sweet scones have a light texture with a soft crumb. Try different types of fruit, such as strawberries––or even chocolate chips––in place of the blueberries.

INGREDIENTS | SERVES 8

3 cups blanched almond flour

¾ cup arrowroot starch or tapioca starch

½ teaspoon baking soda

¼ teaspoon sea salt

¼ cup coconut palm sugar or sugar

⅓ cup butter or Spectrum Organic Shortening

1 large egg, slightly whisked

⅔ cup almond milk

1 teaspoon vanilla extract

½ teaspoon lemon juice or apple cider vinegar

1 cup fresh or frozen blueberries (do not defrost if frozen)

Traditional Scones Versus Almond Flour Scones

Traditional scones are created by shaping the dough into a round loaf and slicing it before baking. These scones, however, are made in a cake pan and then sliced into triangles after they are cooked because almond flour dough is not quite thick enough to support itself baking without a pan. You could use a scone baking pan, but it's just as easy to bake the dough in a cake pan and then slice it.

1. Preheat the oven to 350°F. Line a 9" cake pan with parchment paper and spritz with nonstick cooking spray. Set aside.

2. In a large bowl, whisk the almond flour, arrowroot starch, baking soda, salt, and coconut sugar. Using a fork and knife or a pastry cutter, cut the shortening evenly into the flour mixture until it resembles small peas. Set aside. In a small bowl, mix the egg, almond milk, vanilla extract, and lemon juice.

3. Mix the wet ingredients with the dry ingredients until thoroughly incorporated. Add the blueberries and mix. The batter will be thick. Pour the batter into the cake pan and smooth the top with a spatula.

4. Bake for 25–30 minutes until edges of the scone are golden brown and a toothpick inserted in the middle comes out mostly clean with few crumbs.

5. Remove the scone from oven and set aside to cool for several minutes. Cut the round scone into eight triangular scones.

Per serving: Calories: 415 | Fat: 29 g | Protein: 10 g | Sodium: 172 mg | Fiber: 5 g | Carbohydrates: 32 g | Sugar: 11 g | GI: Low

Banana Walnut Bread

This bread is sweetened only with bananas. Add up to ¼ cup of honey or coconut palm sugar if you prefer your bread a bit sweeter.

INGREDIENTS | MAKES 1 (8½" × 4½") LOAF

2¼ cups blanched almond flour

¾ cup arrowroot starch or tapioca starch

¼ teaspoon sea salt

1¼ teaspoons baking soda

2 tablespoons melted butter or coconut oil

½ teaspoon apple cider vinegar

3 large eggs

2 cups mashed bananas (about 4 medium)

½ cup chopped walnuts

1. Preheat the oven to 350°F. Heavily grease an 8½" × 4½" loaf pan with nonstick cooking spray or olive oil.

2. In a large bowl, whisk the almond flour, arrowroot starch, sea salt, and baking soda. Make a well in the center of the dry ingredients, and add the melted butter, vinegar, eggs, and bananas. Mix the wet ingredients into the dry ingredients until you have a thick batter. Fold the chopped walnuts into the batter.

3. Pour the batter into the greased loaf pan. Smooth the top of the loaf with a spatula dipped in water.

4. Bake for 40–50 minutes until a toothpick inserted in the center of the loaf comes out clean and the top of the bread is golden brown. Allow to cool in pan for 10 minutes; then place loaf on a wire rack to cool completely. Slice and serve.

Per serving (⅛ loaf): Calories: 356 | Fat: 25 g | Protein: 10 g | Sodium: 297 mg | Fiber: 5 g | Carbohydrates: 27 g | Sugar: 6 g | GI: Moderate

Banana Coconut Bread

This bread can double as a dessert recipe quite nicely. Serve with fresh banana and strawberry slices for a completely yummy treat.

INGREDIENTS | SERVES 8

1¼ cups almond meal

2 teaspoons baking powder

¼ teaspoon baking soda

½ cup fruit purée

¼ teaspoon cinnamon

2 large eggs

3 large ripe bananas, mashed

¼ cup flaxseed flour

½ cup chopped walnuts

1 cup unsweetened coconut flakes

Fruit Purées

Fruit purées are a great way to add sweetness to any recipe. Simply place your favorite fruits into a food processor and pulse quickly. Use in place of syrups and jams.

1. Preheat the oven to 350°F. Grease a loaf pan.

2. Combine the almond meal, baking powder, baking soda, fruit purée, cinnamon, eggs, bananas, and flaxseed flour in a large bowl. Mix well.

3. Fold in the chopped walnuts and coconut flakes (do not overmix). Pour the batter into the prepared pan.

4. Bake for about 45 minutes or until a wooden toothpick inserted into the center comes out dry.

5. Let the bread sit for 5 minutes; then transfer to a wire rack and cool completely.

Per serving (1 slice): Calories: 264 | Fat: 12 g | Protein: 5.5 g | Sodium: 26 mg | Fiber: 6 g | Carbohydrate: 38 g | Sugar: 15 g | GI: Moderate

Carrot Cake Bread

This is a very lightly sweetened, low-glycemic version of carrot cake. This bread would make a perfect breakfast on weekday mornings. Just toast it, and spread it lightly with cream cheese or your favorite low-sugar jam.

INGREDIENTS | MAKES 2 (7½" × 3½") LOAVES

2¼ cups blanched almond flour

¾ cup arrowroot starch or tapioca starch

½ teaspoon ground cinnamon

¼ teaspoon sea salt

1¼ teaspoons baking soda

2 tablespoons melted butter or coconut oil

¾ cup coconut palm sugar or brown sugar

3 large eggs

2 cups shredded carrots

½ cup almond milk or other nondairy milk

½ teaspoon apple cider vinegar

½ cup raisins (optional)

1. Preheat the oven to 350°F. Heavily grease two 7½" × 3½" loaf pans with nonstick cooking spray or olive oil.

2. In a medium bowl, whisk the almond flour, arrowroot starch, cinnamon, sea salt, and baking soda. Set aside. In a large bowl, mix the melted butter, coconut sugar, eggs, carrots, almond milk, and apple cider vinegar. Stir the whisked dry ingredients into the wet ingredients. Fold in the raisins, if desired.

3. Divide the batter evenly between the pans. Bake for 35–40 minutes until a toothpick inserted in the middle comes out clean and the tops of the loaves are golden brown.

4. Allow the loaves to cool on a wire rack for one hour before slicing and serving. Wrap leftover bread in plastic wrap and store in zippered bags in the freezer for up to one month.

Per serving (⅛ loaf): Calories: 186 | Fat: 10 g | Protein: 5 g | Fiber: 2 g | Carbohydrates: 20 g | Sugar: 11 g | GI: Moderate

Chocolate-Glazed Doughnuts

Just because you're eating grain-free doesn't mean you should give up doughnuts. This recipe uses honey as the sweetener. You can use coconut palm sugar if you prefer.

INGREDIENTS | SERVES 4

1¼ cups blanched almond flour

2 tablespoons cocoa powder

¼ teaspoon sea salt

¼ teaspoon baking soda

½ teaspoon ground cinnamon

2 large eggs

¼ cup melted butter, coconut oil, or light-tasting olive oil

4 tablespoons honey

½ teaspoon vanilla extract

Quick Chocolate Icing

In a microwave-safe bowl, mix ½ cup of chocolate chips with a high cocoa content and 1½ tablespoons of coconut oil. Melt on high power for 15 seconds at a time until the chips are melted and can be whisked with the oil. Dip each doughnut into the chocolate glaze and set on parchment paper to cool completely. Add toasted chopped nuts or unsweetened flaked coconut as a garnish.

1. Preheat the oven to 350°F. Heavily grease a large doughnut pan with nonstick cooking spray or light-tasting olive oil.

2. In a large bowl, whisk the almond flour, cocoa powder, sea salt, baking soda, and cinnamon. Make a well in the center of the dry ingredients, and add the eggs, butter, honey, and vanilla. Stir the wet ingredients into the dry ingredients until you have a thick dough.

3. Spoon the dough evenly into four doughnut circles in the pan. You can also put the dough into a zip-top plastic bag, cut off a 1" tip at an edge of the bag, and pipe the dough into the pan.

4. Bake for 10–12 minutes until the doughnuts are dark brown and a toothpick inserted in the middle comes out clean. Do not overbake the doughnuts; they can dry out quickly. Glaze with chocolate icing, if desired.

Per serving: Calories: 410 | Fat: 31 g | Protein: 11 g | Sodium: 264 mg | Fiber: 5 g | Carbohydrates: 27 g | Sugar: 18 g | GI: Moderate

Grain-Free "Corn Bread"

If you need a quick bread to serve with dinner or a hot bowl of soup, this is the perfect recipe. This bread is best the day it's made, but it's perfect for stuffing by day two.

INGREDIENTS | SERVES 9

1½ cups blanched almond flour

⅓ cup arrowroot starch or tapioca starch

⅓ cup plus 1 tablespoon coconut flour

½ teaspoon baking soda

½ teaspoon sea salt

¾ cup almond milk or coconut milk

¼ cup butter or coconut oil, melted

3 large eggs

3 tablespoons honey or coconut palm sugar

Coconut oil or jam

What Can You Substitute for Coconut Flour?

Coconut flour is a unique ingredient. It is extremely porous, meaning it soaks up liquids like a sponge. This property makes it hard to replace in recipes. To make a plain almond flour bread with no coconut flour, mix 1½ cups blanched almond flour, ½ teaspoon baking soda, ½ teaspoon salt, 4 tablespoons honey, and 4 eggs. Place in a greased 8" × 8" baking dish. Bake 25 minutes at 350°F until golden brown and a toothpick inserted in the middle comes out clean.

1. Preheat the oven to 350°F. Line an 8" × 8" baking dish with parchment paper and grease with olive oil or nonstick cooking spray.

2. In a large bowl, whisk the almond flour, arrowroot starch, coconut flour, baking soda, and sea salt.

3. Make a well in the center of the dry ingredients, and add the almond milk, melted butter, eggs, and honey. Gently stir the wet ingredients into dry ingredients until you have a thick batter. Pour the batter into the baking dish.

4. Bake for 20–25 minutes until golden brown and a toothpick inserted in the middle comes out clean. Cool in pan for 5–10 minutes and serve warm with butter or coconut oil and jam.

Per serving: Calories: 234 | Fat: 16 g | Protein: 7 g | Sodium: 235 mg | Fiber: 5 g | Carbohydrates: 18 g | Sugar: 7 g | GI: Low

Almond Flour Loaf Bread

Many people miss sandwich bread when they cannot eat grains or gluten. This high-protein sandwich bread is supplemented with ground flaxseeds.

INGREDIENTS | MAKES 1 (7½" × 3½") LOAF

1½ cups blanched almond flour

¾ cup arrowroot starch or tapioca starch

¼ cup ground flaxseeds

½ teaspoon sea salt

½ teaspoon baking soda

4 large eggs

1 teaspoon honey

1 teaspoon apple cider vinegar

Pan Size Matters

When baking gluten-free recipes of any kind, use the correct pan size listed if you can. It's especially important in bread and cake recipes. For this almond flour loaf, the bread will rise much higher in a 7½" × 3½" loaf pan than it would in a larger loaf pan.

1. Preheat the oven to 350°F. Grease the loaf pan generously with olive oil or nonstick cooking spray and set aside.

2. In a medium mixing bowl, whisk the almond flour, arrowroot starch, flaxseeds, sea salt, and baking soda.

3. In a smaller bowl, whisk the eggs, honey, and vinegar.

4. Pour the wet ingredients into dry ingredients and stir until you have a wet batter. Pour the batter into the loaf pan. Bake for 30–35 minutes until a toothpick inserted into the middle of the loaf comes out clean.

5. Allow the bread to cool in pan for 5 minutes and then move to a wire rack to cool completely. Wait until bread has cooled completely before slicing with a sharp, serrated bread knife.

Per serving (⅛ loaf): Calories: 218 | Fat: 14 g | Protein: 8 g | Sodium: 261 mg | Fiber: 4 g | Carbohydrates: 17 g | Sugar: 2 g | GI: Low

Almond Flour Irish Soda Bread

Not only is this loaf fun to make, it looks lovely and has just a hint of sweetness. Feel free to vary the seasonings and add-ins for a different flavor.

INGREDIENTS | SERVES 8

2 cups blanched almond flour

¾ cup arrowroot starch or tapioca starch

1½ teaspoons baking soda

¼ teaspoon sea salt

¼ teaspoon caraway seeds

½ cup raisins

2 large eggs

2 tablespoons honey

1 tablespoon apple cider vinegar

1 tablespoon water

1 large egg white mixed with 1 tablespoon warm water

Coarse gray sea salt (optional)

Alternatives

Instead of using raisins and caraway seeds, try these alternatives: For a Greek-inspired loaf, use ½ cup of chopped and seeded kalamata olives and 1–2 teaspoons of crushed rosemary; for an Italian-inspired loaf, use ¾ cup of finely chopped sun-dried tomatoes and 3 teaspoons of julienned fresh basil.

1. Preheat the oven to 350°F. Line an 8" cake pan with parchment paper and then grease with olive oil or nonstick cooking spray.

2. In a large bowl, whisk the almond flour, arrowroot starch, baking soda, sea salt, caraway seeds, and raisins. In a smaller bowl, whisk the eggs, honey, vinegar, and water. Mix the wet ingredients into the dry ingredients and stir until you have a thick dough.

3. Wet your hands with olive oil or water and pour the dough into the pan. Shape the dough gently with your wet hands into a pretty round loaf. Using a very sharp, serrated knife, gently slice a cross into the top of the loaf.

4. Lightly brush the top of the loaf with the egg white mixture. Bake for 25 minutes until a toothpick inserted in the center of the loaf comes out clean. Sprinkle with coarse gray sea salt, if desired.

5. Allow the bread to cool for 10 minutes in the pan and then transfer to a wire rack to finish cooling completely. Slice bread and serve with butter.

Per serving (1 slice): Calories: 266 | Fat: 15 g | Protein: 8 g | Sodium: 335 mg | Fiber: 4 g | Carbohydrates: 28 g | Sugar: 10 g | GI: Moderate

Savory Coconut Flour Popovers

Popovers are a cross between muffins and pancakes, in a baked form. This savory bread is easy to make and very attractive when taken right from the oven to the table for dinner.

INGREDIENTS | SERVES 6

4 large eggs, room temperature
½ cup almond milk
½ teaspoon sea salt
2 tablespoons coconut flour
Butter or coconut oil and jam

1. Preheat the oven to 400°F. Place a muffin tin in the oven while it's preheating to get it very hot.

2. In a large bowl, whisk the eggs, almond milk, sea salt, baking soda, and coconut flour until bubbly. You don't want to break up the protein in the eggs too much.

3. When the oven has reached the correct temperature, carefully remove the muffin tin with oven mitts. Grease the muffin pan with nonstick cooking spray or brush with olive oil. Fill the pan two-thirds with batter. Place it in the oven immediately and bake for a full 25 minutes without opening the oven door.

4. Remove the pan from the oven after 25 minutes and prick the popovers with a sharp knife in the middle to allow the steam to escape. Allow the popovers to cool for about 5 minutes and then serve hot with butter or coconut oil and jam.

Per serving: Calories: 62 | Fat: 4 g | Protein: 5 g | Sodium: 253 mg | Fiber: 2 g | Carbohydrates: 3 g | Sugar: 1 g | GI: Very low

Rosemary Basil Crackers or Crispy Pizza Crust

This versatile recipe can make crispy, crunchy crackers or a cracker-like pizza crust. Both are delicious and incredibly easy to make.

INGREDIENTS | MAKES 30 SMALL CRACKERS OR 1 (12") PIZZA CRUST

1¾ cups plus additional blanched almond flour

½ teaspoon sea salt

1 teaspoon dried, crushed rosemary

1 teaspoon dried basil

2 tablespoons olive oil

1 large egg or equivalent egg replacer

1. Preheat the oven to 350°F.

2. In a medium mixing bowl, whisk the almond flour, sea salt, rosemary, and basil.

3. Make a well in the center of dry ingredients and add the olive oil and egg, mixing thoroughly until you have a stiff dough.

4. Place a 12" × 16" sheet of parchment paper on a large baking sheet. Lightly sprinkle almond flour over the parchment paper and place the dough in the middle, on top of the flour. Place a sheet of plastic wrap gently over the dough as a barrier between the dough and the rolling pin. Roll to ¼" thickness or roughly into a 10" × 14" rectangle. Score the crackers by gently rolling a pizza cutter over the dough in a crisscross pattern to create about 30–40 (1") squares. For a pizza crust, roll the dough into an 11" × 11" circle.

5. For the crackers, bake for 12–15 minutes until crackers are lightly golden brown around the edges. Remove the pan from the oven and allow the crackers to cool for 20 minutes before breaking them apart. Cool completely on the parchment paper and store any leftover crackers in an airtight container for up to 1 week on the counter. Baked crackers will freeze well for up to 2 months in an airtight container.

6. For pizza, prebake the crust for 10 minutes until it's just crispy. Add toppings and bake an additional 10–12 minutes until the toppings have heated through. Allow to cool for 5 minutes and then cut and serve with salad. Cut pizza into 6–8 slices.

Per serving (⅙ recipe): Calories: 239 | Fat: 21 g | Protein: 8 g | Sodium: 208 mg | Fiber: 3.5 g | Carbohydrates: 7 g | Sugar: 1 g | GI: Very low

Almond Flour Savory Crescent Rolls

This versatile almond flour pastry makes delicious crescent rolls, pie crusts, or single-serving sweet pies.

INGREDIENTS | SERVES 10

3 cups blanched almond flour

¼ teaspoon baking soda

½ teaspoon sea salt

4 tablespoons cold butter (cut into cubes), or chilled coconut oil

1 teaspoon honey

2 large eggs

Melted butter or coconut oil (optional)

Apple Spice Hand Pies

In a medium bowl, mix 3 peeled, cored, and diced apples, ½ teaspoon cinnamon, ¼ teaspoon nutmeg, ⅓ cup brown sugar. Mix and roll out pastry as directed in the following recipe steps. Cut pastry into 4–6" circles using a cookie cutter. Place 2 tablespoons of the apple filling on one side of each circle, leaving ½". Fold the other half of the dough over the filling and crimp the edges closed with a fork. Brush a little melted butter or coconut oil on top of each pie and sprinkle with cinnamon and sugar. Bake 15–20 minutes until pies are golden-brown. Allow to cool 10–15 minutes before eating.

1. Preheat the oven to 400°F. Line a large cookie sheet with parchment paper and set aside.

2. In a large bowl, whisk the almond flour, baking soda, and sea salt. Cut in the butter or coconut oil with a pastry blender, until it resembles small peas throughout the mixture. Make a well in the center of the dry ingredients and add the honey and eggs. Stir the wet ingredients into the dry ingredients until you have a stiff dough.

3. Shape the dough into two large balls. Refrigerate the balls 10–15 minutes before using. Sprinkle additional blanched almond flour onto the parchment paper or plastic wrap to help keep the dough from sticking. Place the dough on a floured surface. Top with a sheet of parchment paper or plastic wrap and roll the dough out into a 12" circle. Using a pizza cutter, cut into eight triangles.

4. Roll up the triangles starting from the wide end to the point, so they look like crescent rolls. Place each roll about 2" apart on baking sheet. If desired, brush the rolls with melted butter or coconut oil.

5. Bake for 12–15 minutes until golden brown and slightly puffy.

Per serving: Calories: 249 | Fat: 22 g | Protein: 8 g | Sodium: 175 mg | Fiber: 3.5 g | Carbohydrates: 8 g | Sugar: 2 g | GI: Very low

CHAPTER 5

Fruit and Vegetable Salads

Floret Salad

Broccoli is one of the most nutrient-dense green vegetables.
Try this floret salad to maximize taste while boosting your health.

INGREDIENTS | SERVES 2

⅔ cup fresh cauliflower florets
⅔ cup fresh broccoli florets
2 tablespoons chopped red onion
8 ounces bacon, cooked and chopped
5 teaspoons raw honey
¼ cup walnut oil or olive oil
2 tablespoons whole cashews

Broccoli: Superfood

Broccoli is one of the most healthful vegetables you can eat. Ounce for ounce, broccoli has more vitamin C than an orange and as much calcium as a glass of milk. Broccoli is packed with fiber to promote digestive health and it is quite rich in vitamin A.

1. In a medium bowl, combine the cauliflower, broccoli, red onion, and bacon.

2. In a small bowl, whisk the raw honey and walnut oil.

3. Combine the honey mixture with the florets and toss.

4. Top with the cashews just before serving.

Per serving: Calories: 930 | Fat: 79 g | Protein: 35 g | Sodium: 1,299 mg | Fiber: 2 g | Carbohydrate: 22 g | Sugar: 10 g | GI: Low

Greek Salad

Olives are a rich source of oleic acid, a heart-healthy monounsaturated fat. While various types of olives are commonly used in Mediterranean dishes, Greek salads often feature kalamata olives.

INGREDIENTS | SERVES 4

4 cups chopped romaine lettuce

1 large tomato, seeds removed and chopped

1 small cucumber, sliced

1 medium green bell pepper, seeded and cut into rings

½ cup feta cheese

¼ cup red wine vinegar

Juice of 1 lemon

1 tablespoon Italian seasoning

Salt and pepper, to taste

¼ cup extra-virgin olive oil

2 teaspoons capers

16 kalamata olives

1. Place the lettuce, tomato, cucumber, bell pepper, and feta in a large bowl.

2. To make the dressing, whisk the vinegar, lemon juice, Italian seasoning, salt, and pepper in a small bowl; mix in the olive oil.

3. Coat the vegetables with the dressing.

4. Place the salad on plates. Top with capers and olives.

Per serving: Calories: 228 | Fat: 7 g | Protein: 5 g | Sodium: 799 mg | Fiber: 3 g | Carbohydrates: 20 g | Sugar: 1 g | GI: Low

Feta Is "Betta"

Greek shepherds have been making feta cheese for centuries. Originally made from goat's or sheep's milk, feta today is produced from pasteurized cow's milk. In Greece, feta cheese is served in restaurants and homes as a garnish on various types of fresh salads.

Cucumber Salad with Yogurt and Dill

This cool and refreshing salad pairs well with a spicy grilled meat for a relaxing summer barbecue.

INGREDIENTS | SERVES 2

2 large cucumbers

1 cup plain low-fat yogurt

1 tablespoon white wine vinegar

2 tablespoons finely chopped fresh dill

Salt and pepper, to taste

1. Wash and peel the cucumbers; chop into ¼"-thick slices.

2. In a medium bowl, combine the cucumber with the yogurt, vinegar, dill, salt, and pepper.

3. Serve chilled.

Per serving: Calories: 109 | Fat: 2 g | Protein: 8 g | Sodium: 625 mg | Fiber: 2 g | Carbohydrates: 14 g | Sugar: 5 g | GI: Low

Making a Cucumber Raita

This recipe may be modified to make raita, an Indian cuisine condiment. Chop the cucumber into ¼" cubes. Substitute 2 tablespoons chopped mint leaves for the dill; add a minced garlic clove and cayenne pepper to taste.

Mediterranean Tomato Salad

Use juicy tomatoes for this recipe, such as heirloom or beefsteak. You can substitute orange bell pepper for the yellow if needed.

INGREDIENTS | SERVES 4

2 cups sliced tomatoes

1 cup peeled and chopped cucumber

⅓ cup diced yellow bell pepper

¼ cup sliced radishes

¼ cup chopped flat-leaf parsley

1 garlic clove, finely minced

1 tablespoon lemon juice

3 tablespoons extra-virgin olive oil

2 cups torn baby spinach leaves

Salt and pepper, to taste

1. Toss the tomatoes, cucumbers, bell pepper, radishes, and parsley in a large salad bowl.

2. Sprinkle the garlic, lemon juice, and oil over the salad. Toss to coat. Salt and pepper to taste. Split the spinach among four plates and top with the salad. Serve immediately.

Per serving: Calories: 131 | Fat: 10 g | Protein: 2.5 g | Sodium: 71 mg | Fiber: 2.5 g | Carbohydrate: 7 g | Sugar: 3 g | GI: Low

Baby Vegetable Salad

Use the smallest vegetables available for this salad. Garnish with spicy prosciutto and sweet fennel.

INGREDIENTS | SERVES 4

¼ cup olive oil

2 cloves garlic, minced

12 tiny fresh white onions, peeled

1 pound tiny haricots verts (French green beans)

1 bulb fennel, trimmed and thinly sliced

5 ounces small white button mushrooms

8 baby carrots

¼ cup Champagne vinegar

¼ cup shredded fresh basil

¼ cup shredded fresh parsley

Salt and pepper, to taste

½ cup stemmed, loosely packed watercress

1 head lettuce, shredded

½ pound currant or grape tomatoes

½ pound Black Forest ham, chopped

1. In a large sauté pan, heat the olive oil over medium-low and sauté the garlic, onions, haricots verts, fennel, mushrooms, and carrots until the haricots verts and carrots are crisp-tender, about 4–5 minutes.

2. Stir in the Champagne vinegar, basil, and parsley. Sprinkle with salt and pepper to taste.

3. When the vegetables are at room temperature, arrange the watercress and lettuce on serving plates and spoon on the vegetables. Add tomatoes. Sprinkle with the ham and serve.

Per serving: Calories: 346 | Fat: 20 g | Protein: 19 g | Sodium: 634 mg | Fiber: 5 g | Carbohydrates: 18 g | Sugar: 3 g | GI: Low

Arugula and Fennel Salad with Pomegranate

Pomegranates pack a high dose of beneficial health-promoting antioxidants. They are in peak season October through January; you can also substitute dried cranberries.

INGREDIENTS | SERVES 4

2 large navel oranges

1 pomegranate

4 cups arugula

1 cup thinly sliced fennel

4 tablespoons olive oil

Salt and pepper, to taste

Fennel Facts

Fennel, a crunchy and slightly sweet vegetable, is a popular Mediterranean ingredient. Fennel has a white or greenish-white bulb and long stalks with feathery green leaves stemming from the top. Fennel is closely related to cilantro, dill, carrots, and parsley.

1. Cut the tops and bottoms off the oranges and then cut away the remaining peel. Slice each orange into 10–12 small pieces.

2. Remove the seeds from the pomegranate.

3. Place the arugula, orange pieces, pomegranate seeds, and fennel slices into a large bowl.

4. Coat the salad with olive oil and season with salt and pepper as desired.

Per serving: Calories: 224 | Fat: 15 g | Protein: 3 g | Protein: 3 g | Sodium: 609 mg | Carbohydrates: 24 g | Sugar: 15 g | GI: Low

Lentil Salad

This is a salad with a burst of protein. Serve it as a side or as a main lunch course.

INGREDIENTS | SERVES 4

1 (1-pound) bag lentils (green, yellow, or red)

1 medium onion, peeled and chopped

½ cup wine vinegar

Salt, to taste

1 medium carrot, peeled and diced

2 stalks celery, chopped

2 medium tomatoes, sliced

1 cup French Dressing (see recipe in Chapter 2)

A Note about Lentils

Like other legumes, lentils are an excellent source of dietary fiber and protein. Due to their small size, lentils cook faster than other beans and legumes. Dried lentils can keep well in the pantry for up to 1 year.

1. Cover the lentils with water in a medium saucepan and add the onions and wine vinegar. Bring to a boil, lower the heat, and simmer until the lentils are soft, about 45 minutes. Sprinkle with salt.

2. Toss with the diced carrot and chopped celery and then arrange the tomatoes around the mound of lentils. Sprinkle with French Dressing and serve warm or at room temperature.

Per serving: Calories: 287 | Fat: 20 g | Protein: 7 g | Protein: 27 g | Sodium: 631 mg | Carbohydrates: 25 g | Sugar: 6 g | GI: Very low

Portobello Mushroom Salad with Gorgonzola, Peppers, and Bacon

The hot Gorgonzola cheese sets this salad apart as an impressive main course or lunch.

INGREDIENTS | SERVES 4

2 large Portobello mushrooms

½ cup French Dressing (see recipe in Chapter 2)

4 strips bacon

4 ounces Gorgonzola cheese, crumbled

½ cup mayonnaise

2 cups chopped romaine lettuce

½ cup chopped roasted red pepper

Mushroom Choices

There are many varieties of mushrooms available. Brown mushrooms have a robust flavor. White button mushrooms are delicious in sauces, and the big ones work well when stuffed or grilled. Get wild mushrooms from a reputable mycologist. Never guess if a wild mushroom that you find in the woods is safe. It may be poisonous!

1. Marinate the mushrooms for 1 hour in the French Dressing. Fry the bacon in a small frying pan over medium heat until crisp; set it on paper towels and crumble it.

2. On a hot grill or in a broiler, grill the mushrooms for 3 minutes per side. Cut them in strips.

3. While the mushrooms are cooking, heat the Gorgonzola and mayonnaise in a small saucepan on low until the cheese melts.

4. Place the mushrooms on the bed of lettuce. Sprinkle with the bacon. Drizzle with the cheese mixture and garnish with roasted red peppers.

Per serving: Calories: 365 | Fat: 31 g | Protein: 11 g | Protein: 12 g | Sodium: 413 mg | Carbohydrates: 12 g | Sugar: 3 g | GI: Very low

Fig and Parmesan Curl Salad

This mixture may sound a bit different, and it is! In addition to being unique, it is also delicious.

INGREDIENTS | SERVES 2

4 fresh figs, cut into halves, or 4 dried figs, plumped in 1 cup boiling water and soaked for ½ hour

2 cups stemmed fresh baby spinach

¼ cup olive oil

Juice of ½ lemon

2 tablespoons balsamic vinegar

1 teaspoon honey

1 teaspoon dark brown mustard

Salt and pepper, to taste

4 large curls Parmesan cheese

1. When the figs (if dried) are softened, prepare the spinach and arrange on serving dishes.

2. In a bowl, whisk the olive oil, lemon juice, balsamic vinegar, honey, mustard, salt, and pepper. Place Parmesan curls over the figs and spinach; drizzle with the dressing.

Per serving: Calories: 284 | Fat: 16 g | Protein: 10 g | Sodium: 1,368 mg | Carbohydrates: 30 g | Sugar: 22 g | GI: Low

A Hidden Gem

Figs are a wonderfully nutritious food. Not only are they high in fiber and minerals, they also add tons of flavor to any recipe. Some cultures even claim that figs have medicinal value and healing potential.

Apple Coleslaw

This coleslaw recipe is a refreshing, sweet alternative to traditional coleslaw with mayonnaise. Additionally, the sesame seeds give it a nice, nutty flavor.

INGREDIENTS | SERVES 4

2 cups packaged coleslaw mix

1 unpeeled tart apple, chopped

½ cup chopped celery

½ cup chopped green bell pepper

¼ cup flaxseed oil

2 tablespoons lemon juice

1 teaspoon sesame seeds

1. In a medium bowl, combine the coleslaw mix, apple, celery, and green pepper.

2. In a small bowl, whisk the remaining ingredients. Pour over the coleslaw mixture and toss to coat.

Per serving: Calories: 158 | Fat: 14 g | Protein: 1 g | Sodium: 20 mg | Fiber: 2.5 g | Carbohydrate: 8.5 g | Sugar: 3 g | GI: Low

Seeds Versus Nuts

Nuts have a higher omega-6 to omega-3 ratio. Seeds, on the other hand, have a much different profile. Seeds have a lower saturated-fat content and are more easily digested by individuals with intestinal issues.

Orange Salad

This bright, orange-colored salad with the zesty flavor of fresh lime is a perfect fall side dish.

INGREDIENTS | SERVES 4

3 cups cubed butternut squash, drizzled with olive oil and roasted

2 medium carrots, peeled and shredded

2 cups diced papaya

2 tablespoons shredded fresh ginger

Juice of 1 lime

1 tablespoon honey, or to taste

1 tablespoon olive oil

½ teaspoon sea salt

Freshly ground black pepper

1. Combine the squash, carrots, and papaya in a large salad bowl. Set aside.

2. In a small bowl, mix the ginger, lime juice, honey, olive oil, salt, and pepper until well combined.

3. Toss the dressing with the salad ingredients and serve.

Per serving: Calories: 142 | Fat: 3.5 g | Protein: 2 g | Sodium: 621 mg | Fiber: 5 g | Carbohydrate: 29 g | Sugar: 13 g | GI: Moderate

Root Vegetable Salad

This root salad has a nice texture and color. It will go well with any traditional fall or winter dish and will make your home smell like a holiday meal.

INGREDIENTS | SERVES 4

1 rutabaga, peeled and cubed
1 turnip, peeled and cubed
6 parsnips, peeled and cubed
3 tablespoons olive oil
1 tablespoon cinnamon
3 cloves garlic, chopped
1 tablespoon ground ginger
1 teaspoon ground black pepper

Root Vegetables

Roots are underappreciated parts of plants. These underground vegetables are Paleo approved and recommended as they are high in vitamin A and are a nice form of carbohydrate fuel, particularly after exercising.

1. Preheat the oven to 400°F.

2. Place the rutabaga, turnip, and parsnips in a roasting pan and drizzle with olive oil.

3. Sprinkle them with the cinnamon, garlic, ginger, and pepper.

4. Toss them in the pan to coat and roast for 40–50 minutes or until a toothpick slides easily through the vegetables.

Per serving: Calories: 247 | Fat: 11 g | Protein: 4 g | Sodium: 79 mg | Fiber: 11 g | Carbohydrate: 36 g | Sugar: 15 g | GI: Moderate

Kale and Sea Vegetables with Orange-Sesame Dressing

This salad is a great appetizer for an Asian-themed meal.

INGREDIENTS | SERVES 4

¼ cup wakame seaweed

½ cup sea lettuce

3 cups kale

½ teaspoon lemon juice

¼ cup fresh squeezed orange juice

6 tablespoons plus 1 teaspoon sesame seeds

1 tablespoon kelp powder

Sea Vegetables

Sea vegetables are among the most nutritious and mineral-rich foods on Earth. Ocean water contains all the mineral elements known to humans. For example, both kelp and dulse, different types of seaweed, are excellent sources of iodine, which is an essential nutrient missing in most diets. Sea vegetables are dried and should be reconstituted by soaking them in water before eating.

1. Soak the wakame and sea lettuce in water for 30 minutes. Rinse the vegetables and discard the water.

2. Remove the stems from the kale. Roll the kale leaves and chop them into small pieces.

3. Sprinkle the lemon juice onto the kale and massage it by hand to create a wilting effect.

4. Place the orange juice, 6 tablespoons of sesame seeds, and kelp powder into a blender and blend until smooth.

5. Toss the dressing with the kale and sea vegetables in a large bowl until well covered. Sprinkle the remaining sesame seeds on top.

Per serving: Calories: 90 | Fat: 5 g | Protein: 4 g | Sodium: 64 mg | Fiber: 3 g | Carbohydrate: 9 g | Sugar: 2 g | GI: Very low

Spring Greens with Berries

The acid in the lime juice breaks down the fat in the olive oil to make a flavorful dressing.

INGREDIENTS | SERVES 2

1 jalapeño
4 tablespoons lime juice
4 tablespoons olive oil
¼ teaspoon ground cumin
4 cups mixed baby greens
2 cups fresh blackberries or raspberries
¼ cup thinly sliced red onion

1. Slice the jalapeño and remove the seeds and stem. Mince the pepper flesh.

2. Place the lime juice, olive oil, cumin, and 2 teaspoons of the minced jalapeño into a blender and blend until smooth.

3. Toss the dressing with the greens, berries, and onions and serve as a side salad.

Per serving: Calories: 363 | Fat: 28 g | Protein: 5.5 g | Sodium: 242 mg | Fiber: 9.5 g | Carbohydrate: 21 g | Sugar: 6 g | GI: Low

Minty Blueberry Melon Salad

Seedless watermelons sometimes have small white seeds scattered among the flesh. Use a fork to remove any noticeable seeds from the cubed watermelon before making the salad.

INGREDIENTS | SERVES 4

1½ cups cantaloupe, 1" cubes
1 cup seedless watermelon, 1" cubes
¾ cup blueberries
1 cup green grapes, halved
1 tablespoon minced mint leaves
1 teaspoon minced flat-leaf parsley

1. Gently toss the cantaloupe, watermelon, blueberries, and grapes in a large salad bowl.

2. Add the mint and parsley to the salad. Toss to mix. Serve immediately or chill in the refrigerator for up to 2 hours.

Per serving: Calories: 65 | Fat: 0.5 g | Protein: 1.5 g | Sodium: 12 mg | Fiber: 1.5 g | Carbohydrate: 16 g | Sugar: 10 g | GI: Low

American Fruit Salad

This classic fruit salad is the perfect accompaniment for breakfast or lunch.

INGREDIENTS | SERVES 4

½ cup cubed cantaloupe

½ cup cubed honeydew melon

½ cup cubed watermelon

½ cup red grapes

½ cup quartered strawberries

1. Toss all the fruits gently in a large bowl.

2. Chill the fruit salad before serving.

3. Serve the salad family-style or divide it among four small plates.

Per serving: Calories: 38 | Fat: 0 g | Protein: 1 g | Sodium: 8 mg | Fiber: 1 g | Carbohydrate: 9.5 g | Sugar: 8 g | GI: Low

Grape Types

Grapes are broken into two major categories: wine grapes and table grapes. Wine grapes are red and green grapes with a high sugar content to make wine. Table grapes are red and green grapes with a lighter and slightly less sweet flavor than wine grapes, making them popular for culinary purposes.

Sweet and Fruity Salad

Always rinse fresh produce under cool water. This will help remove things you don't want to eat such as pesticides, fertilizers, and bacteria.

INGREDIENTS | SERVES 1

2 cups shredded romaine lettuce

4 cherry tomatoes

½ cup sliced Gala apple

2 tablespoons golden raisins

2 tablespoons diced mandarin oranges

Combine all the ingredients in a large bowl and enjoy.

Per serving: Calories: 135 | Fat: 1 g | Protein: 3 g | Sodium: 18 mg | Fiber: 5 g | Carbohydrate: 33 g | Sugar: 9 g | GI: Low

Shaved Fennel Salad with Orange Sections and Toasted Hazelnuts

Tangelos, mandarin oranges, or any easily sectioned citrus will work wonderfully with this recipe.

INGREDIENTS | SERVES 6

3 bulbs fennel
6 large oranges
1 teaspoon finely chopped hazelnuts
⅓ cup fresh orange juice
2 tablespoons extra-virgin olive oil
1 tablespoon fresh orange zest

1. Finely slice the fennel bulbs. Remove the peel and pith from the oranges. With a small paring knife, remove each section of the oranges and slice away the membrane.

2. Form a mound of shaved fennel on each serving plate and arrange the oranges on top. Sprinkle with the nuts; then drizzle with the orange juice and oil. Finish with a sprinkle of zest.

Per serving: Calories: 172 | Fat: 5 g | Protein: 3 g | Sodium: 61 mg | Fiber: 7 g | Carbohydrate: 32 g | Sugar: 19 g | GI: Moderate

Pineapple Onion Salad

This sweet and tangy recipe does not keep well, so make sure to throw it together right before eating. If you prefer a little more zing, add another tablespoon of lime juice and a sprinkle of cayenne pepper.

INGREDIENTS | SERVES 4

1 cup cubed fresh pineapple
½ cup chopped red onion
3 cups mixed baby greens
1 tablespoon lime juice

1. Place the pineapple chunks in a large salad bowl. Mix the onions and baby greens into the pineapple.

2. Sprinkle the salad lightly with lime juice. Toss to coat and serve immediately.

Per serving: Calories: 28 | Fat: 0 g | Protein: 0 g | Sodium: 1 mg | Fiber: 1 g | Carbohydrate: 5.5 g | Sugar: 4 g | GI: Low

Fire-Kissed Cantaloupe Salad

Garnish this light and spicy salad with fresh cilantro or a slice of mango. Serve it as a side to any filling meat dish.

INGREDIENTS | SERVES 4

2 tablespoons mango juice
1 tablespoon walnut oil or olive oil
⅛ teaspoon chili powder
⅛ teaspoon sweet Hungarian paprika
⅛ teaspoon ground red pepper
¼ teaspoon sea salt
3 cups cubed cantaloupe
½ cup diced red onion

1. Whisk mango juice, oil, chili powder, paprika, and red pepper in a small bowl. Whisk until the salt dissolves and the oil is emulsified.

2. Put the cantaloupe and red onion into a large mixing bowl. Pour the dressing over salad. Toss well to mix and coat. Cover the salad and let it chill in the refrigerator for 15 minutes. Remove the bowl from the refrigerator, toss the salad gently to mix, and serve.

Per serving: Calories: 291 | Fat: 27 g | Protein: 1.5 g | Sodium: 41 mg | Fiber: 1.5 g | Carbohydrate: 11 g | Sugar: 6 g | GI: Low

Fruit Skewers with Dip

A forkless version of the fruit salad, this appetizer can be made with a variety of seasonal fruits.

INGREDIENTS | SERVES 4

4 kiwi fruit, sliced in ½" pieces
8 large strawberries, sliced in half
2 medium pears, cut into ½" pieces
1 large orange, sliced into ½" pieces
1 cup plain low-fat yogurt
Juice of 1 lime
2 teaspoons finely chopped fresh mint leaves

1. Arrange the cut fruit pieces on eight wooden skewers, alternating fruit types.

2. In a small bowl, mix the yogurt, lime juice, and mint.

3. Serve the fruit skewers with the yogurt dip.

Per serving: Calories: 159 | Fat: 2 g | Protein: 5 g | Sodium: 33 mg | Fiber: 7.5 g | Carbohydrates: 35 g | Sugar: 17 g | GI: Moderate

Fresh Herbed Yogurt

Herbs and citrus make yogurt taste great. For a different flavor, try using fresh basil leaves and the juice of half a lemon. You may also use other low GI fresh fruits like bananas and apples.

Red Pepper and Fennel Salad

Fennel has a fantastic licorice flavor that blends nicely with nuts. The red pepper adds a flash of color and a bit of sweetness to the mix.

INGREDIENTS | SERVES 2

⅓ cup pine nuts, toasted

3 tablespoons sesame seeds, toasted

2 tablespoons olive oil

1 medium red bell pepper, seeded and halved

6 leaves romaine lettuce, shredded

½ bulb fennel, diced

1 tablespoon walnut oil

Juice from 1 lime

Ground black pepper, to taste

Walnut Oil

Walnut oil cannot withstand high heat, so it's best to add it to food that has been cooked or is served raw, such as a salad. If you choose to cook with walnut oil, use a lower flame to avoid burning it.

1. Preheat the broiler.

2. In a medium skillet, sauté the pine nuts and sesame seeds in olive oil over medium heat for 5 minutes.

3. Grill the pepper under the broiler until the skin is blackened, and the flesh has softened slightly, about 5–8 minutes.

4. Place the pepper halves in a paper bag to cool slightly. When cool enough to handle, remove the skin and slice the pepper into strips.

5. Combine the red pepper slices, lettuce, and fennel in a large salad bowl.

6. Add the walnut oil, lime juice, and black pepper to taste. Mix the dressing well with the salad. Add the nut mixture and serve.

Per serving: Calories: 456 | Fat: 43 g | Protein: 7 g | Sodium: 37 mg | Fiber: 6 g | Carbohydrate: 17 g | Sugar: 5 g | GI: Low

Crunchy Fruit Salad

When you're in the mood for a sweet treat, this crunchy salad will fulfill that sugar craving and replenish glycogen storage after your workouts.

INGREDIENTS | SERVES 2

½ fresh pineapple, peeled, cored, and cubed

1 medium fresh papaya, cubed

1 medium, ripe banana, sliced

½ cup halved seedless grapes

1 tablespoon raw honey

¼ cup chopped cashews

¼ cup unsweetened coconut flakes

Combine all the ingredients, toss, and serve.

Per serving: Calories: 346 | Fat: 16 g | Protein: 6 g | Sodium: 11 mg | Fiber: 6.5 g | Carbohydrate: 53 g | Sugar: 29 g | GI: Moderate

Seasonal Fruits

It is always best to eat foods that are native to your area and in season. Imported fruits have traveled long distances and their freshness factor cannot be guaranteed. Your hunter-gatherer ancestors only had foods that were in season at the time of the hunt. They did not have the luxury of bringing in fruits from a neighboring area. Your body is made to change with the seasons.

Broccoli, Pine Nut, and Apple Salad

This quick little salad will tide you over to your next meal. The broccoli and apple taste great together and the toasted pine nuts add a bit of a crunch.

INGREDIENTS | SERVES 2

4 tablespoons olive oil

¾ cup pine nuts

2 cups broccoli florets

2 cups diced green apples

Juice of 1 lemon

1. Heat the olive oil in a small frying pan and sauté the pine nuts over medium heat until golden brown, about 3–4 minutes.

2. Mix the broccoli and apples in a medium bowl. Add the pine nuts and toss.

3. Squeeze the lemon juice over the salad and serve.

Per serving: Calories: 621 | Fat: 53 g | Protein: 15 g | Sodium: 34 mg | Fiber: 7 g | Carbohydrate: 31 g | Sugar: 9 g | GI: Low

Antioxidant Fruit and Nut Salad

Fruit salad can be eaten any time, but it is particularly good for breakfast. Berries are full of antioxidants, and walnuts have one of the best omega profiles among nuts to reduce inflammation. This is a winning combination.

INGREDIENTS | SERVES 2

½ cup sliced strawberries

½ cup raspberries

½ cup blackberries

½ cup blueberries

½ cup dried mulberries

½ cup chopped walnuts

Combine all the ingredients and enjoy.

Per serving: Calories: 282 | Fat: 20 g | Protein: 6.5 g | Sodium: 5.5 mg | Fiber: 8.5 g | Carbohydrate: 24 g | Sugar: 20 g | GI: Moderate

CHAPTER 6

Simple Sides

Hot German Potato Salad

Serve this with grilled brats and sautéed kale for a balanced low glycemic meal.

INGREDIENTS | SERVES 6

6 medium baking potatoes

1 small red onion, peeled and diced

3 stalks celery, diced

1 small green bell pepper, seeded and diced

¼ cup apple cider vinegar

½ cup water

¼ cup light olive or vegetable oil

2 tablespoons sugar

½ teaspoon celery seeds

¼ cup minced fresh flat-leaf parsley

6 strips bacon, cooked until crisp, drained, and crumbled

1 teaspoon salt

½ teaspoon freshly ground black pepper

1. Scrub the potatoes; cut them into ¼" slices and add to a greased 6-quart slow cooker. Add the onion, celery, and bell pepper; stir to mix.

2. In a small bowl, combine the vinegar, water, oil, sugar, and celery seeds. Whisk to mix and then pour into the slow cooker.

3. Cover and cook on low for 4 hours or until the potatoes are cooked through.

4. Stir in the parsley and crumbled bacon. Season with salt and pepper. Serve hot.

Per serving: Calories: 461 | Fat: 26 g | Protein: 12 g | Sodium: 937 mg | Fiber: 4 g | Carbohydrates: 45 g | Sugar: 7 g | GI: Moderate

Swap Bacon for Sausage

You can omit the oil and bacon and instead add 8 ounces of diced smoked sausage. The fat that renders from the sausage should be sufficient to offset the vinegar; however, if you think it's too tart when you taste the dish for seasoning, you can stir in a little vegetable oil when you add the salt and pepper.

Stuffed Zucchini Boats

Zucchini acts as the perfect vessel for this tempting vegetarian appetizer. A finger food topped with cheese and marinara sauce is a sure crowd-pleaser.

INGREDIENTS | SERVES 2

2 large zucchini

1 teaspoon olive oil

Salt and pepper, to taste

4 ounces ground turkey

¼ cup marinara sauce

2 ounces part-skim ricotta

1 tablespoon shredded Parmesan

Low-Fat Option

To reduce the total calories and fat in the zucchini boats, choose low-fat or fat-free ricotta. The recipe calls for ground turkey since it is leaner than ground beef. Vegetarians or those looking for a meat-free meal can substitute the ground turkey with ground soy "meat."

1. Set the oven rack at the upper-middle position and turn the broiler to high.

2. Slice each zucchini in half lengthwise. Using a spoon, remove the seeds from the halves, creating a hollow center.

3. Rub the zucchini with oil and season with salt and pepper to taste. Place on a baking sheet with the open side facing up. Broil 8 minutes or until the zucchini are fork-tender.

4. Brown the ground turkey in a medium pan over medium heat.

5. Heat the marinara sauce in a small saucepan.

6. Remove the zucchini from the oven and transfer them to a platter.

7. Combine the ground turkey and marinara sauce. Spread a thin layer of ricotta across zucchini; top with the meat sauce. Sprinkle with the Parmesan.

Per serving: Calories: 272 | Fat: 11 g | Protein: 20 g | Sodium: 1,333 mg | Fiber: 4 g | Carbohydrates: 27 g | Sugar: 11 g | GI: Low

Marinated Baby Artichoke Hearts

Here's where frozen artichoke hearts work perfectly! They save you the time and energy of cutting out the choke and removing the leaves of fresh artichokes, and they are delicious marinated.

INGREDIENTS | SERVES 4

2 (9- or 10-ounce) boxes frozen artichoke hearts
½ cup white wine vinegar
¼ cup olive oil
1 teaspoon Dijon-style mustard
½ teaspoon ground coriander seeds
Salt and freshly ground black pepper, to taste

1. Thaw and cook the artichokes according to package directions. Drain.

2. Whisk the rest of the ingredients in a bowl large enough to hold the artichokes. Add the warm artichokes and cover with the dressing. Cover and marinate for 2–4 hours. Serve as an antipasto.

Per serving: Calories: 142 | Fat: 15 g | Protein: 1 g | Sodium: 430 mg | Fiber: 6 g | Carbohydrates: 4 g | Sugar: 1 g | GI: Very low

Stuffed Celery

This unique take on stuffed celery is wonderful, replacing peanut butter or cream cheese with luxurious, buttery Brie.

INGREDIENTS | SERVES 12

Wide ends of 6 celery stalks, cut in half
5 ounces Brie cheese, softened
2 tablespoons capers
3 tablespoons chopped walnuts, toasted

1. Lay the celery pieces on a cool serving plate. Remove the skin from the Brie and mash with a fork. Mix in the capers.

2. Stuff each piece of celery with the filling and garnish with toasted walnuts.

Per serving: Calories: 66 | Fat: 6 g | Protein: 3 g | Protein: 3 g | Sodium: 131 mg | Carbohydrates: 1 g | Sugar: 0.5 g | GI: Low

Pickled String Beans

This cold green bean appetizer is a delicious and healthful start to your meal. Fresh dill has a wonderful aroma and adds the finishing touch to this dish.

INGREDIENTS | SERVES 4

2 cups canned green beans, drained

1 cup canned yellow beans, drained

Juice of 1 lemon

1 teaspoon white wine vinegar

1 teaspoon garlic powder

½ teaspoon dill

2 tablespoons minced onion

1. Combine all the ingredients in a bowl.

2. Serve cold.

Per serving: Calories: 28 | Fat: 0 g | Protein: 2 g | Protein: 10 g | Sodium: 12 mg | Carbohydrates: 6 g | Sugar: 6 g | GI: Very low

Yellow Green Beans

Green beans are not always green. They can be yellow and even purple. Green beans of all colors are rich in vitamins A and C. Despite the different appearance, yellow green beans taste the same as their green counterparts.

Citrus-Steamed Carrots

Figs are the fruit of gods and goddesses. Enjoy them!

INGREDIENTS | SERVES 6

1 pound carrots

1 cup orange juice

2 tablespoons lemon juice

2 tablespoons lime juice

3 fresh figs

1 tablespoon extra-virgin olive oil

1 tablespoon capers

1. Peel and julienne the carrots. In a medium pot, heat the citrus juices on medium-high. Add the carrots, cover, and steam until al dente, about 10–12 minutes. Remove them from the heat and let cool.

2. Cut the figs into wedges. Mound the carrots on serving plates and arrange the figs around the carrots. Sprinkle the olive oil and capers on top, and serve.

Per serving: Calories: 93 | Fat: 2.5 g | Protein: 1.5 g | Sodium: 94 mg | Fiber: 3 g | Carbohydrate: 18 g | Sugar: 11 g | GI: Moderate

Texas Caviar

This simple bean salad is enough to feed a small crowd at a potluck or picnic. Serve with grilled meat hot off the barbecue and a fresh green salad.

INGREDIENTS | SERVES 8

1 pound black-eyed peas

1½ cups Italian Dressing (see recipe in Chapter 2)

1 cup white corn

2 cups diced red bell peppers

1½ cups diced onion

1 cup finely chopped green onions

½ cup finely chopped jalapeño peppers

1 tablespoon finely chopped garlic

Salt and Tabasco, to taste

Timesaving Tip

If you need to speed up the prep time, substitute 2 (12-ounce) cans of black-eyed peas for 1 pound of dried peas and use your favorite bottled salad dressing. The final result will turn out just as well.

1. Soak the peas in enough water to cover them for 6 hours or overnight. Drain well.

2. Transfer the peas to a large saucepan. Add water to cover. Place over high heat and bring to a boil. Let the peas boil until tender, about 40 minutes; do not overcook them.

3. Drain the peas well, and transfer them to a large bowl. Stir in the Italian Dressing and let cool.

4. Add all the remaining ingredients and mix well.

Per serving: Calories: 224 | Fat: 13 g | Protein: 3 g | Sodium: 939 mg | Fiber: 8 g | Carbohydrates: 25 g | Sugar: 11 g | GI: Low

Quinoa Apple Salad

Highly nutritious and full of vitamins and fiber, this salad is ideal for breakfast or as a side. Quinoa (pronounced "keen-wah") is a seed that can be used much like a grain and has a texture very similar to couscous.

INGREDIENTS | SERVES 6

4 cups water

1 teaspoon kosher salt

1 cup quinoa

1 cup French Dressing (see Chapter 2)

2 cups peeled and diced jicama

1 green apple, peeled, cored, and diced

½ pound small seedless red grapes

2 cups mixed baby greens

Freshly ground black pepper, to taste

The Homely Legume

Jicama, also known as a Mexican turnip, is a lumpy root vegetable with a unique and versatile taste. The jicama's peel is inedible, but like a potato, it can be fried, baked, boiled, steamed, or mashed—or eaten raw. Try it as a vehicle for guacamole or use its mild flavor and crunchy texture in fruit salad.

1. Bring the water to a boil. Add the salt and wheat berries.

2. Cook the wheat berries until they are crisp-tender, following package directions.

3. Place the cooked wheat berries in a large serving bowl. While still warm, toss with the French Dressing. Add the jicama, apple, and grapes. Toss and chill. Place the mixture on plates over the mixed baby greens. Add pepper to taste.

Per serving: Calories: 256 | Fat: 11 g | Protein: 5 g | Sodium: 579 mg | Fiber: 4.5 g | Carbohydrates: 35 g | Sugar: 12 g | GI: Low

Basic Polenta with Butter and Cheese

In some parts of Italy, polenta is used more than pasta! It is simply cornmeal cooked in boiling water until soft and fluffy like mashed potatoes. When polenta is cooled, it stiffens up, making it useful for frying or grilling. This classic can be used instead of pasta or potatoes. Serve as a base for stews, veggies, or pasta sauces.

INGREDIENTS | SERVES 4

3½ cups water

1 teaspoon salt

1 cup coarsely ground yellow cornmeal

1 tablespoon butter or heart-healthy margarine

2 tablespoons grated Parmesan or fontina cheese

Pepper, to taste

Parsley for garnish

1. In a large saucepan, bring the water to a boil. Add the salt. Add the cornmeal in a thin stream, stirring constantly. Reduce the heat to low; continue to stir for 20 minutes or until the polenta comes away from the pot.

2. Stir in the butter, cheese, and pepper. Garnish with parsley.

Per serving: Calories: 68 | Fat: 4 g | Protein: 2 g | Sodium: 813 mg | Fiber: 3 g | Carbohydrates: 6 g | Sugar: 3 g | GI: Moderate

Cinnamon-Toasted Butternut Squash

This side dish or snack is a great fall dish. It smells amazing and will give you the carbohydrate boost your glycogen storage needs.

INGREDIENTS | SERVES 4

3 cups cubed butternut squash

1 tablespoon ground cinnamon

1 teaspoon nutmeg

1. Preheat the oven to 350°F.

2. Place the squash in a 9" × 11" baking dish. Sprinkle with the cinnamon and nutmeg.

3. Bake for 30 minutes or until tender and slightly brown.

Per serving: Calories: 93 | Fat: 0 g | Protein: 1 g | Sodium: 7 mg | Fiber: 3 g | Carbohydrate: 24 g | Sugar: 12 g | GI: Moderate

Roasted Green Beans with Pine Nuts

Dress up your everyday green beans with toasted pine nuts, crispy prosciutto, and fresh sage.

INGREDIENTS | SERVES 6

2 pounds green beans, trimmed

2 ounces prosciutto or bacon, thinly sliced

2 teaspoons olive oil

4 cloves garlic, minced

2 teaspoons fresh sage, minced

¼ teaspoon salt, divided

Freshly ground black pepper, to taste

¼ cup pine nuts, toasted

1 teaspoon lemon zest

Toasting Nuts and Seeds

Place nuts or seeds in a dry skillet over medium-low heat and cook for 3–5 minutes. Nuts will have a nutty scent and will be slightly browned.

1. Boil water in a large pot. Add the green beans to the pot and simmer until they are crisp-tender, about 4 minutes. Drain the green beans.

2. Spray a large frying pan with cooking spray and place over medium heat. Add the prosciutto and cook, stirring, until crisp, about 3–4 minutes. Transfer the prosciutto to a paper towel to absorb any excess oil.

3. Add the olive oil to the large pan and return to medium heat. Add the green beans, garlic, sage, ⅛ teaspoon salt, and pepper to the pan. Cook until the green beans begin to brown slightly, about 6–8 minutes.

4. Add in the pine nuts, lemon zest, and prosciutto; season with the remaining salt and additional pepper.

Per serving: Calories: 99 | Fat: 5 g | Protein: 5 g | Sodium: 449 mg | Fiber: 5 g | Carbohydrates: 10 g | Sugar: 3 g | GI: Low

Ratatouille with White Beans

This is a classic French dish of stewed vegetables, often including tomatoes and eggplant, served as an appetizer or side dish. Serving it over beans makes it a bit heartier and very satisfying.

INGREDIENTS | SERVES 2

¼ cup olive oil

2 baby eggplants, chopped

1 medium onion, peeled and sliced

2 cloves garlic, minced

1 small zucchini, chopped

2 medium tomatoes, chopped

1 teaspoon dried parsley; if fresh, 1 tablespoon

1 teaspoon dried thyme, if fresh, 1 tablespoon

1 teaspoon dried rosemary, if fresh, 1 tablespoon

Salt and pepper, to taste

1 (13-ounce) can white beans, drained and rinsed

1. Heat the olive oil in a large sauté pan. Sauté the eggplant, onion, garlic, and zucchini for 5 minutes over medium-high heat.

2. Add the tomatoes, herbs, salt, and pepper. Cover and simmer for 10 minutes. In a saucepan, warm the beans. Serve by pouring the vegetables over the beans.

Per serving: Calories: 409 | Fat: 16 g | Protein: 24 g | Sodium: 1,642 mg | Fiber: 31 g | Carbohydrates: 59 g | Sugar: 23 g | GI: Very low

A Provençal Delight

Ratatouille is a versatile vegetable stew that can be served hot (either alone or as a side dish), at room temperature, or even cold as an appetizer on toast or crackers.

Broccoli Rabe with Lemon and Cheese

Broccoli rabe is somewhat bitter and has a real snap to its flavor. It is wonderful when poached in boiling water and then sautéed in oil with a bit of garlic and lemon juice. Serve this recipe over rice or pasta, or on its own.

INGREDIENTS | SERVES 4

1 quart water

1 teaspoon salt

½ cup loosely packed broccoli rabe, ends trimmed

2 tablespoons olive oil

2 cloves garlic, chopped

1 tablespoon lemon juice

Salt and pepper, to taste

2 tablespoons Parmesan

1. In a large saucepan, bring the water to a boil; add the salt and broccoli rabe. Reduce heat and simmer on low for 6–8 minutes. Drain and shock under cold water and dry on paper towels.

2. In a medium frying pan, heat the olive oil on medium-low and sauté the garlic for 5 minutes. Cut the broccoli rabe stems in 2" pieces and add to the garlic and olive oil. Sprinkle with the lemon juice, salt, and pepper. Serve with Parmesan.

Per serving: Calories: 81 | Fat: 8 g | Protein: 2 g | Sodium: 1238 mg | Fiber: 1 g | Carbohydrates: 2 g | Sugar: 0 g | GI: Zero

Wild Rice with Walnuts and Apples

This is a wonderful side dish and is very filling.

INGREDIENTS | SERVES 4

2 cups wild rice, cooked to package directions

2 shallots

1 tart apple, peeled, cored, and chopped

¼ cup olive oil

½ cup walnuts, toasted

Salt and pepper, to taste

While the rice is cooking, sauté the shallots and apple in the olive oil in a medium frying pan on medium for 5 minutes. Mix all the ingredients together in a large bowl and serve immediately.

Per serving: Calories: 417 | Fat: 32 g | Protein: 8 g | Sodium: 347 mg | Fiber: 4 g | Carbohydrates: 31 g | Sugar: 5 g | GI: Very low

Black Beans and Sweet Bell Peppers

This is a simple, delicious meal that can be made early and thrown in the oven 30 minutes before dinner.

INGREDIENTS | SERVES 2

2 large bell peppers

2 tablespoons olive oil

¼ medium red onion, peeled and minced

2 cloves garlic, minced

1½ cups black beans, drained and well rinsed

1 small tomato

1 bunch cilantro, chopped

Salt and pepper, to taste

¼ cup shredded Monterey jack cheese

1. Preheat the oven to 400°F.

2. Slice peppers in half vertically and remove the membranes and seeds. Place the peppers in a baking dish.

3. Heat the oil in a medium frying pan. Sauté the onion for 2–3 minutes on medium until soft and translucent. Add the garlic and sauté for 1 minute.

4. Transfer the onion mixture to a large bowl. Add the beans, tomato, and cilantro, and mix well. Add salt and pepper to season.

5. Stuff each pepper half with the bean mixture. Cover the dish with foil and bake for 35 minutes.

6. Carefully take the dish from the oven and remove the foil. Sprinkle the cheese on each pepper and return dish to the oven, uncovered. Cook until the cheese is completely melted, about 3–5 minutes.

Per serving: Calories: 420 | Fat: 20 g | Protein: 18 g | Sodium: 1,548 mg | Fiber: 13 g | Carbohydrates: 45 g | Sugar: 9 g | GI: Moderate

Lentils with Stewed Vegetables

This dish can be served as a main course alongside roasted cauliflower and brown rice, or as a flavorful side.

INGREDIENTS | SERVES 4

¼ cup olive oil

1 medium onion, peeled and chopped

1 small piece fresh ginger, peeled and coarsely chopped

5 garlic cloves, chopped

5 cups water, divided

1½ teaspoons curry powder

½ teaspoon ground turmeric

½ teaspoon ground cumin

1 cup lentils

2 medium carrots, peeled, quartered lengthwise, then sliced crosswise

¼ teaspoon crushed red pepper flakes

1 teaspoon salt

1 cup green peas

4 cups fresh spinach

1. Place the olive oil in a large pot over medium heat. Cook the onion, stirring occasionally, until golden brown, about 3–5 minutes.

2. In a blender, purée the ginger, garlic, and ⅓ cup water. Add the purée to the cooked onion and continue cooking and stirring until all water is evaporated, about 5 minutes.

3. Turn the heat to low and add the curry powder, turmeric, and cumin. Stir in the lentils and the remaining water and simmer, covered, occasionally stirring, for about 30 minutes.

4. Add the carrots, red pepper flakes, and salt, and simmer, covered, stirring occasionally, until the carrots are tender, about 15 minutes.

5. Stir in the peas and spinach and simmer, uncovered, about 20 minutes.

Per serving: Calories: 361 | Fat: 14 g | Protein: 16 g | Sodium: 654 mg | Fiber: 19 g | Carbohydrates: 43 g | Sugar: 6 g | GI: Moderate

Baked Apples

You will feel as if you're eating apple pie when you eat these, and your house will smell like Thanksgiving dinner.

INGREDIENTS | SERVES 6

6 Pink Lady apples
1 cup unsweetened coconut flakes
Ground cinnamon, to taste

1. Preheat the oven to 350°F.

2. Remove the cores to within ½" of the bottom of the apples.

3. Place the apples in a medium baking dish.

4. Fill the cores with coconut flakes and sprinkle with cinnamon.

5. Bake for 10–15 minutes. Apples are done when they are completely soft and brown on top.

Per serving: Calories: 159 | Fat: 9.5 g | Protein: 1 g | Sodium: 6.5 mg | Fiber: 4.5 g | Carbohydrate: 21 g | Sugar: 5 g | GI: Low

Roasted Kale

This is a simple recipe that yields a crisp, chewy kale that is irresistible. You can also slice up some collard greens or Swiss chard as a substitute for kale, or mix them all together for a tasty medley.

INGREDIENTS | SERVES 2

6 cups kale
1 tablespoon extra-virgin olive oil
1 teaspoon garlic powder

1. Preheat the oven to 375°F.

2. Wash and trim the kale by pulling the leaves off the tough stems or running a sharp knife down the length of the stem.

3. Place leaves in a medium bowl; toss with the olive oil and garlic powder.

4. Roast for 5 minutes; turn the kale over and roast another 7–10 minutes, until the kale turns brown and becomes paper-thin and brittle.

5. Remove from the oven and serve immediately.

Per serving: Calories: 160 | Fat: 8 g | Protein: 6 g | Sodium: 249 mg | Fiber: 4 g | Carbohydrate: 20 g | Sugar: 0 g | GI: Zero

Roasted Peppers

Many people don't know that peppers become very sweet when roasted.

INGREDIENTS | SERVES 6

2 tablespoons olive oil

2 medium green bell peppers

2 medium yellow bell peppers

2 medium red bell peppers

6 cloves garlic, minced

Freshly cracked black pepper, to taste

1. Pour the olive oil in a stainless steel bowl. Dip the peppers into the olive oil, and then roast or grill them on an open flame (reserve the bowl with the oil in it) for 2–3 minutes on each side over medium-high heat. Shock the peppers in ice water and remove the skins.

2. Julienne the peppers and add them to the bowl with the olive oil, along with the garlic and black pepper.

3. Let the peppers sit at room temperature in a serving bowl until ready to serve.

Per serving: Calories: 76 | Fat: 4.5 g | Protein: 1.5 g | Sodium: 1 mg | Fiber: 2.5 g | Carbohydrate: 9 g | Sugar: 1 g | GI: Low

Roasted Asparagus

Use thicker asparagus to withstand the heat of the grill. Be sure to remove the woody end of the stalks first.

INGREDIENTS | SERVES 6

2 bunches asparagus

1 tablespoon extra-virgin olive oil

Lemon juice, to taste (optional)

Freshly cracked black pepper, to taste

Preheat the grill to medium. Toss the asparagus in the oil, drain it on a rack, and season with lemon juice and pepper. Grill the asparagus for 1–2 minutes on each side (cook to desired doneness). Serve immediately.

Per serving: Calories: 30 | Fat: 2 g | Protein: 1 g | Sodium: 1 mg | Fiber: 1 g | Carbohydrate: 2 g | Sugar: 1 g | GI: Very low

Asparagus

Asparagus is low in calories and sodium, and offers numerous vitamins and minerals, most notably folate and potassium. The stalks also offer a blast of inflammation-fighting antioxidants.

Mediterranean Green Beans

This simple recipe can be served hot or at room temperature. Add any leftovers to your salads.

INGREDIENTS | SERVES 4

1 pound fresh green beans, ends trimmed, cut into 1" pieces

2 teaspoons minced fresh rosemary

1 teaspoon lemon zest

1 tablespoon olive oil

Freshly cracked black pepper, to taste

Taking Care of Your Produce

Store unwashed fresh green beans in a plastic bag in the refrigerator. When you are ready to use them, wash the beans under cold running water. Washing fruits and vegetables right before you use them keeps them fresher and prevents mold from spoiling the final product.

1. Fill a medium saucepan with cold salted water and bring the water to a boil on high. Add the beans and cook until they are a vibrant green, just about 4 minutes.

2. Drain the beans and transfer to a large bowl. Add the remaining ingredients and toss to coat evenly. Serve warm or at room temperature.

Per serving: Calories: 70 | Fat: 3.5 g | Protein: 2 g | Sodium: 22 mg | Fiber: 3.5 g | Carbohydrate: 9 g | Sugar: 2 g | GI: [there is no GI study for Green Beans]

Chipotle-Lime Mashed Sweet Potatoes

Sweet potatoes are a great food for after a workout. This dish will be a favorite at any family table.

INGREDIENTS | SERVES 10

3 pounds sweet potatoes

1½ tablespoons coconut oil

1¼ teaspoons chipotle powder

Juice from ½ large lime

Alternatives to Sweet Potatoes

If you don't like sweet potatoes, you can easily substitute some lower glycemic-load vegetables such as rutabagas, turnips, or beets. Additionally, cauliflower makes a great fake "mashed potato" substitute.

1. Peel the sweet potatoes and cut them into cubes.

2. Steam the cubes until soft, approximately 5–8 minutes. Transfer them to a large bowl.

3. In a small saucepan, heat the coconut oil and whisk in the chipotle powder and lime juice.

4. Pour the mixture into the bowl with the sweet potato cubes and mash them with a fork or potato masher. Serve immediately.

Per serving: Calories: 135 | Fat: 2 g | Protein: 2.5 g | Sodium: 75 mg | Fiber: 4 g | Carbohydrate: 27 g | Sugar: 13 g | GI: Moderate

Wild Rice Pilaf

Wild rice is a perfect side dish for someone following a gluten-free diet. Naturally gluten-free, it is actually in the grass family of botanicals. Wild rice has a rustic earthy flavor that's a nice alternative to plain white rice.

INGREDIENTS | SERVES 6

2 cups uncooked wild rice

2 tablespoons butter

½ cup finely chopped onion

½ teaspoon salt

½ teaspoon ground black pepper

2 (14-ounce) cans gluten-free chicken broth

½ cup water

1 (4-ounce) can sliced mushrooms with liquid

1 teaspoon dried thyme

1 teaspoon dried oregano

1. Pour the rice into a mesh colander and rinse.

2. Add the butter to a large frying pan and heat until sizzling. Add the onion and wild rice. Cook over medium-high heat for 3–4 minutes until the rice has a slightly nutty, toasty aroma and the onions are translucent.

3. Grease a 4-quart slow cooker with nonstick cooking spray. Add the toasted rice and onions to the slow cooker. Add the remaining ingredients and mix well.

4. Cover and cook on high for 3 hours or on low for 6 hours until the rice has absorbed most of the liquid. If rice is not absorbing the liquids fast enough, vent the lid of the slow cooker with a chopstick or wooden spoon handle. Serve hot.

Per serving: Calories: 261 | Fat: 5.5 g | Protein: 10 g | Sodium: 480 mg | Fiber: 4 g | Carbohydrates: 45 g | Sugar: 2 g | GI: Moderate

Carrot Nutmeg Pudding

Carrots are often served as a savory side dish. In this recipe, the carrots have just a little bit of sugar added to bring out their natural sweetness.

INGREDIENTS | SERVES 4

4 large carrots, peeled and grated

2 tablespoons butter

½ teaspoon salt

½ teaspoon freshly grated nutmeg

2 tablespoons sugar

1 teaspoon vanilla

1 cup milk

3 eggs, beaten

1. Add the carrots and butter to a large glass microwavable bowl. Cook on high for 3–4 minutes until the carrots are slightly softened.

2. Stir in the remaining ingredients and pour into a greased 2.5-quart slow cooker. Cook on high for 3 hours or on low for 6 hours. Serve hot or cold.

Per serving: Calories: 200 | Fat: 12 g | Protein: 7.5 g | Sodium: 424 mg | Fiber: 2 g | Carbohydrates: 17 g | Sugar: 13.5 g | GI: Moderate

Butternut Squash with Walnuts and Vanilla

Butternut squash has a very mild, slightly sweet flavor. Often people who don't like sweet potatoes enjoy this alternative side dish. Many grocery stores now sell butternut squash that has been peeled and cut into cubes, which can make meal preparation a breeze.

INGREDIENTS | SERVES 4

1 butternut squash (about 2 pounds), peeled, seeds removed, and cut into 1" cubes

½ cup water

½ cup brown sugar

1 cup chopped walnuts

1 teaspoon cinnamon

4 tablespoons butter

2 teaspoons grated ginger

1 teaspoon vanilla

1. Grease a 4-quart slow cooker with nonstick cooking spray. Add the cubed butternut squash and water to the slow cooker.

2. In a small bowl, mix the brown sugar, walnuts, cinnamon, butter, ginger, and vanilla. Sprinkle this mixture evenly over the squash.

3. Cook on high for 4 hours or on low for 6–8 hours, or until the butternut squash is fork-tender.

Per serving: Calories: 468 | Fat: 30 g | Protein: 6 g | Sodium: 16 mg | Fiber: 5 g | Carbohydrates: 48 g | Sugar: 30 g | GI: Moderate

Sweet Potato Gratin with Leeks and Onions

The combination of sweet and savory makes this a fascinating, unique, delicious dish.

INGREDIENTS | SERVES 6

2 leeks, white part only, rinsed and chopped

2 large sweet onions, peeled and finely chopped

2 stalks celery with tops, finely chopped

4 tablespoons olive oil

4 medium sweet potatoes, peeled and sliced thinly

1 teaspoon dried thyme

1 teaspoon salt

½ teaspoon ground black pepper

3 cups milk

1½ cups gluten-free corn-bread crumbs

2 tablespoons butter or margarine, cut in small pieces

Instead of . . .

Instead of gluten-free corn bread, you can use crushed corn tortillas as a topping. Several brands such as Utz and Food Should Taste Good actually list "This is a gluten-free food" on some of their products. If you have any questions about a product, call the company to ask about their gluten cross-contamination prevention policies.

1. In a skillet over medium heat, add the leeks, onions, celery, and olive oil. Sauté for 3–5 minutes, until softened.

2. Grease a 4-quart slow cooker with nonstick cooking spray.

3. Layer the sweet potato slices in the slow cooker with the sautéed vegetables. Sprinkle the thyme, salt, and pepper on each layer as you go along. Finish with a layer of potatoes.

4. Add the milk until it meets the top layer of potatoes. Then add the corn-bread crumbs. Dot with the butter or margarine.

5. Cover and cook on high for 4 hours or on low for 8 hours, until the potatoes are fork-tender. In the last hour of cooking, vent the lid of the slow cooker with a chopstick or wooden spoon handle to allow excess condensation to escape.

Per serving: Calories: 405 | Fat: 18.5 g | Protein: 10 g | Sodium: 710 mg | Fiber: 5 g | Carbohydrates: 51 g | Sugar: 14.5 g | GI: Moderate

Slow-Cooked Collard Greens

This is a Southern staple that goes perfectly with barbecue chicken or ribs.

1 meaty smoked ham hock, rinsed

1 large carrot, peeled and chopped

1 large onion, peeled and chopped

1 (1-pound) package fresh chopped collard greens, with tough stems removed

1 teaspoon minced garlic

½ teaspoon crushed red pepper

¼ teaspoon ground black pepper

6 cups gluten-free chicken broth

1 cup water

Make It Vegetarian

If you prefer, you can make these hearty greens without the ham hock. Simply leave it out, use vegetable broth instead of chicken broth, and add 1 (15-ounce) can of diced tomatoes (or your favorite salsa) and a few tablespoons of olive oil. Cook as directed and serve with the vegetable broth ladled over each serving.

1. Place the ham hock, carrots, and onions in a 6-quart slow cooker.

2. Add the collard greens. Sprinkle the greens with the garlic, red pepper, and black pepper.

3. Pour the broth and water over the collard greens.

4. Cover and cook on low for 8 hours. To serve, remove the greens to a serving bowl. Remove the meat from the ham hock and discard the fat and bones. Chop the meat and add it to the greens. Ladle 1–2 cups broth over the greens.

Per serving: Calories: 193 | Fat: 7.5 g | Protein: 17.5 g | Sodium: 1,580 mg | Fiber: 2.5 g | Carbohydrates: 14.5 g | Sugar: 1.2 g | GI: Low

Harvard Beets

Beets are richly flavored, beautiful vegetables to serve at the dinner table. For those unaccustomed to their taste, this sweet-and-sour recipe is a good place to start.

INGREDIENTS | SERVES 6

½ cup sugar

1 tablespoon cornstarch

¼ cup water

¼ cup white vinegar

¼ teaspoon ground cloves

2 (14-ounce) cans sliced or whole beets, drained (or 4 cups peeled and sliced fresh beets)

1. Grease a 2.5-quart slow cooker with nonstick cooking spray.

2. Add sugar, cornstarch, water, vinegar, and cloves to the slow cooker and whisk them. Add the drained beets.

3. Cover and cook on high for 3 hours. Serve hot or cold.

Per serving: Calories: 80 | Fat: 0 g | Protein: 1 g | Sodium: 254 mg | Fiber: 2 g | Carbohydrates: 19 g | Sugar: 15 g | GI: Moderate

Beets and Football

The origins of Harvard Beets is uncertain, but beets cooked in a sugar and vinegar solution have been eaten for hundreds of years in many different countries. The addition of cornstarch as a thickening agent is unique to America, specifically the Northeast. One theory behind the name "Harvard Beets" is that the beets shared a similar color to Harvard's football team jerseys.

Sweet-and-Sour Red Cabbage

Cabbage is often overlooked, which is unfortunate considering how nutritious it is. The tart apples, sugar, and apple cider vinegar give the cabbage a tangy pickled flavor. Try this recipe as a side to roast pork.

INGREDIENTS | SERVES 6

1 large head red cabbage, sliced

2 medium onions, chopped

6 small tart apples, cored and quartered, and peeled (if preferred)

2 teaspoons salt

1 cup hot water

1 cup apple juice

⅓ cup sugar

⅔ cup apple cider vinegar

½ teaspoon caraway seeds

6 tablespoons butter, melted

1. Place the cabbage, onions, apples, and salt into a greased 4-quart slow cooker.

2. In a bowl, whisk the water, apple juice, sugar, vinegar, and caraway seeds. Pour over the cabbage.

3. Drizzle the butter over everything and cover the slow cooker. Cook on high for 3–4 hours or on low for 6–8 hours. Stir well before serving.

Per serving: Calories: 300 | Fat: 12 g | Protein: 3 g | Sodium: 793 mg | Fiber: 6.5 g | Carbohydrates: 49 g | Sugar: 38 g | GI: Moderate

Stuffed Tomatoes

A vegetarian lunch option that is packed with flavor.

INGREDIENTS | SERVES 3

3 large beefsteak tomatoes

6 small button mushrooms, sliced

4 cloves garlic, minced

6 pieces sun-dried tomatoes, chopped

1 teaspoon ground black pepper

½ teaspoon paprika

1 teaspoon thyme

8 leaves fresh basil, torn

1. Preheat the oven to 350°F.

2. Hollow out the tomatoes, reserving the tomato pulp. Place the tomatoes in a small baking dish.

3. Mix the tomato pulp with the mushrooms, garlic, sun-dried tomatoes, pepper, paprika, thyme, and basil.

4. Fill the tomatoes with the mixture and bake for 25 minutes.

Per serving: Calories: 116 | Fat: 2.5 | Protein: 7.5 g | Sodium: 162 mg | Fiber: 5.5 g | Carbohydrate: 23 g | Sugar: 2 g | GI: Low

Fingerling Potatoes with Herb Vinaigrette

Fingerling potatoes are small new potatoes. It's fun to use fingerling potatoes, because often they are small enough that they do not have to be chopped or diced. This dish is also delicious served cold as a potato salad.

INGREDIENTS | SERVES 4

2 pounds red or yellow fingerling potatoes, scrubbed

1 teaspoon salt

¼ cup lemon juice

⅓ cup extra-virgin olive oil

1 small shallot, minced (about 2 tablespoons)

1½ teaspoons minced fresh thyme leaves

1 tablespoon minced fresh basil leaves

1 tablespoon minced fresh oregano leaves

½ teaspoon Dijon mustard

1 teaspoon sugar

1. Place the potatoes in a medium pot and cover with cold water. Bring to a boil and add salt to the water. Cook the potatoes for 6–8 minutes until fork-tender.

2. Drain the potatoes and place them in a greased 4-quart slow cooker.

3. In a small bowl, whisk the lemon juice, olive oil, shallot, thyme, basil, oregano, mustard, and sugar. Drizzle the vinaigrette over the potatoes.

4. Cook on low for 4 hours or on high for 2 hours.

Per serving: Calories: 329 | Fat: 18 g | Protein: 4 g | Sodium: 615 mg | Fiber: 6 g | Carbohydrates: 39 g | Sugar: 4 g | GI: Moderate

CHAPTER 7

Vegetarian and Vegan Main Dishes

Vegetable Stew with Cornmeal Dumplings

The naturally gluten-free cornmeal dumplings perfectly complement the fall vegetables in this hearty stew, making it a complete meal in one pot.

INGREDIENTS | SERVES 6

1 teaspoon olive oil

3 russet potatoes, peeled and diced

3 medium carrots, peeled and cut into ½" chunks

2 stalks celery, diced

1 medium onion, peeled and diced

2 rutabagas or turnips, peeled and diced

1 cup cauliflower florets

2 quarts low sodium vegetable stock or Basic Vegetable Stock (see Chapter 11)

1 tablespoon fresh thyme

1 tablespoon fresh parsley

⅔ cup water

2 tablespoons canola oil

½ cup cornmeal

2 teaspoons baking powder

½ teaspoon salt

1. Heat the olive oil in a nonstick skillet over medium heat. Add all of the vegetables. Sauté until the onions are soft and translucent, about 3–5 minutes. Add to a 4-quart slow cooker.

2. Add the stock, thyme, and parsley. Stir. Cook for 4–6 hours on high or 8 hours on low until the vegetables are fork-tender. Stir.

3. In a medium bowl, mix the water, oil, cornmeal, baking powder, and salt. Drop in ¼-cup mounds in a single layer on top of the stew. Cover and cook on high for 20 minutes without lifting the lid. The dumplings will look fluffy and light when fully cooked.

Per serving: Calories: 204 | Fat: 6 g | Protein: 4 g | Sodium: 436 mg | Fiber: 5.5 g | Carbohydrates: 35 g | Sugar: 6 g | GI: Moderate

Herbivore Versus Omnivore

To make this a nonvegetarian meal, use beef stock instead of vegetable broth and add 1 pound of diced, browned stew beef to the vegetables.

Cheese Soufflé

This recipe is a wonderful way to use up bits of cheese that are in your refrigerator or left over from a dinner party. Plus, it is an excellent dish for lunch or supper.

INGREDIENTS | SERVES 2

2 tablespoons butter

¼ cup Parmesan

2 shallots, minced

1 tablespoon brown rice flour

Salt and pepper, to taste

⅛ teaspoon nutmeg

⅛ teaspoon cayenne pepper

½ cup 2% milk, warmed

¾ cup grated Cheddar cheese (you may substitute or add blue, Gorgonzola, or Gruyère)

3 egg yolks

4 egg whites, beaten stiff

1. Preheat the oven to 375°F. Prepare two 2-cup individual soufflé dishes by using 1 tablespoon of butter for greasing the insides and then sprinkling the Parmesan around the bottom and up the sides.

2. Melt the remaining tablespoon of the butter in a frying pan and mix in the shallots. Cook for 3 minutes over medium high heat; then stir in the brown rice flour and seasonings. Cook and stir until well blended, an additional 2 minutes. Whisk in the warm milk. Continue to whisk and stir until very thick.

3. Remove from the heat and stir in the cheese. Beat the egg yolks and add 1 tablespoon of the hot cheese mixture into the yolks; then whisk in the rest. Fold in the beaten egg whites. Pour into the soufflé dishes.

4. Bake for 20 minutes or until brown and puffed. Serve immediately.

Per serving: Calories: 580 | Fat: 42 g | Protein: 40 g | Sodium: 2,189 mg | Fiber: 0 g | Carbohydrates: 8 g | Sugar: 4.5 g | GI: Very low

Cheese Fondue with Crudités

This is an interactive party dish. Use fresh raw vegetables such as broccoli, cauliflower, peppers, zucchini, onion wedges—whatever you like! You can poach the broccoli and cauliflower for easy chewing. Kirsch is a German brandy made from cherries.

INGREDIENTS | SERVES 2

1 clove garlic
⅔ cup dry white wine
½ pound Gruyère cheese, grated
1 tablespoon kirsch brandy
⅛ teaspoon nutmeg
Salt and pepper, to taste
A variety of your favorite vegetables

1. Mash the garlic into a paste. In a chafing dish or large flameproof casserole, whisk together the wine and garlic and cook over medium-high heat for about 3 minutes.

2. Add the cheese, a handful at a time, stirring constantly. When all of the cheese is melted, stir in the kirsch, nutmeg, salt, and pepper.

3. Serve with individual skewers to spear the vegetables and dip them in the fondue.

Per serving (fondue only): Calories: 545 | Fat: 36 g | Protein: 33 g | Sodium: 1,510 mg | Fiber: 0 g | Carbohydrates: 3 g | Sugar: 1 g | GI: Very low

Mediterranean Chickpea Bake

This flavorful dish can be enjoyed as a side dish or as a main course.

INGREDIENTS | SERVES 4

5 tablespoons olive oil
1 large onion, finely chopped
4 cloves garlic, minced
1 large tomato, chopped
2 teaspoons ground cumin
1 teaspoon paprika
2 large bunches fresh spinach, washed
2 cups cooked chickpeas
Salt and pepper, to taste

1. Heat the olive oil in a medium frying pan on medium.

2. Fry the onion and garlic for 2–3 minutes, until the onion starts to become translucent; then add the tomato, cumin, and paprika. Continue cooking for 5 minutes.

3. Add the spinach and chickpeas to the pan.

4. Reduce the heat and cover with a lid. Cook, stirring frequently, until the spinach is wilted and the chickpeas are tender. Add salt and pepper to taste.

Per serving: Calories: 352 | Fat: 20 g | Protein: 13 g | Sodium: 587 mg | Fiber: 9 g | Carbohydrates: 35 g | Sugar: 5 g | GI: Low

Mini Veggie Burgers

These are quite good and easy to make.

INGREDIENTS | SERVES 4

1 (13-ounce) can red kidney beans, drained and rinsed

½ cup dried gluten-free bread crumbs or crushed tortilla chips (more if beans are very wet)

½ cup chopped red onion

2 tablespoons barbecue sauce

1 egg

1 teaspoon oregano, rosemary, thyme, basil, or sage

Salt and pepper, to taste

½ cup cooked brown rice

2 tablespoons olive oil

1. Pulse all the ingredients, except for the rice and canola oil, in the food processor or blender. Turn into a medium bowl.

2. Add the brown rice to the bean mixture.

3. Form the mixture into mini burgers. Heat oil to 300°F and fry the burgers until they are very hot. Serve on gluten-free rolls or over a bed of chopped romaine lettuce.

Per serving: Calories: 251 | Fat: 10 g | Protein: 11 g | Sodium: 1,689 mg | Fiber: 8 g | Carbohydrates: 34 g | Sugar: 4 g | GI: Very low

The Praises of Brown Rice

Unlike white rice, which is rice with its outer layers removed, brown rice has lost only the hard outer hull of the grain by the time it gets to the store. As a result, brown rice contains many more nutrients than its more processed relative. Also, the fiber in brown rice decreases your risk for colon cancer and helps lower cholesterol!

Baked Ricotta Casserole with Hot Peppers and Vegetables

This is a very tasty way to get your children to consume the calcium they need.

INGREDIENTS | SERVES 4

1 tablespoon olive oil

½ cup chopped red onion

1 medium zucchini, chopped

1 medium carrot, peeled and grated

2 jalapeños, seeded and minced

2 beaten eggs

1 pound ricotta

2 tablespoons grated Parmesan

1 teaspoon dried oregano

½ cup fresh basil

½ teaspoon salt

½ teaspoon pepper

1 cup tomato sauce

1 tablespoon capers or green peppercorns

1. Heat the olive oil in a nonstick frying pan over medium heat. Sauté the onion, zucchini, carrots, and peppers in olive oil for 5 minutes. Preheat the oven to 350°F.

2. Mix the beaten eggs with the cheeses, herbs, salt, and pepper. Stir in the vegetables. Prepare a gratin pan with nonstick spray. Add the cheese and vegetables. Spread the top with tomato sauce and bake for 30 minutes. Garnish with capers.

Per serving: Calories: 316 | Fat: 21 g | Protein: 19 g | Sodium: 906 mg | Fiber: 3 g | Carbohydrates: 13 g | Sugar: 6 g | GI: Low

Cutting Down on Salt

Ricotta has a naturally high salt content, so you may want to keep that in mind when adding additional salt for flavoring.

Winter Root Vegetable Soufflé

This recipe puts to good use all of the wonderful root vegetables available in the winter and provides an alternative to simply mashing them with butter.

INGREDIENTS | SERVES 4

1 teaspoon salt

½ large Vidalia onion, peeled and cut into big chunks

2 medium carrots, peeled and chopped

2 medium parsnips, peeled and chopped

2 baby turnips, peeled and cut into pieces

4 eggs, separated, whites reserved

1 teaspoon dried sage

2 tablespoons chopped fresh parsley

1 tablespoon brown rice flour or almond flour

½ teaspoon Tabasco, or to taste

½ cup 2% milk

Soufflé Tip

It's okay to have a soufflé flop, especially in the case of cheese and vegetable soufflés. A dessert soufflé should never fall. If, as directed, you start the soufflé with the oven at 400°F and then reduce the temperature, you are more likely to produce a high soufflé!

1. Set the oven to 400°F. Add the salt to a pot of cold water; place the cleaned vegetables in the pot and cover it. Bring to a boil, reduce the heat, and simmer until the vegetables are very tender when pierced with a fork.

2. Drain and cool slightly. Place the vegetables in the blender and purée. With the blender running on medium speed, add the egg yolks, one at a time. Then add the sage, parsley, flour, Tabasco, and milk. Pour into a bowl.

3. Prepare a 2-quart soufflé dish with nonstick spray. Beat the egg whites until stiff. Fold the egg whites into the purée. Coat a soufflé dish with nonstick spray. Pour into the soufflé dish.

4. Bake the soufflé for 20 minutes at 400°F. Reduce the heat to 350°F and bake for 20 minutes more. Don't worry if your soufflé flops just before serving, it will still be light and delicious.

Per serving: Calories: 189 | Fat: 6 g | Protein: 9 g | Sodium: 704 mg | Fiber: 6 g | Carbohydrates: 25 g | Sugar: 10 g | GI: Moderate

Eggplant Soufflé

Smooth and creamy in texture, this is an Indian favorite. Oftentimes the eggplant is simply puréed and spiced—this is more of a fusion dish.

INGREDIENTS | SERVES 4

1 large or 2 medium eggplants
1–2 teaspoons water
1 tablespoon peanut oil
2 cloves garlic, minced
1 small white onion, minced
4 eggs, separated
Salt and pepper, to taste
1 teaspoon curry powder, or to taste

1. Preheat the oven to 400°F.

2. Wrap the eggplant in aluminum foil packages with 1 teaspoon water added to each. Roast the eggplant for 1 hour, or until very soft when pricked with a fork. Cool, cut in half, scoop out the flesh, and discard the skin.

3. Heat the peanut oil in a medium frying pan and sauté the garlic and onion on medium until softened, about 8–10 minutes. Mix with the eggplant and purée in the food processor or blender until very smooth. Mix in the egg yolks and pulse, adding salt, pepper, and curry powder. Place in a 1-quart soufflé dish, prepared with nonstick spray.

4. Beat the egg whites until stiff. Fold into the eggplant mixture. Bake until puffed and golden, about 45 minutes.

Per serving: Calories: 126 | Fat: 9 g | Protein: 9 g | Sodium: 596 mg | Fiber: 3 g | Carbohydrates: 13 g | Sugar: 4 g | GI: Low

Pumpkin Risotto

This is a fine main course or a side dish, depending on what else you are serving.

INGREDIENTS | SERVES 4

1 small pumpkin (about 3 pounds)
1 tablespoon butter or margarine
1 cup basmati rice
4 cups vegetable broth
⅛ teaspoon ground cloves
1 teaspoon dried sage or 4 fresh sage leaves, torn
Salt and pepper, to taste

Rice Texture

The rice you use in risotto should give the dish a creamy texture, but be careful not to overcook it. There should also be a firmness to the inside part of the grain of rice.

1. Peel the pumpkin and remove the seeds. Dice the pumpkin to make 2 cups. Melt the butter or margarine in a large flameproof casserole over medium heat. Add the rice and stir to coat. Mix in the pumpkin.

2. Stirring constantly, slowly pour ½ cup of broth into the rice mixture. Continuing to stir, add the cloves, sage, salt, and pepper.

3. When the rice has absorbed the broth, the pot will hiss. Continue to add broth a little at a time, about every 4–5 minutes, until the rice has absorbed all of it. If still dry, add water, as with the broth, a little at a time.

4. Serve hot or at room temperature.

Per serving: Calories: 116 | Fat: 3 g | Protein: 2 g | Sodium: 579 mg | Fiber: 4 g | Carbohydrates: 24 g | Sugar: 4 g | GI: Low

Paleo Spaghetti

This is a great alternative to traditional pasta. Serve with sauce and turkey meatballs for a great Paleolithic take on Nonna's spaghetti and meatball recipe!

INGREDIENTS | SERVES 4

1 large spaghetti squash

Pasta Alternative

Spaghetti squash is a fantastic carbohydrate source for all you pasta addicts out there. This squash looks like spaghetti when the meat is peeled from the skin. It has the relative texture of pasta. And, most important, it is quite filling.

1. Preheat the oven to 350°F.

2. Cut the squash in half lengthwise.

3. Place cut-side down in a baking dish with ¼" water.

4. Cook 30 minutes, turn the squash over, and cook it until it is soft all the way through, approximately 10 minutes.

5. Shred with a fork and serve.

Per serving: Calories: 94 | Fat: 0 g | Protein: 2 g | Sodium: 1.5 mg | Fiber: 0 g | Carbohydrate: 20 g | Sugar: 4 g | GI: Low

Spinach with Baked Eggs and Cheese

This is an excellent brunch, lunch, or supper. Everyone loves it, and even after a tough day, it's easy to put together.

INGREDIENTS | SERVES 4

1½ cups gluten-free cornbread crumbs

3 (10-ounce) packages of frozen spinach, thawed, moisture squeezed out

2 tablespoons butter, melted

½ cup shredded Swiss cheese

½ teaspoon nutmeg

½ teaspoon sea salt

½ ground black pepper

1 cup heavy cream

8 eggs

Herbs and Spices

People often confuse herbs with spices. Herbs are green and are the leaves of plants—the only herb (in Western cooking) that is a flower is lavender. Frequently used herbs include parsley, basil, oregano, thyme, rosemary, and mint. Spices are roots, tubers, barks, or berries. These include pepper, cinnamon, nutmeg, all-spice, cumin, turmeric, ginger, cardamom, and coriander.

1. Grease a 4-quart slow cooker with nonstick cooking spray. Sprinkle cornbread crumble on the bottom of the slow cooker.

2. In a medium bowl, mix the spinach, butter, cheese, nutmeg, salt, and pepper together. Stir in the cream. Spread the spinach-cheese mixture on top of the cornbread crumbs.

3. Using the back of a spoon, make 8 depressions in the spinach mixture. Break open the eggs and place one egg in each hole.

4. Cover and cook on low for 3 hours or on high for 1½–2 hours until the yolks are cooked through, but not hard. Serve with gluten-free toast and fresh fruit.

Per serving: Calories: 763 | Fat: 56 g | Protein: 41 g | Sodium: 1,170 mg | Fiber: 1 g | Carbohydrates: 23 g | Sugar: 2 g | GI: Low

"Crustless" Quiche Lorraine

Ham is often quite salty, so take that into consideration when deciding how much salt you add to the egg mixture in this recipe. The gluten-free "crust" is optional; the quiche is just as delicious without it.

INGREDIENTS | SERVES 4

4 slices gluten-free bread, toasted

4 teaspoons butter

2 cups grated Swiss cheese

½ pound cooked ham, cut into cubes

6 large eggs

1 tablespoon mayonnaise

½ teaspoon Dijon mustard

1 cup heavy cream

Salt and freshly ground black pepper, to taste (optional)

Dash of cayenne pepper (optional)

1. Preheat the oven to 350°F. Grease a 2- or 3-quart baking dish with nonstick cooking spray or olive oil.

2. Butter each slice of toast with 1 teaspoon butter. Tear the toast into pieces and arrange the pieces butter-side down in the baking dish to form a "crust."

3. Spread half of the cheese over the toast pieces, and then spread the ham over the cheese, and top the ham layer with the remaining cheese.

4. In a medium bowl, beat the eggs with the mayonnaise, mustard, cream, salt, pepper, and cayenne pepper, if using. Pour the egg mixture on top of the ingredients in the baking dish. Cover with foil and bake for 30–35 minutes until the egg mixture is cooked through. Remove the foil and bake another 5–6 minutes to melt and toast the cheese.

Per serving: Calories: 763 | Fat: 56 g | Protein: 41 g | Sodium: 1,950 mg | Fiber: 1 g | Carbohydrates: 23 g | Sugar: 2 g | GI: Low

Cheddar Baked Hominy

Hominy is a wonderful, naturally gluten-free alternative to wheat pasta. Try it in this variation on macaroni and cheese. Try serving it with steamed mixed vegetables.

INGREDIENTS | SERVES 6

1½ cups milk

2 tablespoons cornstarch

1½ tablespoons butter

2 cups shredded Cheddar cheese, divided

1 (29-ounce) can white or yellow hominy, drained

1 large egg, beaten

½ teaspoon sea salt

1 teaspoon freshly ground black pepper

1 teaspoon garlic

¼ cup gluten-free bread crumbs or crushed tortilla chips

1. Preheat the oven to 350°F. Grease a 2- or 3-quart casserole dish with nonstick cooking spray or olive oil.

2. In a small bowl, whisk the milk and cornstarch.

3. Melt the butter in a medium saucepan over medium heat until sizzling. Add the milk mixture. Whisk constantly for about 5–6 minutes until the mixture thickens.

4. When thickened, add 1¼ cups cheese. Stir together until you have a thick cheesy sauce. Add the hominy and mix thoroughly into the sauce. Add the beaten egg. Stir in the salt, pepper, and garlic.

5. Pour the mixture into the casserole dish and sprinkle the bread crumbs or crushed tortilla chips on top. Bake for 30–35 minutes until casserole is golden brown and the cheese sauce is bubbling along the edges.

6. During the last 10 minutes of baking, sprinkle the remaining cheese on top of casserole.

Per serving: Calories: 255 | Fat: 18 g | Protein: 13 g | Sodium: 502 mg | Fiber: 0 g | Carbohydrates: 9 g | Sugar: 3 g | GI: low

Easy Vegetarian Lasagna with Spinach

You don't need to precook the noodles in this dish. This recipe feeds a crowd, so make it for a family gathering or potluck dinner. Serve with green salad.

INGREDIENTS | SERVES 10

28 ounces fat-free ricotta

10 ounces frozen cut spinach, defrosted and drained

1 large egg

½ cup shredded part-skim mozzarella

8 cups (about 2 jars) marinara sauce

½ pound uncooked gluten-free lasagna noodles

1. Preheat the oven to 350°F. Grease a 9" × 13" baking dish or large casserole dish with nonstick cooking spray or olive oil.

2. In a medium bowl, mix the ricotta, spinach, egg, and mozzarella .

3. Ladle a quarter of the marinara sauce along the bottom of the casserole dish; the bottom should be thoroughly covered in sauce. Add a single layer of lasagna noodles on top of the sauce, breaking the noodles to fit if necessary.

4. Ladle an additional quarter of the sauce over the noodles, covering all of the noodles. Top with half of the cheese mixture, pressing firmly with the back of a spoon to smooth. Add a single layer of lasagna noodles on top of the cheese, breaking the noodles if necessary.

5. Ladle another quarter of the sauce on top of the noodles, and top with the remaining cheese. Press another layer of noodles onto the cheese and top with the remaining sauce. Make sure the noodles are entirely covered in sauce.

6. Place a large sheet of foil over the lasagna and bake for 40–50 minutes until the sauce is bubbly and the noodles are cooked through. Remove the casserole from the oven and allow it to cool for 10–15 minutes before serving.

Per serving: Calories: 287 | Fat: 7 g | Protein: 9 g | Sodium: 850 mg | Fiber: 6.5 g | Carbohydrates: 45 g | Sugar: 18 g | GI: Moderate

Cheesy Toast Casserole

This warm, hearty cheese-filled casserole goes perfectly with Tomato Soup (see recipe in this chapter).

INGREDIENTS | SERVES 4

5 cups gluten-free bread cubes, day-old and toasted

4 large eggs, beaten

1½ cups milk

1 tablespoon Dijon mustard

2½ cups shredded Cheddar cheese, divided

½ teaspoon salt

½ teaspoon ground black pepper

Flavor Variations

Feel free to play with the flavors in this casserole! Here are a few ideas: add 1½ cups of cubed ham or browned ground beef into the entire casserole to make it a more substantial meal. Use stone ground mustard or honey mustard for a different tang. Try using swiss cheese, mozzarella, or even Jarlsberg cheese in place of the cheddar.

1. Preheat the oven to 350°F. Grease a 3-quart casserole dish with nonstick cooking spray or olive oil.

2. In a large bowl, mix the bread cubes, eggs, milk, mustard, and half of the cheese.

3. Pour the mixture into the casserole dish. Top with remaining cheese, salt, and pepper.

4. Bake for 35–40 minutes until casserole is golden-brown. Cool for 5 minutes.

Per serving: Calories: 645 | Fat: 32 g | Protein: 36 g | Sodium: 1,402 mg | Fiber: 2 g | Carbohydrates: 51 g | Sugar: 7 g | GI: Low

Old-Fashioned Sweet Potato Hash Browns

These sweet potato hash browns are likely to become a family favorite. They are easy to make and packed with flavor your entire family will love.

INGREDIENTS | SERVES 6

3 tablespoons coconut oil

3 medium sweet potatoes, peeled and grated

1 tablespoon cinnamon

1. Heat the coconut oil in large sauté pan on medium-high.

2. Cook the sweet potatoes in the hot oil for 7 minutes, stirring often.

3. Once brown, sprinkle the potatoes with cinnamon and serve.

Per serving: Calories: 116 | Fat: 7 g | Protein: 1.5 g | Sodium: 36 mg | Fiber: 2 g | Carbohydrate: 13 g | Sugar: 4 g | GI: Moderate

Gazpacho

Gazpacho is best made the day before so that the flavors will penetrate all the vegetables. It should be served chilled.

INGREDIENTS | SERVES 6

1 (28-ounce) can chopped tomatoes, no salt added

1 green bell pepper, seeded and chopped

3 medium tomatoes, peeled and chopped

1 cucumber, peeled and chopped

1 small onion, peeled and chopped

2 tablespoons olive oil

½ teaspoon ground black pepper

½ teaspoon paprika

¼ teaspoon cayenne pepper

1 teaspoon chopped chives

2 teaspoons chopped parsley

½ clove garlic, minced

4½ teaspoons lemon juice

1. Blend canned tomatoes in the blender until smooth. Pour into a large bowl.

2. Add the remaining ingredients to the bowl.

3. Refrigerate at least 12 hours before serving.

Per serving: Calories: 113 | Fat: 5 g | Protein: 3 g | Sodium: 297 mg | Fiber: 3.5 g | Carbohydrate: 15 g | Sugar: 3 g | GI: Low

Red Beans and Rice

You can add an additional boost to the flavor of this dish by substituting spicy tomato-vegetable juice for the broth or water.

INGREDIENTS | SERVES 6

1 tablespoon olive oil

1 cup converted long-grain rice

1 (15-ounce) can red beans, rinsed and drained

1 (15-ounce) can pinto beans, rinsed and drained

½ teaspoon salt

1 teaspoon Italian seasoning

½ tablespoon dried onion flakes

1 (15-ounce) can diced tomatoes

1¼ cups gluten-free vegetable broth or water

1. Grease a 4-quart slow cooker with nonstick spray. Add the oil and rice; stir to coat the rice in the oil.

2. Add the red beans, pinto beans, salt, Italian seasoning, onion flakes, tomatoes, and vegetable broth or water to the slow cooker. Stir to combine. Cover and cook on low for 6 hours or until the rice is tender.

Per serving: Calories: 442 | Fat: 3.5 g | Protein: 21 g | Sodium: 421.5 mg | Fiber: 18 g | Carbohydrates: 82.5 g | Sugar: 8 g | GI: Moderate

Tomato Soup

Tomato Soup is one of the most famous comfort foods. This recipe is not made with cream or butter, yet has an old fashioned taste you'll love.

INGREDIENTS | SERVES 4

4 cups chopped fresh tomatoes

1 medium onion, sliced

4 whole cloves

2 cups organic, no-salt-added chicken broth

2 tablespoons olive oil

2 tablespoons almond flour

Juice from 1 lime

1. In a stockpot, over medium heat, combine the tomatoes, onion, cloves, and chicken broth.

2. Bring to a boil, and gently boil for about 20 minutes to blend all of the flavors.

3. Remove from the heat and strain into a large bowl. Discard the solids.

4. In the now-empty stockpot, combine the olive oil with the almond flour. Stir until the mixture thickens.

5. Gradually whisk in the tomato mixture to avoid clumps. Add the lime to taste.

Per serving: Calories: 113 | Fat: 7 g | Protein: 4 g | Sodium: 286 mg | Fiber: 2 g | Carbohydrate: 10 g | Sugar: 2 g | GI: Low

Carrot Lemon Soup

This is a great anytime soup and can be served either hot or cold.

1. Peel and dice the carrots and onions. Mince the garlic.

2. Heat the oil in a large stockpot over medium heat and lightly sauté the carrots, onions, and garlic for 3–5 minutes.

3. Add the stock and simmer for approximately 1 hour. Add the ginger, lemon juice, and zest. Season with pepper.

4. Chill and serve with finely chopped scallions as garnish.

Per serving: Calories: 153 | Fat: 7 g | Protein: 3 g | Sodium: 62 mg | Fiber: 5 g | Carbohydrate: 16 g | Sugar: 5 g | GI: Moderate

Lemon Know-How

The thought of lemons may make your cheeks pucker, but it's well worth the powerful dose of cold-fighting vitamin C. The average lemon contains approximately 3 tablespoons of juice. Allow lemons to come to room temperature before squeezing to maximize the amount of juice extracted.

Pumpkin Soup

This is a perfect autumn soup to celebrate the harvest season. If you're short on time or pumpkins are out of season, substitute 1 (15-ounce) can of puréed pumpkin for the fresh pumpkin.

INGREDIENTS | SERVES 6

2 cups large-diced fresh sugar pumpkin, seeds reserved separately

Salt

3 leeks, sliced

1½ teaspoons minced fresh ginger

1 tablespoon olive oil

½ teaspoon grated fresh lemon zest

1 teaspoon fresh lemon juice

2 quarts canned low-sodium vegetable stock or Basic Vegetable Stock (see Chapter 11)

Freshly ground black pepper, to taste

½ teaspoon sea salt

1 tablespoon extra-virgin olive oil, for drizzling

Zesting

If you don't have a zester, you can still easily make lemon zest. Simply use your cheese grater, but be careful to grate only the rind and not the white pith, which tends to be bitter.

1. Preheat the oven to 375°F.

2. Clean the pumpkin seeds thoroughly, place them on a baking sheet, and sprinkle with salt. Roast for approximately 5–8 minutes, until light golden.

3. Place the diced pumpkin in a baking dish with the leeks, ginger, and olive oil; roast for 45 minutes to 1 hour, until cooked al dente.

4. Transfer the cooked pumpkin to a large stockpot and add the zest, juice, stock, and pepper; place over low heat and let simmer for 30–45 minutes.

5. To serve, ladle into serving bowls. Drizzle with extra-virgin olive oil and sprinkle with toasted pumpkin seeds.

Per serving: Calories: 100 | Fat: 4 g | Protein: 3 g | Sodium: 62 mg | Fiber: 1.5 g | Carbohydrate: 10 g | Sugar: 3 g | GI: Moderate

Butternut Squash Soup

This soup is a scrumptious treat on a cool fall day. Warm family and friends with a delightful blend of aroma and flavor.

INGREDIENTS | SERVES 4

1 tablespoon olive oil

1 medium onion, peeled and chopped

1 pound butternut squash, peeled, seeded, and chopped

½ cup flax meal

32 ounces low-sodium chicken broth

1 cup almond milk

½ teaspoon ground cinnamon

¼ teaspoon ground cloves

¼ teaspoon ground nutmeg

1. In a soup pot or Dutch oven, heat olive oil on medium-high. Sauté the onion and butternut squash in oil for 5 minutes.

2. Add the flax meal and chicken broth, and increase heat to high.

3. Bring to a boil, then turn to low, and simmer for 45 minutes.

4. In batches, purée the squash mixture in a blender or food processor and return to the pot.

5. Stir in the almond milk, cinnamon, cloves, and nutmeg.

Per serving: Calories: 182 | Fat: 9 g | Protein: 8.5 g | Sodium: 495 mg | Fiber: 5.5 g | Carbohydrate: 20 g | Sugar: 9 g | GI: Moderate

Cream of Cauliflower Soup

Cauliflower is a fantastic vegetable in Paleolithic diet recipes. Blended cauliflower can be used as a thickener in recipes that normally called for potatoes or root vegetables. Best of all, cauliflower won't spike your insulin levels.

INGREDIENTS | SERVES 4

1 large head cauliflower, chopped

3 stalks celery, chopped

1 medium carrot, peeled and chopped

2 cloves garlic, minced

1 onion, peeled and chopped

2 teaspoons ground cumin

½ teaspoon ground black pepper

1 tablespoon chopped parsley

¼ teaspoon dill

1. In a soup pot or Dutch oven, combine the cauliflower, celery, carrot, garlic, onions, cumin, and pepper.

2. Add enough water to cover the ingredients in the pot. Bring to a boil over high.

3. Reduce heat to low. Simmer about 8 minutes or until the vegetables are tender.

4. Stir in the parsley and dill before serving.

Per serving: Calories: 56 | Fat: 0.5 g | Protein: 3 g | Sodium: 83 mg | Fiber: 5 g | Carbohydrate: 10 g | Sugar: 2 g | GI: Very low

Sautéed Brussels Sprouts

Brussels sprouts will no longer be boring when they are spiced up with bacon and garlic. These are a great appetizer or side dish for any main meal.

INGREDIENTS | SERVES 4

4 cups fresh Brussels sprouts

2 tablespoons olive oil

½ cup minced shallots

½ cup sliced mushrooms

4 cloves garlic, minced

3 ounces uncured, nitrate-free bacon, diced

1. In a large pot add 1 cup of water and steam Brussels sprouts over medium-high until tender, about 10 minutes.

2. Heat the olive oil in a medium frying pan on medium. Sauté the shallots, mushrooms, and garlic until caramelized, approximately 5 minutes. Remove from pan.

3. In the same pan, cook the bacon until crisp.

4. Add the Brussels sprouts mixture to the bacon and cook over medium heat for 5 minutes. Remove from heat and serve.

Per serving: Calories: 141 | Fat: 7.5 g | Protein: 5 g | Sodium: 37 mg | Fiber: 4 g | Carbohydrate: 19 g | Sugar: 5 g | GI: Moderate

Colcannon

A traditional Irish potato and cabbage recipe, this side dish is an incredibly healthful way to include more vitamin-rich leafy green vegetables in your diet.

INGREDIENTS | SERVES 6

2½ pounds russet potatoes (about 4 large), peeled and cut into large chunks

1 teaspoon salt

6 tablespoons butter

3 cups chopped green cabbage (or kale, chard, or other leafy green)

1 cup whole milk

3 green onions, sliced

A Frugal Main Dish

Colcannon is often eaten with boiled ham or Irish bacon and is a staple in some Irish homes. The greens used for the dish are normally kale or cabbage, depending on what's available seasonally. Both of these greens are extremely affordable and healthful food sources and can also be stretched in soups and stews. An old Irish holiday tradition was to serve Colcannon with small gold coins hidden in it.

1. Add the potatoes to a medium pot on the stove. Cover with cold water and add salt. Bring to a boil. Cook the potatoes over medium-high heat until they are fork-tender, about 10–15 minutes. Drain the potatoes and add them to a greased 4-quart slow cooker.

2. Add the butter and chopped greens to the slow cooker. Stir them into the potatoes.

3. Cover and cook on low for 4–5 hours or on high for 2½–3 hours.

4. An hour before serving, stir the milk into the potatoes, and mash the potatoes into the greens with a fork. Sprinkle with green onions about 15 minutes before serving.

Per serving: Calories: 266 | Fat: 13 g | Protein: 5 g | Sodium: 430.5 mg | Fiber: 5.5 g | Carbohydrates: 33.5 g | Sugar: 6 g | GI: Moderate

CHAPTER 8

Chicken and Turkey

Chicken Cacciatore

This classic Italian dish, also called hunter's stew, is cooked slowly until the chicken is falling off the bone.

INGREDIENTS | SERVES 6

3 tablespoons olive oil

1 whole chicken, cut up

1 cup chopped onion

1 cup chopped red bell pepper

3 cloves garlic, minced

2 (15-ounce) cans stewed tomatoes

¾ cup dry white wine

1 tablespoon Italian seasoning

Salt and pepper, to taste

1 bay leaf

3 tablespoons capers

Timesaving Tip

A recipe like this that contains a good amount of liquid and a longer cooking time at a lower temperature turns out well when made in a slow cooker. The slow-cooker technique requires very little active cooking time.

1. Heat the olive oil in a medium frying pan. Brown the chicken thoroughly, about 10 minutes. Remove the chicken from the pan. Add the onion, red bell pepper, and garlic to the hot pan; sauté until onion is tender, about 3–5 minutes.

2. Stir in the tomatoes, wine, Italian seasoning, salt, pepper, and bay leaf. Add the chicken back into the pan with the sauce and bring to a boil.

3. Reduce heat to low, cover, and simmer for 40–45 minutes. Stir in the capers. Remove the bay leaf from the sauce before serving.

Per serving: Calories: 464 | Fat: 32 g | Protein: 25 g | Sodium: 383 mg | Fiber: 3 g | Carbohydrates: 14 g | Sugar: 4 g | GI: Low

Baked Chicken Wings

Cayenne pepper is known for its metabolism-boosting properties. Blended with paprika and garlic, cayenne is sure to kick up the heat in these chicken wings.

INGREDIENTS | SERVES 4

12 chicken wings

3 tablespoons gluten-free soy sauce

½ tablespoon garlic powder

1 teaspoon paprika

1 teaspoon cayenne pepper

2 teaspoons agave nectar

Salt and pepper, to taste

1 tablespoon olive oil

1. Wash the chicken wings and pat dry.

2. Combine the remaining ingredients, except the olive oil, in a bowl. Add the wings and coat with the mixture. Cover and refrigerate for 1–2 hours or overnight.

3. Preheat the oven to 425°F. Cover a baking dish with aluminum foil. Drizzle the foil with olive oil. Place wings in one layer in the baking dish.

4. Bake for 40 minutes or until golden brown. Turn the wings over after 20 minutes to allow even cooking.

Per serving: Calories: 211 | Fat: 14 g | Protein: 18 g | Sodium: 2,199 mg | Fiber: 0 g | Carbohydrates: 3 g | Sugar: 3 g | GI: Very low

Broiled Herb-Crusted Chicken Tenders

Chicken tenders are always popular with kids, but try this recipe for entertaining adults, too. The skewers make the chicken tenders easy and fun for kids to eat with their hands and also make these chicken tenders a convenient appetizer for a party.

INGREDIENTS | SERVES 4

1 pound chicken tenders

¼ cup olive oil

2 teaspoons dried thyme

2 teaspoons dried sage

Salt and pepper, to taste

1. Preheat the broiler to 400°F. Rinse the chicken tenders and pat dry. Mix the olive oil, herbs, salt, and pepper. Dip the chicken tenders in this mixture.

2. Skewer each piece of herbed chicken tender and broil on a baking sheet for 3 minutes per side. Serve with your choice of dipping sauce.

Per serving: Calories: 170 | Fat: 17 g | Protein: 4 g | Sodium: 511 mg | Fiber: 0 g | Carbohydrates: 2 g | Sugar: 0 g | GI: Zero

Chicken Salad

This salad is the perfect lunch made with extra chicken from last night's dinner.

INGREDIENTS | SERVES 4

1 head romaine lettuce

¼ cup red wine vinegar

2 cloves garlic, minced

2 tablespoons Dijon mustard

1 teaspoon dried rosemary

Salt and pepper, to taste

¼ cup olive oil

¼ cup diced carrot

1 medium red bell pepper, seeded and minced

¼ cup sliced radish

2 cups shredded cooked chicken breast

1. Wash the romaine lettuce, remove the core, and chop the leaves into 1" pieces.

2. Combine the vinegar, garlic, mustard, rosemary, salt, and pepper in a small bowl. Whisk the olive oil into the vinegar mixture.

3. Place the romaine, carrot, bell pepper, radish, and chicken in a large bowl. Pour the dressing over the salad and toss to coat.

Per serving: Calories: 281 | Fat: 17 g | Protein: 24 g | Sodium: 532 mg | Fiber: 2 g | Carbohydrates: 9 g | Sugar: 3 g | GI: Low

Not Your Typical Chicken Salad

Using herbs and vegetables brightens up the typical deli-style chicken salad. The purpose of carrots, radishes, bell peppers, and herbs is to bring color to your plate, add crunch, and increase the number of essential vitamins and the amount of fiber.

Marinated Chicken and Brown Rice Salad with Water Chestnuts

Some salads, though not fattening, are still very filling. This is one!

INGREDIENTS | SERVES 4

½ cup red wine vinegar

1 cup low-fat mayonnaise

1 teaspoon Dijon-style mustard

½ teaspoon celery salt

4 (4-ounce) boneless, skinless chicken breasts

2 cups cooked brown rice

4 scallions, chopped

1 medium carrot, peeled and julienned

1 (8-ounce) can water chestnuts, drained and sliced

Salt and pepper, to taste

1 bag mixed greens

1. Mix the red wine vinegar, mayonnaise, mustard, and celery salt in a small bowl. Spread 4 teaspoons of the mixture on the chicken breasts, being careful not to contaminate the dressing with a spoon that touched the chicken.

2. Combine the rest of the dressing with the cooked rice. Mix in the scallions, carrot, water chestnuts, salt, and pepper. Set aside.

3. Grill the chicken for about 4–5 minutes per side on high. Let rest for 5 minutes and slice.

4. Place the mixed greens on serving plates, mound the rice, and decorate with the warm chicken.

Per serving: Calories: 333 | Fat: 21 g | Protein: 5 g | Sodium: 889 mg | Fiber: 3 g | Carbohydrates: 33 g | Sugar: 8 g | GI: Low

What Is a Water Chestnut?

A water chestnut is not a nut at all; it's a tuber. Commonly referred to as a Chinese water chestnut, it gets its name from a resemblance to a chestnut's shape and color. Water chestnuts grow in freshwater ponds, lakes, and slow-running streams in Japan, China, Thailand, and Australia. These tubers add a crunchy texture to stir-fries, salads, and stuffing.

Greek Chicken Paninis

This salad tastes like a Greek salad with chicken stuffed into a sandwich and then pressed in a Panini grill for a quick and easy meal.

INGREDIENTS | SERVES 1

3 ounces boneless, skinless chicken breast, thinly sliced

Salt and pepper, to taste

1 tablespoon olive oil

Juice of 1 lemon

½ teaspoon oregano

2 slices gluten-free bread

2 tablespoons crumbled feta cheese

¼ cup thinly sliced cucumber

¼ cup chopped tomato

¼ cup chopped romaine lettuce

1. Season the chicken with salt and pepper as desired. Add the olive oil to a small frying pan and sauté the chicken over medium heat. While cooking, add lemon juice and oregano to the chicken. Cook until completely done, about 8 minutes.

2. Preheat a Panini press for grilling. Layer chicken, feta cheese, cucumber, tomato, and romaine and place the other piece of gluten-free bread on top. Grill in the Panini press for about 2–3 minutes until bread is hot and toasty.

Per serving: Calories: 480 | Fat: 22 g | Protein: 30 g | Sodium: 1,148 mg | Fiber: 4 | Carbohydrates: 43 g | Sugar: | GI: Moderate

Grilled Chicken Sandwich

Citrus fruit is the perfect marinade. The acids tenderize the chicken while adding a fresh, tangy flavor.

INGREDIENTS | SERVES 1

Juice of 1 orange

Juice of 1 lemon

1 teaspoon olive oil

½ teaspoon lemon pepper

Salt, to taste

1 boneless, skinless chicken breast

1 teaspoon butter

2 slices gluten-free bread or a gluten-free multigrain hamburger bun

1 slice low-fat Swiss cheese

3 leaves romaine lettuce

2 slices tomato

1. Blend orange juice, lemon juice, oil, lemon pepper, and salt in a small dish. Marinate the chicken breast in the citrus blend, covered and refrigerated, for 4–6 hours or overnight.

2. Grill the chicken breast for 10 minutes or until the juices run clear and the chicken is completely cooked. Meanwhile butter each side of bun and place it on the grill, buttered side facing down, to lightly toast.

3. Place the grilled chicken breast, cheese, lettuce, and tomato on the gluten-free bread or gluten-free bun and serve.

Per serving: Calories: 551 | Fat: 22 g | Protein: 61 g | Sodium: 2,432 mg | Fiber: 7 g | Carbohydrates: 27 g | Sugar: 16 g | GI: Low

Chicken Breasts with Orange Glaze and Oranges

This is an excellent way to cook chicken. The flavors complement each other and make a delicious meal.

INGREDIENTS | SERVES 2

2 tablespoons marmalade

2 tablespoons orange juice

1 tablespoon gluten-free soy sauce

1 teaspoon hot pepper sauce

1 teaspoon dried thyme leaves

1 teaspoon ground cardamom

1 tablespoon sesame oil

½ pound bone-in chicken breast, halved, skin removed

1 orange, sliced thinly, skin on

1½ cups cooked brown rice

1. Preheat the oven to 350°F.

2. Mix the marmalade, orange juice, soy sauce, hot pepper sauce, thyme, cardamom, and sesame oil. Paint the mixture on the chicken.

3. Roast the chicken, surrounded by orange slices, on a medium baking pan for 35 minutes. Serve over rice.

Per Serving (excluding rice): Calories: 225 | Fat: 6 g | Protein: 22 g | Sodium: 656 mg | Fiber: 1 g | Carbohydrates: 26 g | Sugar: 7 g | GI: Low

Chicken Breast with Snap Peas and White Beans

The snap peas and white beans add to the protein in this recipe and provide a shot of energy that will last for hours. Aside from being a convenient one-pot meal, this is a delectable dish!

INGREDIENTS | SERVES 2

½ pound boneless, skinless chicken

Salt and pepper, to taste

2 cloves garlic, chopped

1 ounce olive oil

10 fresh scallions, chopped

1 cup snap peas, chopped

1 tablespoon fresh rosemary, or 1 teaspoon dried

4 fresh basil leaves, or 1 teaspoon dried

2 tablespoons dry white vermouth

1 cup canned whole tomatoes, drained

1 (13-ounce) can white beans, drained and rinsed

1 teaspoon red pepper flakes, or to taste

1. Cut the chicken in large chunks; sprinkle with salt and pepper. In a large frying pan, sauté the chicken and garlic in the olive oil over medium heat.

2. Add the scallions and toss with the snap peas; cook for 4 minutes.

3. Stir in the rest of the ingredients; cover and simmer for 10 minutes and serve.

Per serving: Calories: 571 | Fat: 23 g | Protein: 54 g | Sodium: 797 mg | Fiber: 12 g | Carbohydrates: 44 g | Sugar: 5 g | GI: Very low

Poached Mediterranean Chicken with Olives, Tomatoes, and Herbs

Poaching a skinless, boneless chicken breast is a calorie-conscious and practical mode of cooking. The chicken does not dry out as it does when grilled or broiled, and no oil is necessary.

INGREDIENTS | SERVES 2

1 cup low-salt chicken broth

1 large fresh tomato, cored and chopped

4 ounces pearl onions, fresh or frozen

4–6 cloves Roasted Garlic (see sidebar)

10 spicy black olives, such as kalamata or Sicilian

10 green olives, pitted (no pimientos)

½ teaspoon dried, crumbled oregano leaves

1 teaspoon dried, crumbled mint leaves

4 fresh basil leaves, torn

2 (4-ounce) boneless, skinless chicken breasts

Salt and pepper, to taste

½ teaspoon lemon zest

4 sprigs parsley

1. Make the poaching liquid by placing all of the ingredients except for the chicken, salt and pepper, lemon zest, and parsley in a large saucepan. Bring to a boil; reduce heat and simmer for 5 minutes.

2. Add the chicken, salt, and pepper. Simmer for another 8 minutes and add the lemon zest. Sprinkle with parsley and serve.

Per serving: Calories: 330 | Fat: 12 g | Protein: 43 g | Sodium: 1,523 mg | Fiber: 3 g | Carbohydrates: 11 g | Sugar: 4 g | GI: Zero

How to Make Roasted Garlic

You can easily make your own roasted garlic in the oven. Simply cover a small baking sheet with aluminum foil and place 2–4 whole (unpeeled) heads of garlic on the pan. Drizzle 2 tablespoons of olive oil over the garlic and bake at 350°F for about 45 minutes. Allow to cool for 5–10 minutes and then gently squeeze garlic cloves out of the "paper" surrounding them. Use in any recipe called for roasted garlic or even spread on gluten-free toast!

Chicken and Vegetable Frittata

Eggs and chicken make this satisfying meal high in protein and a complete one-pot dish.

INGREDIENTS | SERVES 4

1 teaspoon butter

3 shallots, sliced

2 cloves garlic, minced

Salt and pepper, to taste

8 ounces chicken breast, diced

1 cup broccoli florets

1 cup sliced zucchini

1 cup sliced yellow squash

12 asparagus spears, chopped into 1" pieces

8 eggs

½ cup low-fat milk

¼ cup grated Parmesan cheese

1. Preheat the oven to 350°F. Melt the butter in a small sauté pan over medium heat and sauté the shallots and garlic until soft, about 3 minutes. Be careful not to burn the garlic.

2. Salt and pepper the diced chicken breast as desired. Add the chicken to the pan with the shallots and garlic and sauté until the chicken is cooked, about 10–12 minutes.

3. Grease a round casserole dish. Place all the vegetables and chicken with the shallots in the greased dish.

4. Whisk the eggs, milk, and cheese and pour over the contents in the dish.

5. Bake at 350°F for 20–25 minutes, until the eggs are set but not brown.

Per serving: Calories: 286 | Fat: 14 g | Protein: 32 g | Sodium: 901 mg | Fiber: 5 g | Carbohydrates: 9 g | Sugar: 5 g | GI: Low

Lemon Chicken

A classic citrus chicken with fresh herbs. It has the perfect amount of lemon, so it's not too sour.

INGREDIENTS | SERVES 6

⅓ cup lemon juice

2 tablespoons lemon zest

3 cloves garlic, minced

2 tablespoons chopped fresh thyme

2 tablespoons chopped fresh rosemary

2 tablespoons olive oil

1 teaspoon salt

1 teaspoon fresh ground black pepper

3 pounds bone-in chicken thighs

1. To make the marinade, combine the lemon juice, lemon zest, garlic, thyme, rosemary, olive oil, salt, and pepper in a small bowl. Place the chicken in a large bowl and pour the marinade on top. Let marinate in the refrigerator for 2 hours.

2. Preheat the oven to 425°F. Place the marinated chicken in one layer in a large baking dish. Spoon the leftover marinade over the chicken.

3. Bake until the chicken is completely cooked through, about 50 minutes. The internal temperature will be 175°F.

Per serving: Calories: 254 | Fat: 19 g | Protein: 16 g | Sodium: 308 mg | Fiber: 0 g | Carbohydrates: 4 g | Sugar: 0 g | GI: Very low

Fried Chicken with Cornmeal Crust

Coarsely grated cornmeal makes an excellent crust for fried chicken.

INGREDIENTS | SERVES 4

4 (4-ounce) boneless, skinless chicken breasts

½ cup buttermilk

½ cup coarse cornmeal

1 teaspoon baking powder

½ teaspoon salt

Freshly ground black pepper, to taste

Canola or other oil for frying

1. Soak the chicken in buttermilk for 15 minutes. On a piece of waxed paper, mix the cornmeal, baking powder, salt, and pepper. Coat the chicken with the cornmeal mixture.

2. Cover the bottom of a large frying pan with ½" of oil; heat to 350°F. Fry the chicken for 8–10 minutes per side. Drain on paper towels.

Per serving: Calories: 204 | Fat: 29 g | Protein: 26 g | Sodium: 680 mg | Fiber: 1 g | Carbohydrates: 15 g | Sugar: 2 g | GI: Low

Turkey Meatballs

These baked meatballs are delicious and far less fattening than fried meatballs.
Serve with a flavorful sauce such as a tomato-artichoke sauce.

INGREDIENTS | SERVES 4 (16 MEATBALLS)

2 slices gluten-free bread
½ cup 2% milk
2 eggs
½ cup chili sauce
½ cup chopped yellow onion
2 cloves garlic, minced
1 teaspoon dried oregano
½ teaspoon red pepper flakes
¼ cup finely grated Parmesan
1 pound ground turkey meat
1 cup fine, dry gluten-free bread crumbs

1. Preheat the oven to 325°F.

2. Mix all the ingredients, except the bread crumbs, in the food processor or blender, adding the ingredients one by one.

3. Form the mixture into balls and roll them in the bread crumbs. Bake for 35 minutes; turn once.

4. Serve with a tomato-based sauce, such as the Fresh Tomato Sauce for Steak or Chicken (see Chapter 2).

Per serving: Calories: 476 | Fat: 20 g | Protein: 35 g | Sodium: 599 mg | Fiber: 1 g | Carbohydrates: 45 g | Sugar: 3 g | GI: Very low

Duck Breast with Mushroom Sauce over Wild Rice or Polenta

If you know a mycologist or visit some farmers' markets, you can get wonderful wild mushrooms. Otherwise, use the shiitakes or brown mushrooms available in the supermarket.

INGREDIENTS | SERVES 2

2 boneless, skinless duck breasts

2 tablespoons brown rice flour or almond flour

Salt and pepper, to taste

½ teaspoon thyme

⅛ teaspoon cayenne

½ teaspoon Chinese five-spice powder

2 tablespoons olive oil

1 tablespoon butter

4 shallots

1 cup coarsely chopped wild or exotic mushrooms

½ cup gluten-free chicken broth

2 tablespoons applejack or Calvados (French apple brandy)

1 tablespoon fresh rosemary, or 1 teaspoon dried

1 cup wild rice, prepared to package directions

1. Coat the duck breasts in a mixture of flour, salt, pepper, thyme, cayenne, and five-spice powder. In a large frying pan, heat the canola oil over medium-high and sauté the duck for 4–5 minutes per side to brown.

2. Remove the duck to a warm serving platter.

3. Using the same pan, stir in the butter and shallots. Sauté for 3–4 minutes. Add the mushrooms and toss to coat with butter.

4. Stir in the chicken broth, applejack or Calvados, and rosemary. Return the duck to the pan. Cover and cook for 5 minutes.

5. Serve the duck with mushroom sauce over the wild rice.

Per serving: Calories: 640 | Fat: 29 g | Protein: 36 g | Sodium: 1,279 mg | Fiber: 4 g | Carbohydrates: 51 g | Sugar: 3 g | GI: Moderate

Roast Turkey

The signature main course for a holiday meal or a special family dinner.

INGREDIENTS | SERVES 8

1 (8-pound) turkey
10 cloves garlic, crushed
1 bunch fresh tarragon, chopped
⅓ cup olive oil
Salt and freshly ground black pepper, to taste

1. Heat the oven to 450°F. Place the turkey breast-side down on a large cutting board and remove the backbone. Turn it over and place it breast-side up in a large roasting pan.

2. Arrange the garlic and tarragon under the turkey and in the crevices of the wings and legs. Drizzle the turkey with olive oil and season with salt and pepper.

3. Roast for 20 minutes, remove from the oven, turn the oven down to 400°F, baste the turkey with the juices, and return to the oven.

4. Cook until the internal temperature of the turkey is 165°F–170°F on a meat thermometer, generally about 3–3½ hours for an 8-pound turkey. Let the turkey rest before carving.

Per serving: Calories: 190 | Fat: 10 g | Protein: 24 g | Sodium: 311 mg | Fiber: 0 g | Carbohydrates: 1 g | Sugar: 0 g | GI: Very low

Pulled Chicken

This chicken will melt in your mouth after hours in the slow cooker.

INGREDIENTS | SERVES 8

2 pounds chicken breast

1 (16-ounce) can diced tomatoes

1 cup diced sweet onion

4 medium carrots, peeled and cut into large pieces

2 green onions

4 garlic cloves, cut coarsely

1 tablespoon thyme

1 teaspoon chili powder

Combine all the ingredients in a 4–6 quart slow cooker and cook on high for 5 hours. Reduce heat and serve.

Per serving: Calories: 163 | Fat: 3 g | Protein: 24 g | Sodium: 236 mg | Fiber: 2 g | Carbohydrates: 8 g | Sugar: 4 g | GI: Moderate

Chicken Piccata

Chicken is a staple for the Paleolithic eater. This lunchtime treat is a pleasant departure from the ordinary.

INGREDIENTS | SERVES 4

1 cup gluten-free chicken broth

½ cup lemon juice

4 boneless, skinless chicken breasts

3 tablespoons olive oil

1 cup chopped onion

1 garlic clove, minced

2 cups chopped artichoke hearts

3 tablespoons capers

1 teaspoon ground black pepper

Capers

Capers are salted and should be used only occasionally for a dish such as this one. If you decide not to use them, this dish is still full of flavor and will be a delightful treat for your family.

1. Combine the chicken broth, lemon juice, and chicken in a shallow medium dish. Cover and marinate overnight in the refrigerator.

2. Heat the olive oil in a medium sauté pan and cook the onion and garlic over medium heat until softened, about 2 minutes.

3. Remove the chicken from the marinade, reserving the marinade. Add the chicken to the pan and brown each side, 5–10 minutes.

4. Add the artichoke hearts, capers, pepper, and reserved marinade. Reduce heat and simmer until the chicken is thoroughly cooked, another 10 minutes approximately.

Per serving: Calories: 269 | Fat: 13 g | Protein: 35 g | Sodium: 390 mg | Fiber: 1 g | Carbohydrate: 5 g | Sugar: 1 g | GI: Very low

Chicken Enchiladas

If you have been craving a Mexican feast, try this spicy Paleolithic alternative. This recipe has most of the taste of traditional enchiladas without the carbohydrates.

INGREDIENTS | SERVES 8

2 tablespoons olive oil

2 pounds boneless, skinless chicken breast, cut into 1" cubes

4 cloves garlic, minced

½ cup finely chopped onion

2 cups chopped tomatoes

1 teaspoon ground cumin

1 teaspoon chili powder

½ cup fresh cilantro

Juice from 2 limes

1 (10-ounce) package frozen chopped spinach, thawed and drained

8 collard green leaves

1. Heat the olive oil in a medium skillet over medium-high heat. Sauté chicken, garlic, and onion in the hot oil until thoroughly cooked, about 10 minutes.

2. Add tomatoes, cumin, chili powder, cilantro, and lime juice, and simmer for 5 minutes.

3. Add the spinach and simmer for 5 more minutes. Remove from heat.

4. In a separate large pot pan, quickly steam the collard greens with a little water to soften them, about 3 minutes.

5. Wrap the chicken mixture in the collard greens and serve.

Per serving: Calories: 141 | Fat: 5 g | Protein: 22 g | Sodium: 35 mg | Fiber: 2 g | Carbohydrate: 5 g | Sugar: 3 g | GI: Low

Chicken with Sautéed Tomatoes and Pine Nuts

Sautéed tomatoes and pine nuts add a nice, nutty flavor to an ordinary dish. This topping can be added to fish or beef just as easily.

INGREDIENTS | SERVES 2

¼ cup olive oil
1 cup halved cherry tomatoes
¼ cup chopped green chilies
¼ cup cilantro
½ cup pine nuts
2 boneless, skinless chicken breasts

1. Heat the olive oil in a medium skillet on medium-high. Sauté the tomatoes, chilies, cilantro, and pine nuts until golden brown, about 5 minutes. Set aside.

2. In the same pan, cook the chicken 5 minutes on each side.

3. Return the tomato mixture to the pan and cover it. Simmer on low for 5 minutes until the chicken is fully cooked.

Per serving: Calories: 595 | Fat: 45 g | Protein: 44 g | Sodium: 6.5 mg | Fiber: 2 g | Carbohydrate: 8 g | Sugar: 3 g | GI: Low

Pecan-Crusted Chicken

This pecan crust recipe is quite versatile. It works for fish as well as chicken, and other nuts can be substituted for different flavors.

INGREDIENTS | SERVES 4

1 cup finely chopped pecans
2 large eggs, beaten
4 boneless, skinless chicken breasts

1. Preheat the oven to 350°F.

2. Place the pecans in a small shallow bowl and the eggs in a separate small shallow bowl.

3. Dip each chicken breast into the egg and then into the pecans. Place the coated chicken breasts in a shallow baking dish.

4. Bake for 25 minutes.

Per serving: Calories: 377 | Fat: 24 g | Protein: 40 g | Sodium: 32 mg | Fiber: 3 g | Carbohydrate: 4 g | Sugar: 0 g | GI: Low

Zesty Pecan Chicken and Grape Salad

Coating your chicken with nuts adds a crispy skin to keep the breast inside moist and tender.

INGREDIENTS | SERVES 6

¼ cup chopped pecans

1 teaspoon chili powder

¼ cup olive oil

1½ pounds boneless, skinless chicken breasts

1½ cups white grapes

6 cups salad greens

Toasting Nuts for Fresher Flavor and Crispness

To awaken the natural flavor of the nuts, heat them on the stovetop or in the oven for a few minutes. For the stovetop, spread the nuts in a dry skillet, and heat over a medium flame until their natural oils come to the surface. For the oven, spread the nuts in a single layer on a baking sheet, and toast for 5–10 minutes at 350°F, until the oils are visible. Cool nuts before serving.

1. Preheat the oven to 400°F.

2. In a blender, mix the chopped pecans and chili powder. Pour in the oil while the blender is running. When the mixture is thoroughly combined, pour it into a shallow bowl.

3. Coat the chicken with the pecan mixture and place it on racked baking dish; roast for 40–50 minutes, until the chicken is thoroughly cooked. Remove from the oven, let cool for 5 minutes, and thinly slice.

4. Slice the grapes and tear the greens into bite-size pieces. To serve, fan the chicken over the greens and sprinkle with sliced grapes.

Per serving: Calories: 220 | Fat: 13 g | Protein: 21 g | Sodium: 11 mg | Fiber: 1 g | Carbohydrate: 5.5 g | Sugar: 5 g | GI: Low

Shredded Chicken Wraps

Wraps are a great way to get the feel of a tortilla wrap without the forbidden carbohydrates. You can easily substitute your favorite meat or fish for the chicken to vary your lunchtime menu.

INGREDIENTS | SERVES 8

2 boneless, skinless chicken breasts, cooked (baked, poached, or broiled)

2 celery stalks, chopped

¼ cup chopped basil

2 tablespoons olive oil

2 tablespoons lemon juice

1 teaspoon minced garlic

Ground black pepper, to taste

1 head of radicchio or romaine lettuce

1. Shred or finely chop the chicken and place it in a medium bowl.

2. Mix chicken with celery, basil, olive oil, lemon juice, garlic, and pepper.

3. Separate the lettuce leaves and place on eight plates.

4. Spoon the chicken mixture onto the lettuce leaves and roll them up.

Per serving: Calories: 123 | Fat: 3.5 g | Protein: 9 g | Sodium: 14 mg | Fiber: 0.5 g | Carbohydrate: 1 g | Sugar: 0 g | GI: Very low

Grilled Jerk Chicken

This marinated chicken dish is great to make in large quantities for eating throughout the week. It is a fantastic summer dish to cook outside on the grill.

INGREDIENTS | SERVES 4

5 cloves chopped garlic
1 teaspoon ginger powder
1 teaspoon dried thyme
1 teaspoon ground paprika
1 teaspoon ground cinnamon
½ teaspoon ground allspice
½ cup lemon juice
½ cup red wine
4 boneless, skinless chicken breasts

1. Combine the garlic, ginger, thyme, paprika, cinnamon, allspice, lemon juice, and red wine in a large bowl.

2. Add the chicken and marinate for at least 5 hours in the refrigerator.

3. Prepare a charcoal or gas grill.

4. Remove the chicken from marinade and wrap it in aluminum foil. Discard marinade. Place the foil packets on the preheated grill and cook for 12 minutes over medium-high heat.

5. Remove the chicken from aluminum foil and grill it for an additional 5 minutes.

Per serving: Calories: 161 | Fat: 1.5 g | Protein: 35 g | Sodium: 0.5 mg | Fiber: 0 g | Carbohydrate: 2 g | Sugar: 2 g | GI: Low

Coconut-Crumbed Chicken

This is an easy way to add some flavor and crunch to the chicken (it can be easily adapted to use on firm fish and shrimp). It is also a great way for little kids to enjoy eating with their hands.

INGREDIENTS | SERVES 8

1 cup ground almond meal

2 large eggs

2 teaspoons ground black pepper

1 tablespoon Italian seasoning

1 cup ground unsweetened coconut flakes

½ cup flaxseed meal

16 chicken tenderloins

4 tablespoons coconut oil

1. Pour the almond meal into a small shallow bowl. In another small bowl, whisk the eggs, ground pepper, and Italian seasoning. In a third small bowl, combine the coconut flakes with the flaxseed meal.

2. Coat the chicken pieces with the almond meal.

3. Transfer the chicken to the egg mixture; then coat with the coconut mixture.

4. Heat the coconut oil in a large nonstick skillet over medium-high heat.

5. Pan-fry the tenderloins until cooked through, approximately 5 minutes on each side, depending on the thickness of the chicken.

Per serving: Calories: 323 | Fat: 19 g | Protein: 37 g | Sodium: 21 mg | Fiber: 2 g | Carbohydrate: 4 g | Sugar: 2 g | GI: Low

Ginger-Orange Chicken Breast

This recipe is great chilled, sliced, and served on a crispy green salad.

INGREDIENTS | SERVES 4

4 (5-ounce) boneless, skinless chicken breasts

2 tablespoons olive oil

½ teaspoon seasoned salt

Freshly cracked black pepper, to taste

2 cloves garlic, minced

2 tablespoons grated ginger

2 teaspoons orange zest

½ cup pure orange juice

Working with Chicken

Use fresh boneless, skinless breasts; they're available in the meat section at the local grocery. Use a good reputable brand and check the freshness date.

1. Rinse the chicken under cold running water and pat it dry with paper towels. Heat the olive oil in a small nonstick skillet over medium-high. Season the chicken with salt and pepper. Brown the chicken, turning it once, about 8 minutes per side. Transfer the chicken to a plate and keep warm.

2. Add the garlic to the pan and cook for about 1 minute, stirring frequently to prevent burning. Add the ginger, orange zest, and juice, and bring to a simmer. Add the chicken and any reserved juices and heat through, about 4–5 minutes. Cut through the bottom of the chicken to make sure it is cooked. Adjust seasonings to taste. Serve hot with the sauce.

Per serving: Calories: 240 | Fat: 9.5 g | Protein: 34 g | Sodium: 138 mg | Fiber: 0 g | Carbohydrate: 3 g | Sugar: 3 g | GI: Very low

Spicy Chicken Burgers

You can substitute ground turkey or pork for the chicken. Adjust the quantity of pepper flakes to control the spiciness.

INGREDIENTS | SERVES 4

1 pound ground chicken breast
¼ cup finely chopped yellow onion
¼ cup finely chopped red bell pepper
1 teaspoon minced garlic
¼ cup thinly sliced scallions
½ teaspoon hot pepper flakes
Freshly cracked black pepper, to taste

1. Clean and oil the broiler rack. Preheat the broiler to medium.

2. Combine all the ingredients in a medium bowl, mixing lightly. Broil the burgers for 4–5 minutes per side until they are firm through the center and the juices run clear. Transfer to a plate and tent with tinfoil to keep warm. Allow to rest 1–2 minutes before serving.

Per serving: Calories: 145 | Fat: 3 g | Protein: 27 g | Sodium: 20 mg | Fiber: 0 g | Carbohydrate: 1 g | Sugar: 0 g | GI: Very low

Braised Chicken with Citrus

Lemons, oranges, and grapefruits add a wonderful flavor to chicken. Try it, and use the sauce over rice!

INGREDIENTS | SERVES 2

¼ cup orange juice
¼ cup fresh grapefruit juice
1 tablespoon orange Curaçao, or other liqueur
1 teaspoon dried savory
½ teaspoon lemon zest
1 teaspoon extra-virgin olive oil
½ pound boneless, skinless chicken breasts, cut in chunks
Salt and pepper, to taste

Make a poaching liquid with the orange juice, grapefruit juice, Curaçao, savory, lemon zest, and olive oil. Sprinkle the chicken with salt and pepper. Poach for 10 minutes and serve over rice or chilled in a salad.

Per serving: Calories: 274 | Fat: 10 g | Protein: 40 g | Sodium: 1199 mg | Fiber: 0 g | Carbohydrates: 7 g | Sugar: 6 g | GI: Very low

Indian Tandoori-Style Chicken

Garam masala is a combination of spices used in most Indian cooking. A basic recipe contains coriander, cinnamon, cloves, cardamom, and cumin. Try ½ teaspoon of each as a base, and then make changes to suit your taste.

INGREDIENTS | SERVES 4

4 boneless, skinless chicken breast halves, pounded thin

1 tablespoon garam masala

2 cloves garlic, mashed

1 cup low-fat yogurt

Asian Markets

Don't be afraid to ask the manager or owner of an Asian market about items you find unfamiliar. You'll open yourself to discovering such goodies as premade garam masala, tamarind pulp, lemongrass, and other delicious additions for your cooking.

1. In a large glass pan, marinate the chicken breasts overnight in a mixture of garam masala, garlic, and yogurt.

2. Preheat the oven or grill to 400°F. Broil or grill the chicken for 4 minutes per side. The hot oven recreates the clay oven, or tandoori, used in India to bake meats.

Per serving: Calories: 169 | Fat: 6 g | Protein: 28 g | Sodium: 28 mg | Fiber: 0 g | Carbohydrates: 4 g | Sugar: 4 g | GI: Zero

Grilled San Francisco–Style Chicken

This is a quick chef's delight. It's excellent, and everyone at your table will want to know your recipe.

INGREDIENTS | SERVES 4

1 tablespoon olive oil

1 tablespoon Dijon-style mustard

2 tablespoons raspberry white-wine vinegar

1 small (2½–3 pound) chicken, cut in quarters

Celery salt and pepper, to taste

Olive oil, as needed

1. Heat the grill to 400°F. In a small bowl, mix the olive oil, mustard, and vinegar. Sprinkle the chicken with celery salt and pepper.

2. Paint the skin-side of the chicken with the mustard mixture. Spray a few drops of olive oil on the bone side.

3. Grill the chicken, bone-side to the flame, for 15 minutes. Reduce the heat to 325°F; cover and cook for 15 minutes.

Per serving: Calories: 358 | Fat: 20 g | Protein: 16 g | Sodium: 630 mg | Fiber: 1.5 g | Carbohydrates: 17 g | Sugar: 0.5 g | GI: Very low

Duck Breasts Sautéed with Rum-Raisin Sauce

This is a different and delectable take on two holiday classics. Sweet rum-raisin sauce is often used in desserts—this one is not so sweet.

INGREDIENTS | SERVES 4

2 (8-ounce) boneless, skinless duck breasts

Salt and pepper, to taste

2 tablespoons brown rice flour or almond flour

¼ teaspoon ground nutmeg

¼ teaspoon ground cloves

1 tablespoon extra-virgin olive oil

½ cup chicken broth

2 tablespoons golden rum

½ cup golden raisins (sultanas)

1 teaspoon brown rice flour or almond flour

¼ cup light cream

1. Roll the duck breasts in a mixture of salt, pepper, brown rice or almond flour, nutmeg, and cloves. In a medium frying pan, sauté the duck in olive oil over medium heat until they are brown on both sides. Set aside, covered with aluminum foil on a warm platter.

2. Add the chicken broth and rum to the pan the duck was cooked in. Bring to a boil. Add raisins, salt, pepper, and additional brown rice or almond flour. Turn the heat down and simmer for 5 minutes. Add the cream and pour over the duck breasts.

Per serving: Calories: 234 | Fat: 10 g | Protein: 12 g | Sodium: 1,218 mg | Fiber: 1 g | Carbohydrates: 21 g | Sugar: 10 g | GI: Moderate

Duck? Delicious!

While most people believe duck meat to be extremely fattening, it is actually the skin that is fatty, not the meat. Duck meat is actually very lean when prepared without the skin and contains large amounts of protein and iron.

Poached Chicken with Pears and Herbs

Any seasonal fresh fruit will make a dish very special. If you have some fruit brandy or eau de vie (a clear fruit brandy), a splash will also add to the flavor. Pears go very well with all poultry. Try this for a quick treat and double the recipe for company.

INGREDIENTS | SERVES 2

1 ripe pear, peeled, cored, and cut in chunks

2 shallots, minced

½ cup dry white wine

1 teaspoon dried rosemary or 1 tablespoon fresh

1 teaspoon dried thyme or 1 tablespoon fresh

Salt and pepper, to taste

2½ pounds boneless, skinless chicken breasts

Prepare the poaching liquid by mixing the pear, shallots, wine, rosemary, and thyme and bringing the mixture to a boil in a medium saucepan. Salt and pepper the chicken and add it to the pan. Simmer slowly for 10 minutes. Serve with pears on top of each piece.

Per serving: Calories: 307 | Fat: 9 g | Protein: 41 g | Sodium: 1,102 mg | Fiber: 2 g | Carbohydrates: 15 g | Sugar: 5 g | GI: Very low

Baked Chicken Legs

This is so simple—an everyday baked chicken recipe that requires no fuss or hassle.

INGREDIENTS | SERVES 6

6 chicken legs and thighs
2 tablespoons olive oil, divided
2 tablespoons paprika
1½ tablespoons onion powder
1 teaspoon salt

1. Preheat the oven to 400°F. Rinse and pat dry the chicken. Coat the bottom of a large roasting pan with 1 tablespoon olive oil.

2. Coat the chicken pieces lightly with the remaining olive oil. Cover the chicken evenly with paprika, onion powder, and salt. Place the chicken pieces skin-side up inside the pan.

3. Bake the chicken at 400°F for 30 minutes; then lower the temperature to 350°F and cook for 10–15 minutes. The internal temperature of the chicken thighs should be 185°F.

Per serving: Calories: 355 | Fat: 25 g | Protein: 28 g | Sodium: 383 mg | Fiber: 0 g | Carbohydrates: 1 g | Sugar: 0 g | GI: Very low

Chicken Tagine with Black Olives

This tantalizing one-pot meal is bursting with spices, fresh herbs, and Moroccan flavor.

INGREDIENTS | SERVES 6

4 tablespoons cooking oil

1 large onion, peeled and thinly sliced

2 cloves garlic, minced

¼ teaspoon ground cinnamon

1 teaspoon ground ginger

1 teaspoon ground cumin

2 teaspoons chopped cilantro

½ teaspoon ground black pepper

Pinch cayenne pepper

½ teaspoon sea salt

1 large tomato, chopped

3 cups canned chickpeas, drained and rinsed

½ cup water

1 whole chicken, cut up

1 cup black olives, pitted

1. Add the oil to a large, deep pan over medium-high heat; set lid aside. Add the onion to the hot oil, and cook, stirring occasionally, until tender, about 4–5 minutes. Add the garlic, spices, black and cayenne peppers, and salt as desired. Cook, continuously stirring, for 1 minute. Add the tomato, chickpeas, and water, and bring to a boil.

2. Season the chicken pieces with salt. Place the chicken in the sauce, turn down the heat to medium-low, cover, and simmer. Cook for 35 minutes. Add the olives and continue cooking for 10 more minutes.

Per serving: Calories: 619 | Fat: 40 g | Protein: 30 g | Sodium: 545 mg | Fiber: 6 g | Carbohydrates: 33 g | Sugar: 3 g | GI: Low

Skewered Chicken Satay with Baby Eggplants

This combination of grilled vegetables, chicken, and Asian flavors is delicious and complemented by the easy-to-make peanut dipping sauce.

INGREDIENTS | SERVES 4

12 bamboo skewers, soaked in water for 1 hour

1 pound boneless, skinless chicken breast, cut into bite-size chunks

2 baby eggplants, cut in half lengthwise, unpeeled

¼ cup lemon juice

½ cup gluten-free soy sauce, divided

Salt and pepper, to taste

½ cup creamy peanut butter or almond butter (if following a paleo diet)

1 tablespoon pineapple juice

1 teaspoon Tabasco

1 head romaine lettuce leaves (save small white hearts for salad)

1. Skewer the chicken and eggplants on separate skewers. Mix the lemon juice, ¼ cup of soy sauce, salt, and pepper in a bowl. Brush the mixture on the eggplant halves first, and then on the chicken.

2. Set the grill on medium or use the broiler on high.

3. Make the peanut dipping sauce by mixing the peanut butter, remaining soy sauce, pineapple juice, and Tabasco. If the sauce is too thick, add more pineapple juice.

4. Grill the chicken and eggplants for 4–5 minutes per side, turning frequently.

5. Dip the skewered chicken and eggplant in peanut dipping sauce to serve. Use the lettuce leaves as wraps to prevent burning your hands or getting sticky.

Per serving: Calories: 438 | Fat: 24 g | Protein: 51 g | Sodium: 600 mg | Fiber: 2 g | Carbohydrates: 11 g | Sugar: 3 g | GI: Very low

CHAPTER 9

Beef, Pork, and Lamb

Grass-Fed Lamb Meatballs

Meatballs are always a kid favorite. These grass-fed lamb meatballs are high in good fats that contribute to their taste and their health factor.

INGREDIENTS | SERVES 6

¼ cup pine nuts

4 tablespoons olive oil, divided

1½ pounds ground grass-fed lamb

¼ cup minced garlic

2 tablespoons cumin

1. Over medium-high heat in a medium frying pan, sauté the pine nuts in 2 tablespoons of olive oil for 2 minutes until brown. Remove them from the pan and allow them to cool.

2. In a large bowl, combine the lamb, garlic, cumin, and pine nuts, and form the mixture into meatballs.

3. Add the remaining olive oil to the pan and fry the meatballs until cooked through, about 5–10 minutes, depending on size of meatballs.

Per serving: Calories: 148 | Fat: 13 g | Protein: 5 g | Sodium: 201 mg | Fiber: 2.5 g | Carbohydrate: 6.5 g | Sugar: 1 g | GI: Very low

London Broil with Grilled Vegetables

London broil is a lot cheaper than filet mignon and is still very tasty. You can use meat tenderizer or marinade to add to the flavor. This meal is perfect when cooked on the grill with the veggies on skewers.

INGREDIENTS | SERVES 2

2 tablespoons olive oil

1 teaspoon red wine vinegar

1 tablespoon gluten-free steak sauce

1 teaspoon salt, or to taste

1 teaspoon red pepper flakes, or to taste

4 wooden skewers, presoaked for 30 minutes

1 zucchini, cut into 1" chunks

1 medium orange or yellow bell pepper, seeded and cut into quarters

2 medium sweet onions, peeled and cut into thick chunks

4 cherry tomatoes

½ pound London broil, cut into chunks

1. If planning on grilling immediately, preheat grill to 350°F. (Meat and vegetables can also marinate up to 3 hours before grilling.) In a small bowl, mix the olive oil, vinegar, steak sauce, and seasonings. Skewer the vegetables.

2. Brush the vegetables with the dressing. Toss the London broil in the rest of the dressing to coat and skewer it.

3. Heat grill to 350°F and roast the vegetables and meat to the desired level of doneness, generally about 5–7 minutes per side for medium-rare.

Per serving: Calories: 354 | Fat: 12 g | Protein: 39 g | Sodium: 1,203 mg | Fiber: 3 g | Carbohydrates: 26 g | Sugar: 3 g | GI: Very low

Beef Tenderloin with Chimichurri

This is simple enough to make for a weeknight meal or perfect for a sophisticated gourmet dinner party.

INGREDIENTS | SERVES 2

1 cup parsley
3 cloves garlic
¼ cup capers, drained
2 tablespoons red wine vinegar
1 teaspoon Dijon mustard
2 tablespoons olive oil
Salt and pepper, to taste
2 (5-ounce) beef tenderloins

1. In a small bowl whisk together parsley, garlic, capers, vinegar, mustard, and oil. Season with salt and pepper as desired.

2. Heat grill to 350°F. Grill the steaks to medium-rare, about 4–5 minutes per side. Serve with chimichurri.

Per serving: Calories: 435 | Fat: 30 g | Protein: 37 g | Sodium: 1,299 mg | Fiber: 1 g | Carbohydrates: 4 g | Sugar: 1 g | GI: Very low

Corned Beef and Cabbage

The slow cooker is the secret cooking technique of the busy home cook. It requires little attention, and the meat will come out tender and juicy.

INGREDIENTS | SERVES 10

3 pounds corned beef brisket
3 medium carrots, peeled and cut into 3" pieces
3 medium onions, peeled and quartered
1 cup water
½ small head cabbage, cut into wedges

1. Place the beef, carrots, onions, and water in a slow cooker. Cover and cook on low for 8–10 hours.

2. Add the cabbage to the slow cooker; be sure to submerge the cabbage in liquid. Turn the heat up to high, cover, and cook for up to 2–3 hours.

Per serving: Calories: 300 | Fat: 20 g | Protein: 21 g | Sodium: 129 mg | Fiber: 2 g | Carbohydrates: 7 g | Sugar: 3 g | GI: Low

Pot Roast with Vegetables and Gravy

As a family dinner, this can't be beat. The leftovers can be reheated with gravy and served over noodles or toast for a quick lunch or supper.

INGREDIENTS | SERVES 6

3 pounds beef bottom-round roast, trimmed of fat

2 tablespoons olive oil

4 medium sweet onions, peeled and chopped

4 cloves garlic, chopped

4 medium carrots, peeled and chopped

4 celery stalks, chopped

8 small bluenose turnips, peeled and chopped

1" gingerroot, peeled and minced

1 (13-ounce) can gluten-free beef broth

½ cup dry red wine

Salt and pepper, to taste

1–2 tablespoons brown rice flour or almond flour

1. In a large pot, brown the beef in oil on medium-high and set aside. Add the onion, garlic, carrots, celery, turnips, and gingerroot to the pot and cook, stirring until wilted, about 5–6 minutes. Return the beef to the pot and add the rest of the ingredients. Cover and cook over very low heat for 3 hours.

2. To serve, slice the beef across, not with, the grain. Serve surrounded by vegetables and place the gravy on the side or over the top.

Per serving: Calories: 590 | Fat: 24 g | Protein: 67 g | Sodium: 589 mg | Fiber: 2 g | Carbohydrates: 24 g | Sugar: 8 g | GI: Low

Beef Brisket with Onions and Mushrooms

A roast so packed with flavor it will melt in your mouth.

INGREDIENTS | SERVES 4

2 cloves garlic

½ teaspoon salt, plus more to taste

4 tablespoons olive oil, divided

½ bunch rosemary, chopped

1 pound beef brisket

Freshly ground black pepper, to taste

3 large onions, peeled and quartered

3 cups sliced white mushrooms

3 celery stalks, cut into large chunks

2 cups dry red cooking wine

1 (16-ounce) can whole tomatoes, chopped

2 bay leaves

Kitchen Gadgets

The mortar and pestle was originally used in pharmacies to crush ingredients to make medicines. In the culinary world, the mortar and pestle is a very useful tool for crushing seeds and nuts and making guacamole, pesto, and garlic paste.

1. Preheat the oven to 325°F.

2. Place the garlic, ½ teaspoon salt, 2 tablespoons oil, and chopped rosemary leaves in a mortar or a bowl and using a pestle or the back of a spoon, mash them to make a paste.

3. Season the brisket with salt and pepper. Heat the remaining olive oil in a large frying pan, place the brisket in the pan, and sear it over medium-high to make a dark crust on both sides. Place the brisket in a large roasting pan and spread the rosemary paste on it. Place the onions, mushrooms, and celery around the brisket in the pan. Pour the wine and tomatoes over the top and toss in the bay leaves.

4. Tightly cover the pan with foil and place it in the oven. Bake for about 4 hours, basting with pan juices every 30 minutes, until the beef is very tender.

5. Let the brisket rest for 15 minutes before slicing it across the grain at a slight diagonal. Remove the bay leaves before serving.

Per serving: Calories: 633 | Fat: 39 g | Protein: 25 g | Sodium: 1,548 mg | Fiber: 3 g | Carbohydrates: 26 g | Sugar: 15 g | GI: Low

Greek Meatballs

Buckwheat (it is gluten-free!) instead of bread crumbs is used to keep these meatballs flavorful but still maintain a low-glycemic value.

INGREDIENTS | SERVES 10

1 cup cooked buckwheat or quinoa

2 pounds lean ground beef

1 medium onion, peeled and minced

4 cloves garlic, minced

2 tablespoons Italian seasoning

1 bunch fresh mint leaves, chopped

2 teaspoons white vinegar

2 eggs, beaten

Salt and pepper, to taste

½ cup olive oil

Serving Suggestions

Try serving these Greek meatballs with the Cucumber with Yogurt and Dill Salad in Chapter 5, or with steamed broccoli or asparagus.

1. Preheat oven to 325°F. Mix the buckwheat, beef, onion, garlic, Italian seasoning, mint, vinegar, eggs, salt, and pepper in a bowl. Using your fingers, roll the mixture into meatballs.

2. Heat the oil in a medium frying pan over medium-high. Fry the meatballs in the oil in batches. Use a slotted spoon to move the balls in the oil to brown all sides.

3. Place the cooked meatballs on a paper towel to drain.

4. If the meatballs remain raw in the center, place them on a baking sheet and finished cooking them in a 325°F oven for 15–20 minutes.

Per serving: Calories: 209 | Fat: 6.5 g | Protein: 23 g | Sodium: 313 mg | Fiber: 2 g | Carbohydrates: 13 g | Sugar: 0.5 g | GI: Very low

Beef with Bell Peppers

Choose a variety of red, yellow, orange, and green bell peppers to bring vibrant color to this one-pot dinner.

INGREDIENTS | SERVES 4

1 pound lean beef
4 bell peppers, seeded and chopped
3 cloves garlic, minced
Juice of 2 lemons
1 can chickpeas, drained
4 stalks celery, chopped
3 large shallots, sliced
Salt and pepper, to taste

1. Preheat the oven to 350°F.

2. Cut the beef into cubes. Place all the ingredients in a large casserole dish and bake for 30 minutes.

Per serving: Calories: 358 | Fat: 13 g | Protein: 31 g | Sodium: 1,321 mg | Fiber: 8 g | Carbohydrates: 31 g | Sugar: 2 g | GI: Low

Steak and Mushroom Kabobs

These meaty, juicy kabobs are a hit at summer barbecues. They can also be cooked indoors on a well-seasoned grilling pan.

INGREDIENTS | SERVES 3

1 pound sirloin steak
3 tablespoons olive oil
¼ cup balsamic vinegar
1 tablespoon Worcestershire sauce
½ teaspoon salt
2 cloves garlic, minced
Freshly ground black pepper, to taste
½ pound large white mushrooms

1. Cut the steak into 1½" cubes.

2. Combine the oil, vinegar, Worcestershire sauce, salt, garlic, and pepper to make a marinade.

3. Wash the mushrooms and cut them in half. Place the steak and mushrooms in a shallow bowl with the marinade in the refrigerator for 1–2 hours.

4. Place the mushrooms and steak cubes on separate wooden or metal skewers. Grill at 350°F for about 4 minutes per side for medium-rare steak. You may need additional cooking time for the mushrooms.

Per serving: Calories: 321 | Fat: 17 g | Protein: 25 g | Sodium: 401 mg | Fiber: 2 g | Carbohydrates: 16 g | Sugar: 1 g | GI: Low

Boeuf Bourguignon

A well-known classic French beef stew.

INGREDIENTS | SERVES 8

2 pounds stewing beef, cut into ½" cubes

Salt and pepper, to taste

1 tablespoon olive oil

3 cloves garlic, minced

3 medium onions, peeled and quartered

2 cups red wine

¾ pound carrots, peeled and sliced

¾ pound white mushrooms, sliced

1 bunch fresh rosemary, chopped

1 bunch fresh thyme, chopped

Water, as needed

1. Season the beef with the salt and pepper.

2. Add the olive oil to a large frying pan over medium heat. Place the beef in the pan and brown on the outside. Add the garlic and onions and cook until tender, about 3–5 minutes. Add the red wine, bring it to a boil, and then simmer.

3. Add the carrots, mushrooms, and herbs to the pan. Add two cups of water if you want a thinner stew and to keep the stew's sauce from cooking down. Cook for 3 hours, stirring occasionally.

Per serving: Calories: 383 | Fat: 25 g | Protein: 21 g | Sodium: 302 mg | Fiber: 2 g | Carbohydrates: 14 g | Sugar: 4 g | GI: Low

Roasted Pork Tenderloin

When you have a bit more time and want to prepare a meal for a large family gathering, this is the recipe to use. It serves ten easily and will wow your guests with its flavorful punch.

INGREDIENTS | SERVES 10

2½ pounds pork loin

Juice of 1 large orange

3 tablespoons lime juice

2 tablespoons red wine

10 cloves of garlic, minced

2 tablespoons dried rosemary

1 tablespoon ground black pepper

1. Combine all the ingredients in a shallow dish or large zip-top plastic bag. Refrigerate and marinate the pork for at least 2 hours.

2. Remove the pork from the marinade and bring it to room temperature. Preheat the oven to 350°F.

3. Place the marinated ingredients in a roasting pan and cook for 20–25 minutes, or until the internal temperature reaches 165°F. Allow the pork to rest for 5 minutes before carving.

Per serving: Calories: 218 | Fat: 9.5 g | Protein: 30 g | Sodium: 53 mg | Fiber: 0 g | Carbohydrate: 1 g | Sugar: 1 g | GI: Very low

Tomato-Braised Pork

In this recipe, the pork is gently cooked in tomatoes to yield incredibly tender meat. Try serving the pork and sauce over cooked rice or polenta with a salad on the side. Delicious!

INGREDIENTS | SERVES 4

28 ounces canned crushed tomatoes

3 tablespoons tomato paste

1 cup loosely packed fresh basil

½ teaspoon freshly ground black pepper

½ teaspoon marjoram

1¼ pounds boneless pork roast

1. Place the tomatoes, tomato paste, basil, pepper, and marjoram into a greased 4-quart slow cooker. Stir to create a uniform sauce. Add the pork.

2. Cook on low for 7–8 hours or until the pork easily falls apart when poked with a fork.

Per serving: Calories: 226 | Fat: 5 g | Protein: 34 g | Sodium: 176 mg | Fiber: 3 g | Carbohydrates: 10 g | Sugar: 7 g | GI: Low

Mushroom Pork Medallions

You would never guess this meal is Paleo-approved. It tastes so amazing, you will swear it was deep-fried with flour.

INGREDIENTS | SERVES 2

1 pound pork tenderloin
1 tablespoon olive oil
1 small onion, peeled and sliced
¼ cup sliced fresh mushrooms
1 garlic clove, minced
2 teaspoons flax meal
½ cup gluten-free beef broth
¼ teaspoon dried rosemary, crushed
⅛ teaspoon ground black pepper

1. Slice the tenderloin into ½" thick medallions.

2. In a skillet, heat the olive oil over medium-high. Brown the pork in oil for 2 minutes on each side.

3. Remove the pork from the skillet and set it aside.

4. Add the onion, mushrooms, and garlic to the skillet and sauté for 1 minute.

5. Stir in the flax meal until blended.

6. Gradually stir in the broth, rosemary, and pepper. Bring to a boil; cook and stir for 1 minute or until thickened.

7. Lay the pork medallions on top of the mixture. Reduce the heat, cover, and simmer for 15 minutes or until the meat juices run clear.

Per serving: Calories: 196 | Fat: 11 g | Protein: 16 g | Sodium: 325 mg | Fiber: 1 g | Carbohydrate: 3.5 g | Sugar: 0 g | GI: Very low

Country-Style Pork Ribs

These big, meaty ribs are delicious when properly cooked. If you don't have a smoker, add some wood chips to your grill. If you don't have a grill, use a couple of drops of liquid smoke.

INGREDIENTS | SERVES 4

2½ pounds country-style pork ribs

Salt and pepper, to taste

Garlic powder, to taste

Cayenne pepper, to taste

1 cup water

1 teaspoon liquid smoke

2 tablespoons Worcestershire sauce

1 cup barbecue sauce

Liquid Smoke

Liquid smoke is a flavoring for food used to give a smoky, barbecued flavor without the wood chips. It is most often made out of hickory wood, which the manufacturers burn to capture and condense the smoke. They filter out impurities in the liquid and bottle the rest.

1. Preheat oven to 225°F. Sprinkle the ribs with the salt and pepper, garlic powder, and cayenne pepper. Rub the spices into the meat and bone on both sides. Place the ribs in a turkey roasting pan with the water and liquid smoke on the bottom. Sprinkle with the Worcestershire sauce.

2. Cover the ribs tightly with aluminum foil. Roast them for 4–5 hours. They should be "falling off the bone" tender.

3. Remove the foil and brush the ribs with barbecue sauce. Bake for another 15–20 minutes or until dark brown.

Per serving: Calories: 186 | Fat: 7 g | Protein: 5 g | Sodium: 775 mg | Fiber: 0 g | Carbohydrates: 25 g | Sugar: 4 g | GI: Low

Pan-Fried Pork Chops with Apples

Apple and rosemary pair perfectly with pork chops.

INGREDIENTS | SERVES 4

4 boneless pork loin chops

2 teaspoons olive oil, divided

2 tablespoons chopped fresh rosemary

¼ teaspoon salt

½ teaspoon freshly ground black pepper

1 medium Granny Smith apple, cored and quartered

¼ cup golden raisins

¾ cup red wine

1. Rub pork chops lightly with 1 teaspoon olive oil. In a small bowl, combine the rosemary, salt, and pepper. Rub the mixture evenly on both sides of the pork chops.

2. In a hot skillet, add the remaining oil and cook the apple and raisins over medium heat, stirring, for 4 minutes.

3. Add half the wine, stirring continuously, until the liquid evaporates. Add the remaining wine and cook on medium-low for 15 minutes.

4. Season a large pan with nonstick cooking spray. Cook the pork chops on medium for 6 minutes on each side. Serve the chops with the apple mixture.

Per serving: Calories: 273 | Fat: 6 g | Protein: 35 g | Sodium: 163 mg | Fiber: 2 g | Carbohydrates: 15 g | Sugar: 5 g | GI: Low

Country Ham

A country ham is a beautiful thing! Depending on where they come from, country hams are smoked or salt-cured. Both are improved by soaking.

INGREDIENTS | SERVES 20

10-pound country ham, bone-in

10 bay leaves

1 pound plus ½ cup brown sugar, divided

20 whole cloves, bruised

25 peppercorns, bruised

10 coriander seeds, bruised

2 tablespoons dark mustard

½ teaspoon powdered cloves

1½ cups apple cider

Applesauce (optional)

1. Prepare the ham by removing the skin and most of the fat, leaving ¼" fat.

2. Place the ham in a large container and add water to cover it. Add the bay leaves, 1 pound brown sugar, cloves, peppercorns, and coriander seeds; soak for 30 hours.

3. Preheat the oven to 300°F. Pat the ham dry and place it in a roasting pan. Mix the rest of the brown sugar with the mustard and powdered cloves; spread the mixture on the ham.

4. Bake for 3½ hours, basting with the apple cider. You can degrease the pan juices and use the apple cider as a sauce; otherwise, serve the ham with applesauce.

Per serving (not including apple cider): Calories: 467 | Fat: 19 g | Protein: 41 g | Sodium: 2534 mg | Fiber: 1 g | Carbohydrates: 31 g | Sugar: 23 g | GI: Low

Pork Tenderloin with Caraway Sauerkraut

Caraway, a popular flavor in Scandinavian and Eastern European cooking, is excellent with veal and pork. Tenderloin of pork is lean, moist, and delicious. It is very low in calories and a real treat with the sauerkraut.

INGREDIENTS | SERVES 2

1 teaspoon olive oil

8 ounces pork tenderloin

Salt and pepper, to taste

1 teaspoon brown rice flour or almond flour

2 medium red onions, peeled and chopped

¼ cup gluten-free chicken broth

8 ounces sauerkraut, drained

1 teaspoon caraway seeds

1. Heat the oil in a medium frying pan on medium. Sprinkle the pork tenderloin with the salt, pepper, and brown rice flour or almond flour. Sauté the pork over medium heat for 4 minutes; turn the pork and add the onions.

2. Continue to sauté until the pork is lightly browned on both sides and the onions have softened slightly, about 3–5 minutes.

3. Add the chicken broth, sauerkraut, and caraway seeds. Cover and simmer for 25 minutes. Pork should be pink.

Per serving: Calories: 309 | Fat: 15 g | Protein: 36 g | Sodium: 1,335 mg | Fiber: 2 g | Carbohydrates: 4 g | Sugar: 0 g | GI: Zero

Glazed Lean Pork Shoulder

Over a long cooking time, apples and apple cider form a glaze that is both flavorful and light. Use crisp, in-season apples for the best results.

INGREDIENTS | SERVES 8

3 pounds bone-in pork shoulder, excess fat removed

3 apples, thinly sliced

¼ cup apple cider

1 tablespoon brown sugar

1 teaspoon allspice

½ teaspoon cinnamon

¼ teaspoon nutmeg

Place the pork shoulder into a 4-quart slow cooker. Top with the remaining ingredients. Cook on low for 8 hours. Remove the lid and cook on high for 30 minutes or until the sauce thickens.

Per serving: Calories: 218 | Fat: 5 g | Protein: 31 g | Sodium: 69 mg | Fiber: 1 g | Carbohydrates: 10 g | Sugar: 8 g | GI: Low

Hawaiian Fresh Ham, Roasted with Pineapple and Rum

Fresh ham is basically leg of pork. It is a tender white meat and a great fall or winter dish.

INGREDIENTS | SERVES 10

2 cups pineapple juice

1 cup rum

¼ cup brown sugar, or to taste

½ teaspoon ground cloves

Salt and hot red pepper sauce, to taste

6 pounds fresh ham, some fat (about ¼")

1 fresh pineapple, peeled and cut into chunks

1. Preheat the oven to 350°F. In a medium saucepan, reduce the pineapple juice to 1 cup over high heat. Add the rum, brown sugar, cloves, salt, and red pepper sauce.

2. Score the fat left on the ham with a sharp knife and place the ham in a roasting pan. Baste with the pineapple syrup. Roast the ham for 3 hours, basting often. If the bottom of the pan starts to burn, add water.

3. Surround the ham with the fresh pineapple chunks in the last hour of cooking. If the ham gets too brown, tent it with aluminum foil.

4. Serve with the pan drippings on the side and caramelized pineapple chunks, also on the side.

Per serving: Calories: 608 | Fat: 37 g | Protein: 28 g | Sodium: 1,998 mg | Fiber: 2 g | Carbohydrates: 27 g | Sugar: 17 g | GI: Low

Pork Chops with Balsamic Glaze

Shallots, balsamic vinegar, and agave nectar add a balanced touch of sweetness to this savory dish.

INGREDIENTS | SERVES 4

4 (5-ounce) center-cut pork chops
1 teaspoon salt, divided
Freshly ground black pepper, to taste
2 tablespoons olive oil
6 large shallots, peeled and quartered
½ cup balsamic vinegar
2 teaspoons agave nectar

1. Wash and pat dry the pork chops. Season them with ½ teaspoon salt and pepper.

2. Heat the oil in a large frying pan on medium-high. Add the pork and shallots to the pan. Turn the pork over once, to cook about 3 minutes on each side, and stir the shallots occasionally until tender, about 3 minutes. Transfer the pork to a plate, cover it, and set it aside.

3. Add the vinegar, agave nectar, ½ teaspoon salt, and a pinch of pepper to the shallots in the pan. Cook until the liquid begins to thicken, about 1–2 minutes.

4. Turn the heat down to medium-low, return the pork to the pan, and coat the pork well with the sauce. Cook for 3–4 minutes; a thermometer inserted into pork should read 150°F.

5. Remove the pork from the pan, turn the heat up, and allow the remaining sauce to thicken. Pour the sauce over the pork chops before serving.

Per serving: Calories: 288 | Fat: 12 g | Protein: 30 g | Sodium: 642 mg | Fiber: 0 g | Carbohydrates: 10 g | Sugar: 6 g | GI: Very low

Lamb Shanks with White Beans and Carrots

This is a French bistro and comfort meal that most people find delicious on a cool evening.

INGREDIENTS | SERVES 4

4 lamb shanks, well trimmed

Salt and pepper, to taste

1 tablespoon olive oil

1 large yellow onion, peeled and chopped

4 garlic cloves, minced

1 medium carrot, peeled and cut into chunks

2 tablespoons tomato paste

1 cup dry red wine

1 cup gluten-free chicken broth

2 bay leaves

¼ cup chopped parsley

2 (13-ounce) cans white beans, drained and rinsed

1. Sprinkle the lamb shanks with the salt and pepper. In a large frying pan, brown the lamb in the olive oil, adding the onion, garlic, and carrot over medium high heat. Cook for 5 minutes. Stir in the tomato paste, red wine, chicken broth, bay leaves, and parsley.

2. Cover the pot and simmer for 1 hour. Add the white beans and simmer for another 30 minutes. Remove the bay leaves before serving.

Per serving: Calories: 417 | Fat: 12 g | Protein: 31 g | Sodium: 601 mg | Fiber: 6 g | Carbohydrates: 44 g | Sugar: 3 g | GI: Very low

Not Crazy about Lamb?

When people don't like lamb, it's usually the fat, not the lamb, they dislike. When you prepare roast lamb, stew, or shanks, be sure to remove all of the fat.

Grilled Rib Lamb Chops with Garlic and Citrus

Young lamb is a great party dish and is perfect when cooked medium-rare.

INGREDIENTS | SERVES 2

2 teaspoons olive oil

½ lemon, juice and zest

1 tablespoon grapefruit juice

1–2 cloves garlic, minced

1 teaspoon dried rosemary, or 1 tablespoon fresh

Salt and pepper, to taste

8 baby rib lamb chops, about ½" each, well trimmed

2 tablespoons white vermouth, for basting

1. Using a mortar and pestle, mash the olive oil, lemon juice and zest, grapefruit juice, garlic, rosemary, salt, and pepper.

2. Make sure all the fat is removed from the lamb chops. Coat the lamb chops with the garlic mixture and let rest in the refrigerator for 1 hour.

3. Heat the grill to high. Place the chops over a high flame until they are seared on one side. Baste with the vermouth and turn after 3 minutes. Baste again and reduce the heat. Cover the grill and let the chops roast for 8 minutes.

Per serving: Calories: 513 | Fat: 24 g | Protein: 68 g | Sodium: 1,199 mg | Fiber: 0 g | Carbohydrates: 0 g | Sugar: 0 g | GI: Zero

Grilled Lamb Chops with Garlic, Rosemary, and Thyme

These succulent lamb chops are inspired by the typical flavors of Greek cuisine.

INGREDIENTS | SERVES 2

2 cloves garlic

½ teaspoon salt

1 teaspoon chopped fresh rosemary

1 teaspoon chopped fresh thyme

1 tablespoon olive oil

1 teaspoon minced lemon zest

Pepper, to taste

4 (1¼"-thick) lamb chops

1. Mash the garlic cloves into a paste. Add the salt.

2. In a small bowl, stir the garlic paste, rosemary, thyme, oil, and lemon zest, and add pepper to taste. Rub the herb-garlic paste onto the lamb chops and set them aside to marinate for 15 minutes.

3. Grill the lamb chops for 4–5 minutes on each side for medium-rare.

Per serving: Calories: 287 | Fat: 15 g | Protein: 35 g | Sodium: 521 mg | Fiber: 0 g | Carbohydrates: 1 g | Sugar: 0 g | GI: Very low

Easy Leg of Lamb

Although lamb can be an expensive cut of meat, it is often on sale during the holidays. Stock up on several cuts and freeze them when you find good prices.

INGREDIENTS | SERVES 6

1 (4-pound) leg of lamb, bone-in

5 cloves garlic, skin removed, and cut into spears

2 tablespoons olive oil

1 tablespoon dried rosemary

½ teaspoon salt

½ teaspoon ground black pepper

4 cups low-sodium, gluten-free chicken stock

¼ cup gluten-free soy sauce or red wine

1. Make small incisions evenly in the lamb. Place the garlic spears into the small openings.

2. Rub the olive oil, rosemary, salt, and pepper over the lamb. Place the lamb into a greased 4- or 6-quart slow cooker.

3. Pour the stock and soy sauce (or wine) around the lamb. Cook on high for 4 hours or on low for 8 hours.

4. Serve the roast lamb in bowls. Ladle the sauce from the slow cooker over each serving.

Per serving: Calories: 536 | Fat: 24 g | Protein: 66 g | Sodium: 1,195 mg | Fiber: 1 g | Carbohydrates: 8 g | Sugar: 3 g | GI: Very low

Lamb and Root Vegetable Tagine

This exotic dish is a North African–inspired stew with curried root vegetables and apricots.

INGREDIENTS | SERVES 6

2 pounds leg of lamb, trimmed of fat and cut into bite-size chunks

1 tablespoon olive oil

½ medium onion, peeled and chopped

1 clove garlic, minced

½ teaspoon ground black pepper

½ teaspoon salt

1 cup gluten-free chicken stock

½ pound (about 2 medium) sweet potatoes, peeled and cut into 1" chunks

⅓ cup dried apricots, cut in half

1 teaspoon coriander

1 teaspoon cumin

¼ teaspoon cinnamon

1. In a large skillet, brown the cubed lamb in the olive oil over medium-high heat, approximately 1–2 minutes per side. Add the lamb to a greased 4-quart slow cooker. Cook the onion and garlic in the same skillet over medium-high heat for 3–4 minutes until soft and then add them to the slow cooker.

2. Add the remaining ingredients to the slow cooker. Cook on high for 4 hours or on low for 8 hours.

Per serving: Calories: 304 | Fat: 12 g | Protein: 32 g | Sodium: 371 mg | Fiber: 2 g | Carbohydrates: 15 g | Sugar: 6 g | GI: Low

CHAPTER 10

Fish and Seafood

Thai Coconut Scallops

These scallops cook in 10 minutes and taste as if you were cooking all day.
Great for dinner or for special occasions.

INGREDIENTS | SERVES 4

1 tablespoon olive oil
1 pound large scallops
½ medium onion, peeled and chopped
1 (13.5-ounce) can coconut milk
2 tablespoons hot curry powder
1 teaspoon cumin
¼ cup flaked coconut
8–10 leaves fresh basil, slivered

Health Benefits of Scallops

Scallops are rich in omega-3 fatty acids. Additionally, they are a great source of vitamin B_{12}, potassium, magnesium, and selenium, which has been shown to neutralize free radicals in the body.

1. Heat the olive oil in a medium skillet over medium-high heat.

2. Sauté the scallops and onion in olive oil until browned, 5–8 minutes depending on the thickness of scallops.

3. Add the coconut milk, curry powder, cumin, and coconut.

4. Bring the mixture to a light boil and simmer for 10 minutes.

5. Garnish with the basil.

Per serving: Calories: 148 | Fat: 13 g | Protein: 5 g | Sodium: 201 mg | Fiber: 2.5 g | Carbohydrate: 6.5 g | Sugar: 1 g | GI: Very low

Curried Shrimp with Veggies

This curried shrimp and vegetable dish is quick and easy, but quite authentic-tasting. It is sure to please everyone in your family who is fond of Indian cuisine.

INGREDIENTS | SERVES 4

2 tablespoons olive oil

1 tablespoon green curry powder

1 pound medium or large shrimp, peeled and deveined

1 (12-ounce) bag frozen broccoli florets

4 large carrots, peeled and sliced

1 (8-ounce) can coconut milk

1. In a large skillet over medium heat, warm the olive oil and green curry powder.

2. Add the shrimp, broccoli, carrots, and coconut milk.

3. Cook until all vegetables are tender and the coconut milk cooks down to a thick, pastelike consistency (approximately 15 minutes).

Per serving: Calories: 343 | Fat: 21 g | Protein: 22 g | Sodium: 250 mg | Fiber: 6 g | Carbohydrate: 21 g | Sugar: 4.5 g | GI: Moderate

Steamed King Crab Legs

Shellfish is a healthful, flavorful protein source. It is naturally low in fat and has a nice, sweet taste. It is a great alternative to the usual poultry or beef dish.

INGREDIENTS | SERVES 4

2 tablespoons oil

3 cloves garlic, crushed

1 (1") piece fresh gingerroot, crushed

1 stalk lemongrass, crushed

2 pounds Alaskan king crab legs

1 teaspoon ground black pepper

1. Heat the oil in a large pot on medium-high.

2. Add the garlic, ginger, and lemongrass; cook and stir until brown, about 5 minutes.

3. Add the crab legs and pepper. Cover and cook, tossing occasionally, for 15 minutes.

Per serving: Calories: 208 | Fat: 8 g | Protein: 31 g | Sodium: 1,022 mg | Fiber: 0 g | Carbohydrate: 1 g | Sugar: 0 g | GI: Zero

Tuna Salad with a Kick

Tuna is a great lunch or snack. It is naturally low in fat, low in calories, and flavorful.

INGREDIENTS | SERVES 3

2 (7-ounce) cans chunk light tuna in water

20 green olives, chopped

½ cup chopped green onions

3 tablespoons capers

1 jalapeño, finely chopped

1 medium red bell pepper, seeded and chopped

2 tablespoons olive oil

2 tablespoons red chili flakes

Juice of 3 lemons

Lettuce greens (optional)

1. Mix all the ingredients in a large bowl.

2. Serve the tuna salad chilled alone or over lettuce greens.

Per serving: Calories: 267 | Fat: 15 g | Protein: 30 g | Sodium: 1,072 mg | Fiber: 2 g | Carbohydrate: 4.5 g | Sugar: 4 g | GI: Very low

Quick Meals

Organic, no-salt-added tuna is a staple in the Paleolithic chef's kitchen. You can whip up a quick lunch or dinner on a moment's notice, and you'll get plenty of low-fat protein.

Shrimp Cocktail

Shrimp is another flavorful, low-fat shellfish that is a nice addition to the Paleolithic lifestyle.

INGREDIENTS | SERVES 4

6 tablespoons horseradish root, grated

1 tablespoon raw honey

1 (6-ounce) can organic no-salt-added tomato paste

Juice of 1 lemon

½ teaspoon red pepper flakes

1 pound jumbo cooked shrimp, peeled

In a small bowl, blend the horseradish, honey, tomato paste, lemon juice, and red pepper flakes. Serve immediately with the jumbo shrimp.

Per serving: Calories: 152 | Fat: 2 g | Protein: 19 g | Sodium: 238 mg | Fiber: 3 g | Carbohydrate: 16 g | Sugar: 11 g | GI: Low

Shrimp Facts

Shrimp is a great protein source. A single (4-ounce) serving of shrimp contains 24 grams of protein with less than 1 gram of fat. It contains a high level of selenium, vitamin D, and vitamin B12. Selenium has been linked with cancer-fighting properties and is utilized in DNA repair.

Grilled Lemon-and-Dill Swordfish Steaks

This recipe calls for preparation on the grill, but it could easily be cooked in the oven using the broiler.

INGREDIENTS | SERVES 4

4 (4-ounce) swordfish steaks

1 tablespoon olive oil

1 lemon

4 dill sprigs

1. Lightly coat the swordfish steaks with olive oil.

2. Slice the lemons into rings and place them on top of the swordfish steaks.

3. Place a fresh dill sprig on each swordfish steak.

4. Grill over medium-high heat, about 10 minutes, depending on the thickness of the steak.

Per serving: Calories: 134 | Fat: 6.5 g | Protein: 17 g | Sodium: 77 mg | Fiber: 0 g | Carbohydrate: 0 g | Sugar: 0 g | GI: Zero

Grilled Trout

Cooking the fish inside the foil packets keeps it tender and moist.

INGREDIENTS | SERVES 2

2 whole trout, heads removed, cleaned and butterflied
1 teaspoon ground black pepper
2 cloves garlic, minced
½ teaspoon chopped fresh rosemary
1 teaspoon chopped fresh parsley
6 sprigs fresh rosemary
1 lemon, halved; one half thinly sliced

Oily Fishes

There are many fishes that are good sources of beneficial fatty acids. These fish include trout, sardines, swordfish, whitebait, fresh tuna, anchovies, eel, kipper, mackerel, carp, bloater, smelt, and bluefish. The more variety of fish that you try, the better fatty acid profile you will compile.

1. Place each trout on a square piece of aluminum.

2. Season both sides of trout with pepper, garlic, chopped rosemary, and parsley.

3. Fold the fish closed and top with the rosemary sprigs and a few slices of lemon.

4. Squeeze the lemon half over each fish.

5. Wrap each fish securely inside the sheet of aluminum foil.

6. Grill the packets over medium-high heat for 7 minutes on each side or until the fish is flaky.

Per serving: Calories: 176 | Fat: 8 g | Protein: 25 g | Sodium: 62 mg | Fiber: 0 g | Carbohydrate: 0 g | Sugar: 1 g | GI: Zero

Salmon in Parchment with Baby Brussels Sprouts

Cooking the salmon in parchment paper works to keep the fish from drying out, a common problem when cooking fish in the oven. The paper also helps to contain flavors so they are not cooked off.

INGREDIENTS | SERVES 2

2 (4- to 5-ounce) salmon fillets or steaks

2 tablespoons frozen petite Brussels sprouts

2 cloves garlic, crushed

2 dashes lemon juice

1 tablespoon olive oil

1. Preheat the oven to 425°F.

2. Place each piece of salmon on a 12" circle of parchment paper.

3. Cover each salmon piece with a spoonful of Brussels sprouts, a clove of crushed garlic, a squeeze of lemon juice, and a drizzle of olive oil.

4. Fold the paper over into a packet, and seal the edges by crimping and folding like a pastry. Place the packets on a baking sheet.

5. Bake for 15 minutes, or until the fish flakes easily with a fork.

Per serving: Calories: 189 | Fat: 12 g | Protein: 17 g | Sodium: 39 mg | Fiber: 0.5 g | Carbohydrate: 1.5 g | Sugar: 0 g | GI: Zero

Lemon-Thyme Grilled Swordfish

Thyme is a useful spice that adds flavor without overpowering a dish, and it blends well with other spices.

INGREDIENTS | SERVES 4

4 (4-ounce) swordfish steaks
1 cup water
3 tablespoons fresh lemon juice
1 bay leaf
1 teaspoon dried thyme, crushed

1. Preheat the barbecue grill to 350°F.

2. Place the fish in an aluminum foil wrapping each steak separately.

3. Pour the water and lemon juice over the fish. Add the bay leaf.

4. Sprinkle the thyme over the fish and wrap the foil closed.

5. Cook for 10 minutes, or until the fish flakes easily when tested with a fork and is opaque all the way through.

Per serving: Calories: 107 | Fat: 3.5 g | Protein: 17 g | Sodium: 77 mg | Fiber: 0 g | Carbohydrate: 1 g | Sugar: 0 g | GI: Zero

Haddock Fish Cakes

This familiar fish cake has the fresh flavor of haddock. Serve them with a spicy sauce or a fresh spritz of lemon.

INGREDIENTS | SERVES 6

1 pound haddock
2 medium leeks, trimmed and diced
1 medium red bell pepper, seeded and diced
2 egg whites
Freshly cracked black pepper, to taste
1 tablespoon olive oil

1. Finely shred the raw fish with a fork. Combine all the ingredients except the oil in a medium bowl; mix well. Form the mixture into small oval patties.

2. Heat the oil in a medium sauté pan over medium-high heat. Place the haddock in the pan and loosely cover with the lid; sauté the fish cakes for 4–6 minutes on each side. Drain on a rack covered with paper towels; serve immediately.

Per serving: Calories: 97 | Fat: 3 g | Protein: 13 g | Sodium: 67 mg | Fiber: 1 g | Carbohydrate: 5 g | Sugar: 0 g | GI: Very low

Salmon Skewers

Salmon has a wonderful omega profile, being one of the highest sources of omega-3 fatty acid.

INGREDIENTS | SERVES 4

8 ounces salmon fillet

1 medium red onion, peeled and cut into wedges

2 medium red bell peppers, seeded and cut into 2" squares

12 mushrooms

12 cherry tomatoes

Wild-Caught Versus Farm-Raised Salmon

Salmon is one of the best sources of omega-3 fatty acids, but be sure to purchase wild-caught salmon. Farm-raised salmon is not exposed to the colder water; therefore, their fat reserves are not as robust as wild salmon.

1. Preheat grill to 350°F. Cut the salmon into 1"–2" cubes.

2. Thread all the ingredients on metal skewers, alternating the vegetables and meat.

3. Grill over medium-high heat until vegetables are soft and the salmon is light pink, about 10 minutes, depending on the thickness of the salmon steak.

Per serving: Calories: 107 | Fat: 3.5 g | Protein: 15 g | Sodium: 235 mg | Fiber: 2.5 g | Carbohydrate: 6.5 g | Sugar: 6 g | GI: Low

Citrus-Baked Snapper

Snapper is a tasty fish that absorbs the flavors in the recipe quite nicely.

INGREDIENTS | SERVES 4

1 (3-pound) whole red snapper, cleaned and scaled

3½ tablespoons grated fresh gingerroot

3 green onions, chopped

1 tomato, seeded and diced

¼ cup fresh squeezed orange juice

¼ cup fresh squeezed lime juice

¼ cup fresh squeezed lemon juice

3 thin slices lime

3 thin slices lemon

Snapper and Omega-3

Snapper is not the fish that comes to mind when you're thinking about omega-3, but this cold-water fish does have some beneficial DHA fatty acid packed inside. Those with elevated blood triglycerides will benefit greatly from even small amounts of EPA and DHA, which are different types of very healthy omega-3 fatty acids.

1. Preheat the oven to 350°F.

2. Make three slashes across each side of the fish using a sharp knife. This will keep the fish from curling as it cooks.

3. Place the fish in a large, shallow baking dish or roasting pan.

4. Cover each side of the fish with the ginger, green onions, and tomatoes.

5. Combine the juices and drizzle them over the snapper.

6. Place the lime and lemon slices on top of the fish.

7. Cover the pan with aluminum foil and bake until the flesh is opaque and can be flaked with a fork, about 20 minutes.

Per serving: Calories: 271 | Fat: 3.5 g | Protein: 53 g | Sodium: 166 mg | Fiber: 0.5 g | Carbohydrate: 4 g | Sugar: 3 g | GI: Very low

Mackerel with Tomato and Cucumber Salad

According to the USDA Nutrient Database, mackerel contains 2.3 grams of omega-3 for every 100 grams of fish. That makes mackerel the highest EFA(essential fatty acid)-containing fish.

INGREDIENTS | SERVES 4

15 ounces mackerel fillets, drained

1 clove garlic, crushed

1½ tablespoons flaxseed oil

1 tablespoon chopped fresh basil

½ teaspoon ground black pepper

10 cherry tomatoes, halved

½ cucumber, peeled and diced

1 small onion, peeled and chopped

2 cups mixed lettuce greens

1. Place the mackerel in a medium bowl with the garlic and flaxseed oil.

2. Add the basil and pepper to the mackerel mixture and place in a medium frying pan. Sauté over medium heat for 5–8 minutes each side, or until brown.

3. Cut the cooked mackerel into bite-size pieces and add to a large serving bowl.

4. Stir in the cherry tomatoes, cucumber, onion, and lettuce, and serve.

Per serving: Calories: 235 | Fat: 16 g | Protein: 16 g | Sodium: 82 mg | Fiber: 1 g | Carbohydrate: 3.5 g | Sugar: 1 g | GI: Low

Lime-Poached Flounder

Lime brings out the delicate flavor of the fish and complements the zip of the cilantro.

INGREDIENTS | SERVES 6

¾ cup sliced leek

¼ cup cilantro leaves (reserve stems)

1½ pounds flounder fillets

1¾ cups fish stock

2 tablespoons fresh lime juice

½ teaspoon fresh lime zest

¼ teaspoon ground black pepper

1 cup shredded yellow onion

⅔ cup shredded carrot

⅔ cup shredded celery

2 tablespoons extra-virgin olive oil

Using Frozen Fish

Don't fret if you do not have fresh fish available. Using a quality fish frozen at sea is fine. In fact, sometimes the frozen fish is fresher than the fresh!

1. Place the leek slices and cilantro stems in a large skillet; lay the flounder on top.

2. Add the stock, lime juice, lime zest, and pepper. Turn on the heat and bring the mixture to a simmer, cover, and cook for 7–10 minutes, until the flounder is thoroughly cooked. Remove from heat. Strain off and discard the liquid.

3. To serve, lay the shredded onions, carrots, and celery in separate strips on serving plates. Top with the flounder, drizzle with the extra-virgin olive oil, and sprinkle with the cilantro leaves.

Per serving: Calories: 150 | Fat: 6 g | Protein: 18 g | Sodium: 218 mg | Fiber: 1 g | Carbohydrate: 3.5 g | Sugar: 2 g | GI: Low

Fresh Tuna with Sweet Lemon-Leek Salsa

The tuna can be prepared the night before, refrigerated, and either reheated or served at room temperature.

INGREDIENTS | SERVES 6

Tuna

1½ pounds fresh tuna steaks (cut into 4-ounce portions)

¼–½ teaspoon extra-virgin olive oil

Freshly cracked black pepper, to taste

Salsa

1 teaspoon extra-virgin olive oil

3 fresh leeks (light green and white parts only), thinly sliced

1 tablespoon fresh lemon juice

1 tablespoon honey

Tuna Packs a Punch

Tuna is truly a nutrient-dense food. This fish, rich in omega-3 fatty acids, and has anti-inflammation written all over it with heaps of other valuable disease-fighting nutrients as well. Health authorities are urging consumers to eat fish two times per week to reap the significant health benefits.

1. Preheat the grill to medium-high.

2. Brush each portion of the tuna with the oil and drain on a rack. Season the tuna with the pepper and place on the grill; cook for 3 minutes. Shift the tuna steaks on the grill to form an X grill pattern on the fish; cook 3 more minutes.

3. Turn the steaks over and grill 3 more minutes; then change position again to create the grill pattern. Cook to desired doneness.

4. To make the salsa, heat the oil in a medium-size sauté pan on medium; add the leeks. When the leeks are wilted, about 2–3 minutes, add the lemon juice and honey. Plate each tuna portion with a spoonful of salsa.

Per serving: Calories: 171 | Fat: 5.5 g | Protein: 21 g | Sodium: 43 mg | Fiber: 1 g | Carbohydrate: 9.5 g | Sugar: 4.5 g | GI: Low

Salmon and Broccoli Stir-Fry

*This is a quick and easy supper, in addition to being good for you.
You can blanch the broccoli in advance.*

INGREDIENTS | SERVES 2

½ pound broccoli florets

½ pound salmon fillet, skin removed

1 tablespoon canola oil

1 teaspoon sesame oil

1 teaspoon minced gingerroot

2 slices pickled ginger, chopped

1 clove garlic, minced

1 teaspoon gluten-free hoisin sauce

1 cup brown rice (optional)

5 scallions, chopped

1. Blanch the broccoli in boiling water for 5 minutes; drain.

2. Toss the broccoli and salmon over medium-high heat in a large frying pan with the canola oil and sesame oil. Cook, stirring for 3–4 minutes.

3. Add the gingerroot, pickled ginger, garlic, and hoisin sauce, and serve over rice, garnished with scallions.

Per serving: Calories: 631 | Fat: 19 g | Protein: 32 g | Sodium: 95 mg | Fiber: 7 g | Carbohydrates: 82 g | Sugar: 3 g | GI: Moderate

Food Safety

When preparing a dish that lists fish, sea-food, or poultry as one of the ingredients, be sure to keep the fish, seafood, or chicken ice-cold during preparation to ensure food safety. If you will be doing a lot of handling of the ingredient or if the item will be standing on the counter for a long time, keep a bowl of ice nearby to place the ingredients in while you are tending to other steps of the recipe.

Baked Fillet of Sole with Shrimp Sauce and Artichokes

The varieties of sole are daunting. There's gray, lemon, Dover, and more. When you are buying sole, make sure that it smells like fresh milk. Get whatever is cheapest—it will all taste pretty much the same. All the varieties are delicious when they're fresh!

INGREDIENTS | SERVES 2

5 medium shrimp, cooked

1 shallot, chopped

¼ cup mayonnaise

¼ teaspoon dried dill

2 tablespoons orange juice

1 (9-ounce) package frozen artichoke hearts

2 (6-ounce) sole fillets

Salt and pepper, to taste

4 tablespoons fine, dry gluten-free bread crumbs

Artichokes

Artichokes are thistle-like plants, and the part we eat is actually the immature flower head. There are many varieties, but the type commonly available in the United States (usually in markets November through May) are globe artichokes. The soft heart or center of the artichoke can be eaten raw or cooked, sprinkled with olive oil, salt, and pepper.

1. Preheat the oven to 375°F. Add the shrimp, shallot, mayonnaise, dill, and orange juice to the blender, and pulse. Set the sauce aside.

2. Cook the frozen artichokes according to the directions on the package. Place the sole on a baking sheet prepared with nonstick spray. Sprinkle the fillets with salt and pepper. Arrange the artichokes around the sole. Spoon the sauce over all, and sprinkle with bread crumbs.

3. Bake for 15 minutes, or until the sole is hot and bubbling and the artichokes are crisply browned on top.

Per serving: Calories: 368 | Fat: 13 g | Protein: 43 g | Sodium: 1,200 mg | Fiber: 7.5 g | Carbohydrates: 20 g | Sugar: 3.5 g | GI: Very low

Mahi-Mahi Tacos with Avocado and Fresh Cabbage

These California-style tacos can be prepared with any meaty, mild fish or shrimp.

INGREDIENTS | SERVES 4

1 pound mahi-mahi
Salt and pepper, to taste
1 teaspoon olive oil
1 avocado
4 corn tortillas
2 cups shredded cabbage
2 limes, quartered

1. Season the fish with salt and pepper. Heat the oil in a large frying pan on medium. Once the oil is hot, sauté the fish for about 3–4 minutes on each side. Slice or flake the fish into 1-ounce pieces

2. Slice the avocado in half. Remove the seed and, using a spoon, remove the flesh from the skin. Slice the avocado halves into ½"-thick slices.

3. In a small pan, warm the corn tortillas; cook for about 1 minute on each side.

4. Place one-fourth of the mahi-mahi on each tortilla; top with the avocado and cabbage. Serve with lime wedges.

Per serving: Calories: 251 | Fat: 9 g | Protein: 25 g | Sodium: 889 mg | Fiber: 6 g | Carbohydrates: 21 g | Sugar: 2.5 g | GI: Low

Lemon-Garlic Shrimp and Vegetables

The shrimp will sing in this light stir-fry with hints of sweet and sour flavors.

INGREDIENTS | SERVES 2

2 tablespoons gluten-free soy sauce

1 teaspoon lemon zest

1½ tablespoons lemon juice

½ teaspoon agave nectar

½ cup water

Ground black pepper, to taste

1 celery stalk, sliced

1 cup shredded red cabbage

½ medium red bell pepper, seeded and thinly sliced

3 cloves garlic, chopped

½ cup bean sprouts

1 teaspoon sesame oil

½ pound raw shrimp, peeled and deveined

1. Mix the soy sauce, lemon zest, lemon juice, agave nectar, water, and pepper in a small bowl; set aside.

2. Spray a large frying pan with nonstick cooking spray. Place the pan over medium heat.

3. Add the celery and cabbage to the pan; sauté for 1 minute. Add the bell pepper, garlic, and bean sprouts, and sauté until all vegetables are crisp-tender. Transfer the vegetables to a plate and cover.

4. Add the sesame oil to the pan. Once the oil is hot, place the shrimp in the pan and cook until they are opaque. Return the vegetables to the pan with the cooked shrimp.

5. Pour the soy sauce mixture over the shrimp and vegetables and cook for 3–4 minutes, until the sauce has reduced.

Per serving: Calories: 197 | Fat: 4.5 g | Protein: 26 g | Sodium: 1,094mg | Fiber: 2 g | Carbohydrates: 12 g | Sugar: 4.5 g | GI: Very low

Cod with Tomatoes and Garlic

Cooked tomatoes are an excellent source of lycopene, which has antioxidant properties that are important for eye health.

INGREDIENTS | SERVES 6

2 pounds cod fillet

2 tablespoons olive oil, divided

4 teaspoons salt, divided

1 teaspoon ground black pepper, divided

2 large tomatoes, sliced ¼" thick

2 medium onions, peeled and sliced

3 cloves garlic, minced

2 tablespoons capers

1 tablespoon Italian seasoning

1. Preheat the oven to 400°F.

2. Rinse the cod and pat dry. Season the fish with 1 tablespoon olive oil, 3 teaspoons salt, and ½ teaspoon black pepper. Place it in a glass baking dish.

3. In a medium bowl, combine the tomatoes, onions, garlic, capers, Italian seasoning, 1 tablespoon olive oil, 1 teaspoon salt, and ½ teaspoon black pepper.

4. Place the mixture evenly over the top of the cod. Place the dish in the oven and bake for 20 minutes.

Per serving: Calories: 204 | Fat: 6 g | Protein: 31 g | Sodium: 1,742mg | Fiber: 1.5 g | Carbohydrates: 6 g | Sugar: 3 g | GI: Very low

Planked Salmon with Dill Sauce

This is a festive and delicious way to prepare salmon. The use of a cedar plank and juniper berries are reminiscent of Native American cooking.

INGREDIENTS | SERVES 10

1 cedar plank

Grapeseed oil, as needed

3½ pounds salmon fillet, checked for bones

Juice of 1 lemon

8 juniper berries

Salt and pepper, to taste

1 lemon, thinly sliced

1 cup mayonnaise

¼ cup chopped fresh dill weed

1 teaspoon horseradish

Fish Bones

The larger the fish, the more likely you will find bones in a fillet. Before cooking, hold a clean pair of pliers and run the finger of your other hand down the fillet, against the grain. Whenever you feel a bone, press down close to it. It will pop up, and you can then pull it out with the pliers.

1. Presoak the cedar plank in water for 2–6 hours before grilling. When thoroughly soaked, preheat the grill and then lightly oil the side of the cedar plank on which the salmon will lay. Set the salmon on the plank. Sprinkle with the lemon juice and press the juniper berries into the flesh at intervals. Add salt, pepper, and lemon slices.

2. Place the plank over indirect heat on a hot grill and close the lid. Roast for about 15–20 minutes, or until the salmon begins to flake.

3. Mix the rest of the ingredients in a small bowl with more salt and pepper and serve with the fish.

Per serving: Calories: 395 | Fat: 28 g | Protein: 31 g | Sodium: 432 mg | Fiber: 0 g | Carbohydrates: 1 g | Sugar: 0 g | GI: Very low

Jambalaya

This authentic Louisiana favorite is full of flavor and spice.

INGREDIENTS | SERVES 6

1 tablespoon olive oil

2 boneless, skinless chicken breasts, chopped

8 ounces andouille sausage, sliced

12 medium shrimp, peeled and deveined

½ medium onion, peeled and chopped

2 medium green bell peppers, seeded and chopped

2 stalks celery, diced

2 cloves garlic, minced

¼ teaspoon crushed red pepper

1 teaspoon chili powder

2 teaspoons dried oregano

Ground black pepper, to taste

6 ounces brown rice

2½ cans gluten-free chicken broth

1 can diced tomatoes

1 cup water

Tabasco, to taste

1. Pour the oil into a large pot and place on medium-high heat. Sauté the chicken and sausage until browned, about 6–8 minutes. Add the shrimp; cook and stir until shrimp are opaque, about 4 minutes.

2. Add the onion, bell pepper, celery, and garlic; season with crushed red pepper, chili powder, oregano, and black pepper. Cook until the onion is tender.

3. Stir in the rice, broth, tomatoes, and water. Bring to a boil and then reduce heat; simmer until the rice is cooked. Stir in the Tabasco before serving.

Per serving: Calories: 328 | Fat: 14 g | Protein: 22 g | Sodium: 906 mg | Fiber: 3 g | Carbohydrates: 29 g | Sugar: 3 g | GI: Moderate

CHAPTER 11

Soups

Basic Chicken Soup

The major advantage of this soup is that it will be much lower in sodium than canned chicken soups. The only limit is your imagination. Each time you make it, substitute different vegetables and seasonings to tantalize your taste buds.

INGREDIENTS | SERVES 6

5–6 pounds chicken (including giblets)
2 medium carrots
2 stalks celery
4 large yellow onions
¼ bunch parsley
12 cups water
Freshly cracked black pepper, to taste
Kosher salt, to taste

1. Clean, trim, and quarter the chicken. Peel and chop all the vegetables. Chop the parsley.

2. Place the chicken and giblets in a stockpot, add the water, and bring to a boil. Reduce the heat to a simmer and skim off all foam.

3. Add all the remaining ingredients and simmer uncovered for about 3 hours.

4. Remove the chicken and giblets from the stockpot; discard the giblets. Remove the meat from the bones, discard the bones, and return the meat to the broth; serve.

Per serving: Calories: 183 | Fat: 8 g | Protein: 16 g | Sodium: 84 mg | Fiber: 1.5 g | Carbohydrate: 5.5 g | Sugar: 2 g | GI: Low

Basic Vegetable Stock

Another great broth that is low on sodium and high on disease-fighting phytochemicals. Try adding mushrooms for additional flavor.

INGREDIENTS | MAKES 1 GALLON

2 pounds yellow onions

1 pound carrots

1 pound celery

1 bunch fresh parley stems

1½ gallons water

4 stems fresh thyme

2 bay leaves (fresh or dried)

10–20 peppercorns

Homemade Stocks

Homemade stocks give a special quality to any dish. Not only will the flavor of homemade stocks be better than that from purchased bases, but you will have added your own personal touch to the meal. Always cook them uncovered, as covering will cause them to become cloudy.

1. Peel and roughly chop the onions and carrots. Roughly chop the celery (stalks only; no leaves) and the fresh parsley stems.

2. Put the vegetables and water in a stockpot over medium heat; bring to a simmer and cook, uncovered, for 1½ hours.

3. Add the herbs and peppercorns, and continue to simmer, uncovered, for 45 minutes. Adjust seasonings to taste as necessary.

4. Remove from heat and cool by submerging the pot in a bath of ice and water. Place in freezer-safe containers and store in the freezer until ready to use. Remove the bay leaves before serving.

Per serving (1 cup): | Calories: 22 | Fat: 0 g | Protein: 0 g | Sodium: 31 mg | Fiber: 0 g | Carbohydrate: 5.3 g | Sugar: 2 g | GI: Low

Simple Ground Turkey and Vegetable Soup

This soup is easy to throw together with ingredients from the pantry.

INGREDIENTS | SERVES 6

1 tablespoon olive oil

1 pound ground turkey

1 medium onion, peeled and diced

2 cloves garlic, minced

1 (16-ounce) package frozen mixed vegetables

4 cups gluten-free chicken broth

½ teaspoon ground black pepper

½ teaspoon salt

Gluten-free crackers (optional)

1. In a large skillet on medium, heat the olive oil until sizzling. Cook the ground turkey until browned, about 5–6 minutes, stirring to break up the meat. Add the meat to a greased 4-quart slow cooker. Sauté the onion and garlic until softened, about 3–5 minutes. Add to the slow cooker.

2. Add the remaining ingredients. Cover and cook on high for 4 hours or on low for 8 hours. Serve with gluten-free crackers.

Per serving: Calories: 254 | Fat: 11.5 g | Protein: 19 g | Sodium: 1,001 mg | Fiber: 3.5 g | Carbohydrates: 20 g | Sugar: 1 g | GI: Very low

Chicken Stew with Meat Sauce

This easy-to-make chicken stew is sure to please the entire family. Both kids and adults love this delicious recipe. Serve alone or pour over spaghetti squash as a bolognaise-type sauce.

INGREDIENTS | SERVES 4

1 pound (90% lean) ground beef

4 boneless, skinless chicken breasts

1 (6-ounce) can tomato paste

1 (28-ounce) can diced organic tomatoes, no salt added

4 garlic cloves, chopped

4 large carrots, peeled and sliced

2 medium red bell peppers, seeded and diced

2 medium green bell peppers, seeded and diced

1 tablespoon dried thyme

2 tablespoons olive oil

1 tablespoon chili powder

1. In a medium sauté pan, cook the ground beef over medium-high heat until browned, about 5 minutes. Drain and place in the slow cooker.

2. Wipe out the pan and place it over medium-high heat. Brown the chicken breasts (5 minutes per side). Add them to the slow cooker.

3. Combine all the remaining ingredients in the slow cooker.

4. Cook on high for 5 hours.

5. Serve over your favorite steamed vegetable.

Per serving: Calories: 605 | Fat: 18 g | Protein: 74 g | Sodium: 666 mg | Fiber: 10 g | Carbohydrate: 42 g | Sugar: 5 g | GI: Low

Slow Cookers Are Lifesavers

Slow cookers are the greatest appliance for the Paleo enthusiast. These little counter-top cookers allow you to cook easily and in bulk, which is important for a successful Paleolithic dieter.

Sour-Cherry Beef Stew

This recipe was adapted from a traditional non–Paleolithic diet beef stew recipe. You will be surprised at how good this tastes.

INGREDIENTS | SERVES 10

¼ cup almond flour

½ teaspoon nutmeg

1 teaspoon cinnamon

½ teaspoon allspice

½ teaspoon ground black pepper

2 pounds chuck steak, cubed

2 tablespoons olive oil

2 medium onions, peeled and chopped

2 (16-ounce) cans sour cherries (reserve half of the juice)

½ cup red wine

1 (14-ounce) can gluten-free beef broth, unsalted

2 pounds button mushrooms, quartered

½ cup water

Alcohol in Cooking

Alcohol in general is not allowed on the Paleolithic plan, but some chefs find it acceptable to use alcohol while cooking, since most of the alcohol is burned off. This is a nice way to bring some flavor to a dish without worrying about altering the plan significantly. All of the ingredients in this stew fall very low on the glycemic index.

1. Combine the almond flour, nutmeg, cinnamon, allspice, and pepper in a plastic bag.

2. Add the chuck steak to the plastic bag and shake to coat evenly.

3. Heat the olive oil in a large skillet on medium-high.

4. Sear the steak quickly for 1–2 minutes on each side. Remove from the skillet and place in the slow cooker.

5. Using the same skillet, cook the onion on medium heat for 8 minutes.

6. Add the cherries, juice, and red wine to the skillet and cook for 5 more minutes, until the onions are browned.

7. Pour the cherry mixture into the slow cooker.

8. Add the broth, mushrooms, and water. Cook for at least 5 hours on low heat in the slow cooker.

Per serving: Calories: 307 | Fat: 16 g | Protein: 24 g | Sodium: 197 mg | Fiber: 3 g | Carbohydrate: 16 g | Sugar: 2 g | GI: Low

Black Bean Chili with Beef and Corn

This will give your family a meal with a real punch, staying power, and nutrition.

INGREDIENTS | SERVES 4

2 tablespoons olive oil or other cooking oil

½ pound ground beef

1 large red onion, peeled and chopped

2 cloves garlic, minced

1 large red bell pepper, seeded and chopped

1 small hot pepper, seeded and minced

1 teaspoon ground cumin

1 teaspoon dried cilantro or parsley or 1 tablespoon fresh

1 cup frozen corn

2 (13-ounce) cans black beans, drained and rinsed

1 cup crushed tomatoes

Salt and pepper, to taste

Juice of ½ lime

2 ounces shredded Monterey jack cheese

1. In a large, ovenproof casserole, heat the oil over a medium flame. Brown the beef for 6–8 minutes, until it is no longer pink. Move the beef to one side of the casserole dish and sauté the onion, garlic, and peppers for 5 minutes. Stir in the cumin and cilantro and mix well.

2. Preheat the oven to 340°F. Stir in the corn, black beans, tomatoes, salt, and pepper. Sprinkle with lime juice. Stir to mix.

3. Spread the top with cheese and bake for 30 minutes, or until hot and bubbling. Serve with corn bread or corn tortillas.

Per serving: Calories: 429 | Fat: 13 g | Protein: 23 g | Sodium: 612 mg | Fiber: 6 g | Carbohydrates: 69 g | Sugar: 6 g | GI: Low

Legumes

Beans are legumes, as are lentils, peas, soybeans, and peanuts. Not only are legumes good for farmers to grow because their roots produce nitrogen, which fertilizes land, but they are delicious and full of healthful protein for you!

Broccoli Soup with Cheese

There is a lot to love about broccoli soup. Both nourishing and full of fiber, it can be enriched with cream or heated up with spicy pepper jack cheese.

INGREDIENTS | SERVES 4

¼ cup olive oil

1 medium sweet onion, peeled and chopped

2 cloves garlic, chopped

1 large baking potato, peeled and chopped

1 large bunch broccoli, coarsely chopped

½ cup dry white wine

3 cups gluten-free chicken broth

Salt and pepper, to taste

Pinch ground nutmeg

4 heaping tablespoons grated extra-sharp Cheddar

1. Heat the olive oil in a large soup kettle. Sauté the onion, garlic, and potato over medium heat until softened slightly. Add the broccoli, liquids, and seasonings.

2. Cover the soup and simmer over low heat for 45 minutes.

3. Cool slightly. Purée in the blender. Reheat and place in bowls.

4. Spoon the cheese over the hot soup to serve.

Per serving: Calories: 297 | Fat: 19 g | Protein: 8 g | Sodium: 623 mg | Fiber: 3 g | Carbohydrates: 22 g | Sugar: 2 g | GI: Very low

Save the Stalks

When you prepare broccoli, save the stems. They can be grated and mixed with carrots in a slaw, cut into coins and served hot, or cooked and puréed as a side. Broccoli marries well with potatoes and carrots and is good served raw with a dipping sauce.

Cashew-Zucchini Soup

Cashews make this soup thick and creamy and provide a serving of heart-healthy fat.

INGREDIENTS | SERVES 4

5 medium zucchini

1 large Vidalia onion, peeled and chopped

4 cloves garlic, chopped

½ teaspoon salt, plus more to taste

¼ teaspoon ground black pepper, plus more to taste

3 cups vegetable broth

½ cup raw cashews

½ teaspoon dried tarragon

Cashew Nut Butter

To save time, you may substitute cashew nut butter for the whole raw cashews. Enjoy the leftover cashew nut butter as a spread on sandwiches and as a dip for fresh fruit. Remember, nut butters are high in calories, so limit the portion size.

1. Coarsely chop 4 zucchini; set 1 zucchini aside.

2. Spray a large saucepan with nonstick cooking spray. Add the onion to the pan and cook for 5 minutes, until soft and translucent. Add the garlic and cook for 1 minute. Stir in the chopped zucchini, ½ teaspoon salt, and ¼ teaspoon ground pepper, and cook over medium heat, covered, stirring occasionally, for 5 minutes.

3. Add the broth and simmer for 15 minutes.

4. Add the cashews and tarragon. Purée the soup in a blender in one to two batches. Fill the blender halfway to avoid burns from the hot liquid.

5. Return the soup to the pot; season with additional salt and pepper as desired.

Per serving: Calories: 117 | Fat: 8 g | Protein: 6 g | Sodium: 585 mg | Fiber: 3 g | Carbohydrates: 23 g | Sugar: 2 g | GI: Low

Black Bean Soup with Chilies

Soak the black beans overnight and then cook them for 2–3 hours or until tender. Canned beans also work well in this recipe. It's important to adjust the type of chilies to your personal taste. Serrano and Scotch bonnet are among the hottest.

INGREDIENTS | SERVES 4

4 strips bacon

4 cloves garlic, chopped

1 medium sweet onion, peeled and chopped

2 hot chilies, seeded and minced

2 cans black beans or 1 pound black beans

8 ounces gluten-free beef broth

½ cup tomato juice

2 ounces dark rum

Salt and pepper, to taste

Fresh lime wedges, sour cream, chopped cilantro, and pepper jack cheese for garnish

1. In a large pot, fry the bacon over medium heat until crisp, about 3–4 minutes. Remove bacon to a paper towel-lined plate and leave the bacon fat in the pot. Crumble the bacon. Add garlic, onion, and chilies to the pot. Sauté over medium-high heat until softened, about 5 minutes.

2. Stir in the black beans, beef broth, tomato juice, rum, salt, and pepper. Cover and simmer for 1 hour.

3. You may either purée the soup or serve it as is. Garnish with any or all of the suggestions.

Per serving: Calories: 206 | Fat: 5 g | Protein: 11 g | Sodium: 875 mg | Fiber: 7 g | Carbohydrates: 27 g | Sugar: 3 g | GI: Low

Flavor Substitutions

Beans make for a very nutritious meal and can be flavored with a variety of different meats and seasonings. Try flavoring the soup with a ham bone (which you must remove before puréeing or serving) or browned sausage. You could even flavor the beans with dried bay leaves or Italian seasoning.

Chicken and Rice Soup

This comforting soup stands alone as a healthful and satisfying meal.

INGREDIENTS | SERVES 6

3 boneless, skinless chicken breasts
Salt and pepper, to taste
4 tablespoons olive oil
1 small onion, peeled and chopped
2 cloves garlic, minced
3 stalks celery, chopped
2 medium carrots, peeled and chopped
5½ cups gluten-free chicken broth
¾ tablespoon thyme
2 cups shredded cabbage
2 bay leaves
1 cup water
¾ cup long-grain brown rice

Nutrition Note

Chicken and rice soup is a classic American comfort food. This recipe replaces the egg noodles with brown rice and omits the high-glycemic veggies to keep the soup low on the glycemic index and extremely flavorful. This is a guilt-free meal!

1. Wash the chicken and pat dry. Season with salt and pepper and chop into 1"-thick pieces.

2. Heat 2 tablespoons oil in a medium frying pan over medium-high heat and sauté the chicken pieces for 6–8 minutes, until they are well done. Set the chicken aside.

3. Heat the remaining oil in a large pot, and sauté the onion and garlic over medium heat until translucent, about 3–4 minutes. Add the celery and carrot to the pot and cook for 5 minutes.

4. Add the chicken broth, thyme, cooked chicken, cabbage, bay leaves, water, and rice to the pot. Simmer the soup for 30 minutes or until the rice is completely cooked. Remove the bay leaves before serving.

Per serving: Calories: 263 | Fat: 10 g | Protein: 24 g | Sodium: 499 mg | Fiber: 4 g | Carbohydrates: 19 g | Sugar: 2 g | GI: Low

Leek and Potato Soup

There are many versions of this excellent soup, which tastes wonderful either hot or chilled. Some recipes have chunky potatoes, and others are smooth—you can prepare this one whichever way you prefer.

INGREDIENTS | SERVES 4

¼ cup olive oil

2 leeks, coarsely chopped

1 large sweet onion, peeled and chopped

2 large baking potatoes, peeled and chopped

2 cups gluten-free chicken broth

1 teaspoon salt, plus more to taste

1 cup 2% milk

1 cup whipping cream

¼ cup chopped chives

Freshly ground black pepper, to taste

¼ cup chopped watercress for garnish

1. Heat the olive oil in a large soup kettle on medium. Rinse the sand out of the leeks. Add the leeks and onion and sauté for 5 minutes over medium heat.

2. Add the potatoes, chicken broth, and 1 teaspoon salt. Simmer until the potatoes are tender. Set aside to cool.

3. Put the soup through a ricer or purée it in the blender until smooth.

4. Pour the soup back into the pot; add the milk, whipping cream, and chives and reheat. Add salt and pepper to taste. Float the watercress on top for garnish.

Per serving: Calories: 491 | Fat: 33 g | Protein: 8 g | Sodium: 1,345 mg | Fiber: 2 g | Carbohydrates: 40 g | Sugar: 5 g | GI: Moderate

Lentil Soup with Winter Vegetables

This is a substantial soup that will get you through a long winter!

INGREDIENTS | SERVES 4

½ pound bag red or yellow lentils

4 cups vegetable broth

2 cups water

2 parsnips, peeled and chopped

2 medium carrots, peeled and chopped

2 medium white onions, peeled and chopped

4 cloves garlic, chopped

4 small bluenose turnips, peeled and chopped

½ pound deli baked ham, cut in cubes

Put all ingredients in a soup kettle, bring to a boil, cover, and simmer for 1 hour.

Per serving: Calories: 188 | Fat: 5 g | Protein: 18 g | Sodium: 499 mg | Fiber: 9 g | Carbohydrates: 19 g | Sugar: 3 g | GI: Low

Cold Basil and Fresh Tomato Soup

This is a wonderful summer soup served cold or it can be heated on a cold winter's day. It is also good for you! The red tomatoes are full of vitamin C. (The amount of vitamin C in tomatoes increases as they ripen.) This soup also freezes beautifully!

INGREDIENTS | SERVES 4

2 pounds ripe red tomatoes, halved and cored

1 cup gluten-free beef broth

¼ cup red wine

1 teaspoon garlic powder

20 basil leaves

Salt and pepper, to taste

Chopped chives, for garnish

Cheddar or Parmesan cheese (optional)

1. In the blender, purée the tomatoes, beef broth, wine, garlic powder, basil, salt, and pepper. Chill overnight. Add the garnish at the last minute.

2. If serving the soup hot, garnish it with grated Cheddar or Parmesan cheese.

Per serving: Calories: 60 | Fat: 0 g | Protein: 2 g | Sodium: 609 mg | Fiber: 1 g | Carbohydrates: 11 g | Sugar: 3 g | GI: Very low

Mediterranean Seafood Soup

This quick and easy soup will give you a taste of the Mediterranean.

INGREDIENTS | SERVES 2

2 tablespoons olive oil

½ cup chopped sweet onion

2 cloves garlic, chopped

½ bulb fennel, chopped

½ cup dry white wine

1 cup clam broth

2 cups chopped tomatoes

6 littleneck clams, tightly closed

6 mussels, tightly closed

8 raw shrimp, jumbo, peeled and deveined

1 teaspoon dried basil, or 5 leaves fresh basil, torn

Salt and red pepper flakes, to taste

1. In a dutch oven or stock pot, heat the oil over medium-high heat, and add the onion, garlic, and fennel. After 10 minutes, stir in the wine and clam broth and add the tomatoes. Bring to a boil.

2. Drop the clams into the boiling liquid. When the clams start to open, add the mussels. When the mussels start to open, add the shrimp, basil, salt, and pepper flakes. Serve when the shrimp turns pink.

Per serving: Calories: 450 | Fat: 18 g | Protein: 48 g | Sodium: 1,355 mg | Fiber: 1 g | Carbohydrates: 19 g | Sugar: 2 g | GI: Very low

Littleneck Clams

Littleneck clams are the smallest variety of hard-shell clams and can be found on the northeastern and northwestern coasts of the United States. They have a sweet taste and are delicious steamed and dipped in melted butter, battered and fried, or baked.

Savory Fish Stew

This stew is fresh and easy to make and has a whole lot of flavor. The recipe calls for halibut, but just about any meaty whitefish will do.

INGREDIENTS | SERVES 6

1 tablespoon olive oil

1 medium onion, peeled and finely chopped

½ cup dry white wine

3 large tomatoes, chopped

2 cups low-sodium chicken broth

8 ounces clam juice

3 cups fresh spinach

1 pound halibut fillets, cut into 1" pieces

White pepper, to taste

1 tablespoon chopped fresh cilantro

1. Place a large frying pan over medium heat. Add the oil to the pan and sauté the onions for 2–3 minutes. Add wine to deglaze the pan. Scrape the pan to loosen the small bits of onion.

2. Add the tomatoes and cook for 3–4 minutes; then add the broth and clam juice to the pan. Stir in the spinach and allow it to wilt while continuing to stir.

3. Season the fish with pepper, place the fish in the pan, and cook for 5–6 minutes until opaque. Mix in the cilantro before serving.

Per serving: Calories: 157 | Fat: 7 g | Protein: 19 g | Sodium: 321 mg | Fiber: 2 g | Carbohydrates: 7 g | Sugar: 1 g | GI: Very low

Green Pea Soup

This rich and velvety soup will warm you from the inside out.

INGREDIENTS | SERVES 4

2 tablespoons olive oil

1 medium onion, peeled and chopped

3 cloves garlic, minced

4 cups gluten-free chicken stock

3 cups green peas

¾ teaspoon tarragon

¼ tablespoon ground black pepper

2 slices bacon

4 teaspoons sour cream

1. Heat the oil in a pot on medium, and add the onion and garlic. Cook for 5 minutes or until the onion is soft and translucent.

2. Add the chicken stock, peas, and tarragon to the pot. Bring to a boil, and reduce to a simmer for 8 minutes.

3. Remove the soup from the heat, allow it to cool slightly, and then purée the soup in a food processor or blender. Season the soup with the pepper.

4. Place bacon under a broiler and cook until crispy, about 3–5 minutes.

5. Serve the soup garnished with crumbled bacon and sour cream.

Per serving: Calories: 290 | Fat: 14 g | Protein: 14 g | Sodium: 305 mg | Fiber: 5 g | Carbohydrates: 28 g | Sugar: 8 g | GI: Moderate

Cucumber Soup

Some recipes for cucumber soup call for cooking the cucumber.
This one "cooks" it in the acidity of lemon juice.

INGREDIENTS | SERVES 2

1 slender English cucumber, peeled and chopped

Juice of 1 lemon

1 cup nonfat buttermilk

1 cup low-fat yogurt

2 tablespoons fresh dill weed, snipped

Salt and freshly ground white pepper, to taste

1 teaspoon Tabasco (optional)

Garnish of extra snippets of dill or chives

Skin Health

Silica, a chemical known for improving the health and complexion of the skin, is found in cucumber juice. Cucumber is used to treat puffy eyes and ease sunburn. Other compounds in cucumbers are said to prevent water retention and dermatitis. Cool cucumbers are soothing and refreshing.

1. Mix all the ingredients except the garnish and purée them in a blender until smooth. Place the soup in a glass or nonreactive bowl (to avoid staining with the acidic citrus).

2. Let the soup rest in the refrigerator for 4 hours or overnight.

3. Taste and add seasonings if necessary before serving in chilled bowls, topped with garnish.

Per serving: Calories: 145 | Fat: 3 g | Protein: 11 g | Sodium: 1,321 mg | Fiber: 2 g | Carbohydrates: 21 g | Sugar: 12 g | GI: Very low

Creamy Cauliflower Soup

Cauliflower, a cruciferous vegetable, contains compounds that may prevent cancer.

INGREDIENTS | SERVES 4

2 tablespoons olive oil
½ cup finely chopped onion
½ cup chopped celery
1 cup cauliflower florets
4 cups gluten-free chicken stock
1 cup shredded Cheddar cheese
Salt and pepper, to taste
1 cup low-fat milk

1. Heat the oil in a large pot, and sauté the onion and celery until translucent, about 3–4 minutes. Add the cauliflower and chicken stock, and bring to a boil. Reduce heat, cover, and simmer for 25 minutes, stirring occasionally.

2. Purée the soup in a food processor or blender until smooth.

3. Return the soup to the pot and bring the temperature to medium-low heat. Add the cheese, salt, and pepper, continue to cook and stir until the cheese is melted and well integrated.

4. Stir the milk into the soup. Add more chicken stock if the consistency is too thick.

Per serving: Calories: 291 | Fat: 18 g | Protein: 17 g | Sodium: 612 mg | Fiber: 3 g | Carbohydrates: 16 g | Sugar: 4 g | GI: Low

Spinach and Sausage Soup with Pink Beans

This is a hearty and delicious soup. If you don't want to work with fresh spinach, you may use frozen, chopped spinach, or even substitute escarole or kale. Some sausage is so lean that you will need to add a bit of oil when you cook it.

INGREDIENTS | SERVES 4

8 ounces Italian sweet sausage, cut in bite-size chunks

2 cups water, divided

¼ cup olive oil

2 medium white onions, peeled and chopped

4 cloves garlic, chopped

2 stalks celery, chopped, leaves included

2 cups gluten-free beef broth

1 bunch fresh spinach, kale, or escarole, or 1 (10-ounce) package frozen, chopped spinach

1 teaspoon dried oregano

1 teaspoon red pepper flakes

1 (13-ounce) can pink or red kidney beans, drained

Salt, to taste

Grated Parmesan, to taste

1. Place the sausage in a soup kettle. Add ¾ cup water and bring it to a boil; let the water boil off. Add the oil if the kettle becomes dry, and sauté the onions, garlic, and celery for 10 minutes over medium-low heat.

2. Stir in the rest of the ingredients except the cheese; cover and simmer the soup for 35 minutes. Serve in heated bowls. Garnish with grated Parmesan.

Per serving: Calories: 344 | Fat: 20 g | Protein: 19 g | Sodium: 989 mg | Fiber: 5 g | Carbohydrates: 28 g | Sugar: 1 g | GI: Very low

Vegetarian Option

This recipe can easily be transformed into a vegetarian delight. Substitute vegetarian sausage for regular sausage Italian sausage and use vegetable broth instead of beef broth.

Thai Chicken Stew with Vegetables in Coconut Cream

Asian flavorings can provide so many minimal, yet wonderful, additions to rather ordinary foods. This chicken stew is spicy and tastes very rich. It is loaded with vegetables that reduce the GI value of this dish. Try it served over rice.

INGREDIENTS | SERVES 4

2 cloves garlic, minced

1" fresh gingerroot, peeled and minced

2 tablespoons peanut oil

2 medium carrots, peeled and shredded

1 cup canned coconut cream

1 cup gluten-free chicken broth

2 cups shredded napa cabbage

4 (5-ounce) boneless, skinless chicken breasts, cut into bite-size pieces

¼ cup gluten-free soy sauce

2 tablespoons fish sauce

1 teaspoon Thai chili paste (red or green) or red hot-pepper sauce

1 tablespoon sesame oil

½ cup chopped scallion (green part only)

¼ cup chopped cilantro

1. In a large dutch oven or stock pot, sauté the garlic and ginger in the peanut oil over medium-high heat for 3–5 minutes. Add the carrots, coconut cream, and chicken broth, and simmer for 10 minutes. Add the cabbage, chicken, soy sauce, and fish sauce.

2. Whisk in the chili paste. Stir in the sesame oil, scallions, and cilantro. Simmer for 20 minutes.

Per serving: Calories: 540 | Fat: 35 g | Protein: 55 g | Sodium: 778 mg | Fiber: 2 g | Carbohydrates: 16 g | Sugar: 3 g | GI: Low

Coconut Cream, Coconut Milk, Coconut Juice

Contrary to popular belief, coconut milk is not the liquid found inside a whole coconut (that is called coconut juice). Coconut milk is made by mixing water with shredded coconut and then squeezing the mixture through cheesecloth to filter out the coconut pieces. Coconut cream is the same as coconut milk, but it is made with less water and more coconut.

Vegetable Chili

A steaming hot bowl of this spicy chili will satisfy meat eaters and vegetarians alike.

INGREDIENTS | SERVES 8

2 tablespoons olive oil

1 medium onion, peeled and chopped

1 celery stalk, chopped

1 medium green bell pepper, seeded and chopped

1 medium red bell pepper, seeded and chopped

4 cloves garlic, minced

2 tablespoons chopped chipotles in adobo

1 tablespoon ground cumin

1 tablespoon dried oregano

1 tablespoon chili powder

1½ teaspoons salt

1 (28-ounce) can diced tomatoes

3 cups water

1½ cups cooked and drained black beans

3 cups cooked and drained kidney beans

½ cup sour cream

1. Heat the oil in a large pot on medium.

2. Add the onions, celery, peppers, and garlic, and cook for 10 minutes.

3. Add the chipotles, cumin, oregano, chili powder, and salt. Stir the ingredients together, and add the tomatoes and water. Turn heat to low, and simmer, uncovered, for 45 minutes.

4. Add the beans and simmer for 20 minutes more.

5. Serve with a dollop of sour cream.

Per serving: Calories: 230 | Fat: 5 g | Protein: 11 g | Sodium: 501 mg | Fiber: 10 g | Carbohydrates: 37 g | Sugar: 2 g | GI: Moderate

Yellow Pepper and Tomato Soup

Yellow peppers and yellow tomatoes are very sweet and make a wonderful soup!

INGREDIENTS | SERVES 4

¼ cup peanut oil

½ cup chopped sweet onion

2 cloves garlic, minced

1 medium yellow bell pepper, seeded and finely chopped

1½ cups gluten-free chicken broth

4 medium-size yellow tomatoes, cored and puréed

½ teaspoon ground cumin

½ teaspoon ground coriander

Juice of ½ lemon

Salt and pepper, to taste

Garnish of fresh basil leaves, torn

1. In a soup kettle, heat the oil on medium. Sauté the onion, garlic, and yellow pepper. After about 5 minutes, add the chicken broth and tomatoes.

2. Stir in the seasonings, lemon juice, salt, and pepper.

3. Cover and simmer for at least 30 minutes, but as long as 3 hours over low heat. You can purée the soup if you wish or leave some bits of texture in it.

4. Sprinkle with basil and serve hot or cold.

Per serving: Calories: 176 | Fat: 14 g | Protein: 2 g | Sodium: 625 mg | Fiber: 3 g | Carbohydrates: 12 g | Sugar: 3 g | GI: Very low

Colorful Veggies

Yellow fruits and vegetables are loaded with vitamin A, or retinol, which keeps your skin moist and helps your eyes adjust to changes in light. It is important to eat a variety of different colored fruits and vegetables every day.

Egg Drop Soup with Lemon

This is a lovely spicy version of the Chinese staple, made with a variety of Asian sauces. Asian fish sauce is a liquid made from salted fish that is used instead of salt in many Asian recipes. Hoisin sauce is made from crushed soybeans and garlic, has a sweet and spicy flavor, and is a rich brown color.

INGREDIENTS | SERVES 2

1 tablespoon peanut oil
1 clove garlic, minced
2 cups gluten-free chicken broth
Juice of ½ lemon
1 tablespoon gluten-free hoisin sauce
1 teaspoon gluten-free soy sauce
1 teaspoon fish sauce
½ teaspoon chili oil, or to taste
1" fresh gingerroot, peeled and minced
2 eggs

1. Heat the peanut oil in a large saucepan. Sauté the garlic over medium heat until softened, about 5 minutes.

2. Add the chicken broth, lemon juice, hoisin sauce, soy sauce, fish sauce, chili oil, and gingerroot. Stir and cover. Cook over low heat for 20 minutes.

3. Just before serving, whisk the eggs with a fork. Add to the boiling soup and continue to whisk until the eggs form thin strands.

Per serving: Calories: 158 | Fat: 13 g | Protein: 5 g | Sodium: 599 mg | Fiber: 0 g | Carbohydrates: 2 g | Sugar: 2 g | GI: Very low

Slow-Cooker Pork Posole

Posole is a spicy Mexican stew made from pork and hominy. This version is made in a slow cooker. For a milder version, use plain diced tomatoes instead of tomatoes with green chilies. Try serving it with shredded cheese, diced avocados, sliced black olives, pico de gallo, pickled jalapeños, or sour cream.

INGREDIENTS | SERVES 8

2 pounds lean cubed pork

2 cans (14.5-ounce) white or yellow hominy, drained and rinsed

1 can (10-ounce) cubed potatoes, drained and rinsed

2 (15-ounce) cans diced tomatoes with green chilies, not drained

2 cups warm water

1 cup chopped carrots

4 garlic cloves, minced

1 medium onion, peeled and chopped

2 teaspoons cumin

2 teaspoons chili powder

1 teaspoon red pepper flakes

1 teaspoon dried oregano

Add all the ingredients to a greased 4-quart slow cooker. Cook on low for 8 hours or on high for 4 hours.

Per serving: Calories: 412 | Fat: 5 g | Protein: 32 g | Sodium: 82 mg | Fiber: 6 g | Carbohydrates: 61 g | Sugar: 5 g | GI: Moderate

Corn by Any Other Name

Hominy is corn that has been soaked in a weak lye solution. This treatment gives the corn a creamy white texture and a distinctive taste because it removes the germ and the bran of the grain. Roughly ground hominy is known as hominy grits and often served for breakfast.

Chicken Chili Verde

Enjoy this spicy chili over white or brown rice. You can also use a prepared gluten-free chili seasoning mix (such as Carroll Shelby's Chili Kit) in place of the spices in this recipe.

INGREDIENTS | SERVES 8

½ tablespoon olive oil

2 pounds boneless, skinless chicken breast, cubed

2 (28-ounce) cans whole peeled tomatoes, not drained

1 (16-ounce) can chili beans, drained and rinsed

1 (15-ounce) can kidney beans, drained and rinsed

1 (4-ounce) can diced green chili pepper, not drained

1 tablespoon Italian seasoning

1 tablespoon chili powder

2 teaspoons cumin

1 tablespoon sugar

1 medium onion, peeled and minced

3 cloves garlic, minced

½ cup water

1. Heat the oil in a skillet on medium. Add the chicken. Cook, stirring frequently, until the chicken is browned on all sides, about 1–2 minutes per side. Place the browned chicken in a greased 4- to 6-quart slow cooker.

2. Add the remaining ingredients over the chicken in the slow cooker.

3. Cover and cook on high for 3 hours or on low for 6 hours.

Per serving: Calories: 464 | Fat: 10 g | Protein: 41 g | Sodium: 445 mg | Fiber: 15 g | Carbohydrates: 53 g | Sugar: 13 g | GI: Moderate

Using Your Slow Cooker as a Rice Cooker

If you have a second slow cooker, you can use it to make rice while the chili is cooking. To make rice: grease a 2.5-quart or larger slow cooker with butter or nonstick spray. Add 1 cup of raw white rice, ½ teaspoon of salt, and 2 cups of water. Cover and cook on high for 1½–2½ hours until the rice is cooked through, has absorbed the liquid, and is fluffy.

CHAPTER 12

Slow-Cooker Favorites

Rotisserie-Style Chicken

Here is a delicious alternative to buying rotisserie chicken in your grocery store. This flavorful roast chicken is incredibly easy to make in your slow cooker. For a fast weeknight meal, cook the chicken overnight in the slow cooker and serve for dinner the next day.

INGREDIENTS | SERVES 6

1 (4-pound) whole chicken

1½ teaspoons salt

2 teaspoons paprika

½ teaspoon onion powder

½ teaspoon dried thyme

½ teaspoon dried basil

½ teaspoon white pepper

½ teaspoon ground cayenne pepper

½ teaspoon black pepper

½ teaspoon garlic powder

2 tablespoons olive oil

Gravy

If you would like to make a gravy to go with the chicken, follow these directions: After removing the cooked chicken, turn the slow cooker on high. Whisk ⅓ cup of garbanzo bean flour or ⅓ cup of brown rice flour into the cooking juices. Add salt and pepper to taste and cook for 10–15 minutes, whisking occasionally, until the gravy has thickened. Spoon the gravy over the chicken.

1. Rinse the chicken in cold water and pat dry with a paper towel.

2. In a small bowl, mix the salt, paprika, onion powder, thyme, basil, white pepper, cayenne pepper, black pepper, and garlic powder.

3. Rub the spice mixture over the entire chicken. Rub part of the spice mixture underneath the skin, making sure to leave the skin intact.

4. Place the spice-rubbed chicken in a greased 6-quart slow cooker. Drizzle olive oil evenly over the chicken. Cook on high for 3–3½ hours or on low for 4–5 hours.

5. Remove chicken carefully from the slow cooker and place on a large plate or serving platter.

Per serving: Calories: 171 | Fat: 7.5 g | Protein: 23 g | Sodium: 474 mg | Fiber: 0 g | Carbohydrates: 0 g | Sugar: 0 g | GI: Very low

Dijon Beef Roast

Dijon mustard gives this roast a delicious tangy flavor. This recipe is perfect for roast beef sandwiches or for a traditional Sunday meal with mashed potatoes and gravy.

INGREDIENTS | SERVES 6

1 large onion, peeled and thickly sliced
1 (3–4 pound) beef round roast
3–4 tablespoons Dijon mustard
½ teaspoon salt
½ teaspoon ground black pepper
1 tablespoon olive oil
½ cup gluten-free beef broth, or water

1. Place the onion slices in a greased 4-quart slow cooker.

2. Rub the beef roast with the Dijon mustard. Place it on top of the sliced onions.

3. Sprinkle salt and pepper on top of beef roast and drizzle with the olive oil and beef broth.

4. Cover and cook on high for 2½–3 hours or on low for 5–6 hours. Cooking time will vary depending on your preference of doneness (either rare, medium, or well done). For a rarer roast, check the internal temperature (around 145°F) after cooking for 1½ hours on high or 3 hours on low. Serve the roast with the cooked onions and au jus drizzled on top.

Per serving: Calories: 499 | Fat: 24 g | Protein: 54 g | Sodium: 346 mg | Fiber: 1 g | Carbohydrates: 3 g | Sugar: 1 g | GI: Very low

Herbed Tilapia Stew

Any type of whitefish fillets (such as haddock or cod) will also work in this recipe. Fish cooks very, very quickly, even on the low setting, in a slow cooker, so be sure to set a timer. Serve the stew over cooked rice or gluten-free pasta.

INGREDIENTS | SERVES 6

2 pounds frozen boneless tilapia fillets

4 tablespoons butter

1 (14.5-ounce) can diced tomatoes, with juice

4 cloves garlic, minced

½ cup sliced green onions

2 teaspoons fish sauce

2 tablespoons chopped fresh thyme, or 1 teaspoon dried thyme

1. Grease a 4-quart slow cooker with nonstick cooking spray. Place all the ingredients in the slow cooker.

2. Cover and cook on high for 1½–2 hours or on low for 2½–3 hours. Watch the cooking time. If your fish fillets are very thin, you may need to reduce the cooking time.

3. When the fish is cooked through, the fillets will easily separate and flake with a fork. Break the fish up into the tomatoes and cooking liquids.

Per serving: Calories: 208 | Fat: 9 g | Protein: 27 g | Sodium: 180 mg | Fiber: 1 g | Carbohydrates: 4 g | Sugar: 2 g | GI: Very low

Buffalo Chicken Sandwich Filling

Serve this delicious chicken on toasted gluten-free bread with crumbled blue cheese or try gluten-free ranch dressing on top of each sandwich.

INGREDIENTS | SERVES 4

6 boneless, skinless chicken thighs

¼ cup diced onion

1 clove garlic, minced

½ teaspoon freshly ground black pepper

½ teaspoon salt

2 cups gluten-free buffalo wing sauce

1. Place all the ingredients in a greased 4-quart slow cooker. Stir to combine. Cook on high for 2–3 hours or on low for 4–6 hours or until the chicken is easily shredded with a fork. If the sauce is very thin, continue to cook on high uncovered for 30 minutes or until thickened.

2. Shred the chicken and toss with the sauce.

Per serving: Calories: 316 | Fat: 4 g | Protein: 20 g | Sodium: 1,783 mg | Fiber: 1 g | Carbohydrates: 46 g | Sugar: 33 g | GI: Moderate

Scalloped Potatoes with Bacon

This is an ideal dish for the slow cooker. Potatoes cooked slowly over low heat are tender and delicious.

INGREDIENTS | SERVES 8

2 tablespoons cornstarch

1 teaspoon salt

½ teaspoon ground black pepper

2 cups milk

4 cups thinly sliced potatoes (about 6–8 medium potatoes)

½ pound bacon, cooked and crumbled

3 tablespoons butter, cut in small pieces

½ cup shredded Cheddar cheese

½ cup sliced scallions

Make It Dairy-Free

You can easily make this recipe dairy-free by using coconut oil or olive oil in place of the butter, coconut milk or almond milk in place of the dairy milk, and Daiya (soy-free, gluten-free, and dairy-free cheese product) in place of the dairy cheese.

1. Grease a 4-quart slow cooker with nonstick cooking spray.

2. In a small bowl, mix the cornstarch, salt, pepper, and milk.

3. Place one-third of the potatoes in the bottom of the slow cooker. Pour one-third of the milk mixture over the potatoes. Sprinkle one-third of the bacon over the milk. Continue to layer the ingredients, finishing with potatoes.

4. Dot butter over potatoes. Cover the slow cooker and cook on low for 6–8 hours until the potatoes are tender.

5. Thirty minutes before serving, sprinkle the cheese and green onions on top of the potatoes. Allow the cheese to melt and then serve.

Per serving: Calories: 293 | Fat: 21 g | Protein: 8 g | Sodium: 604.5 mg | Fiber: 2 g | Carbohydrates: 17 g | Sugar: 4.5 g | GI: Low

Slow-Cooked Southern Lima Beans with Ham

Lima beans are a Southern favorite and can withstand long cooking periods without being mushy. In this traditional recipe, the lima beans are flavored with bite-size pieces of ham and simmered in a savory tomato-based sauce. Serve over cooked rice or gluten-free pasta.

INGREDIENTS | SERVES 8

1 pound dry lima beans, soaked for 6–8 hours and rinsed with cold water

2 cups diced cooked ham

1 medium sweet onion, peeled and chopped

1 teaspoon dry mustard

1 teaspoon salt

½ teaspoon freshly ground black pepper

2 cups water

1 (15.5-ounce) can tomato sauce

1. Drain and rinse the soaked lima beans. Add them to a greased 4- to 6-quart slow cooker. Add the remaining ingredients. If needed, add water to cover the beans by 1".

2. Cook on high for 4 hours or on low for 8 hours.

Per serving: Calories: 266 | Fat: 3 g | Protein: 20.5 g | Sodium: 1,083.5 mg | Fiber: 12 g | Carbohydrates: 40 g | Sugar: 7.5 g | GI: Low

Hatteras Clam Chowder

This cozy, creamy chowder is thickened only by potatoes. Serve it with a fresh green salad and homemade gluten-free bread.

INGREDIENTS | SERVES 4

4 slices bacon, diced

1 small onion, peeled and diced

2 medium russet potatoes, peeled and diced

1 (8-ounce) bottle clam stock

2–3 cups water

½ teaspoon salt

½ teaspoon freshly ground black pepper

2 (6.5-ounce) cans minced clams, with juice

1. In a 2-quart or larger saucepan, sauté the bacon over medium-high heat until crispy and browned. Add the onion and sauté until translucent, about 3–5 minutes. Add the cooked onions and bacon to a greased 2.5-quart slow cooker.

2. Add the potatoes, clam stock, and enough water to cover (2–3 cups). Add salt and pepper.

3. Cover and cook on high for 3 hours until the potatoes are very tender.

4. One hour before serving, add clams along with broth and cook until heated through.

Per serving: Calories: 253 | Fat: 11.5 g | Protein: 12.5 g | Sodium: 601 mg | Fiber: 2 g | Carbohydrates: 25 g | Sugar: 3 g | GI: Low

Eastern North Carolina Brunswick Stew

Brunswick Stew is a traditional Southern vegetable stew with chicken and pork. Serve it with gluten-free cornbread and sliced tomatoes.

INGREDIENTS | SERVES 10

¼ cup unsalted butter

1 large yellow onion, peeled and diced

2 quarts (8 cups) water

1 pound boneless, skinless chicken breasts

1 pound boneless, skinless chicken thighs

2 cups pulled pork, chopped

1 (15-ounce) can green beans, with liquid

2 (8-ounce) cans baby lima beans, with liquid

2 (28-ounce) cans whole tomatoes, chopped with juice

3 medium potatoes, peeled and diced

1 (15-ounce) can sweet corn

⅓ cup sugar

2 teaspoons salt

1 teaspoon ground black pepper

2 teaspoons hot sauce

1. In a medium skillet, heat the butter until sizzling and cook the onion until softened and fragrant, about 3–5 minutes. Add the onion to a 6-quart slow cooker.

2. Add the remaining ingredients to the slow cooker. Cook on high for 4 hours or on low for 8 hours.

3. One hour before serving, remove the chicken and shred it using two forks. Return the chicken to the soup. Add additional hot sauce, salt, and pepper as needed, to taste.

Per serving: Calories: 430.5 | Fat: 10 | Protein: 38 | Sodium: 1,240.5 mg | Fiber: 9 g | Carbohydrates: 49 g | Sugar: 14 g | GI: Moderate

Virginia, Georgia, or Maybe North Carolina?

The origins of Brunswick Stew have been debated for years. Some say the stew originated in Georgia; others say it began in Virginia. The stew is usually tomato-based with lima beans, corn, okra, and other vegetables. The meats used can vary. Many old recipes call for wild meats such as rabbit and squirrel. In Eastern North Carolina, it's often served in restaurants with shredded pork barbecue, vinegary coleslaw, and corn bread.

Hearty Beef Chili

The key to this hearty chili is keeping the ground beef in larger chunks (instead of breaking it into very small pieces) when you are browning it for the slow cooker. If you prefer a spicier version, add 1 tablespoon of chili powder, 1 teaspoon of cumin, and ½ teaspoon of cayenne pepper.

INGREDIENTS | SERVES 6

1 pound ground beef

1 cup chopped onion

¾ cup chopped green bell pepper

1 clove garlic, minced

1 (16-ounce) can diced tomatoes

1 (16-ounce) can pinto beans

1 (8-ounce) can tomato sauce

2 teaspoons chili powder

½ teaspoon crushed basil

1. Brown ground beef and onion in a large skillet over medium-high heat, approximately 5–6 minutes. Leave the ground beef in larger chunks when cooking, instead of breaking it into very small pieces. Add the cooked beef and onion to a greased 4-quart slow cooker.

2. Add the remaining ingredients. Cover and cook on high for 4 hours or on low for 8 hours.

Per serving: Calories: 235 | Fat: 8 g | Protein: 20 g | Sodium: 581 mg | Fiber: 6 g | Carbohydrates: 20 g | Sugar: 5 g | GI: Low

Where's the Beef?

Some people prefer to use all beef in their chili. For a full beef, bean-free chili, use 2 pounds of ground beef and leave out the pinto beans. Quartered button mushrooms can also add a meaty texture to this chili.

Cabbage and Beef Casserole

This lower-carbohydrate beefy casserole includes cabbage and tomato sauce.

INGREDIENTS | SERVES 6

2 pounds ground beef

1 small onion, peeled and chopped

1 head cabbage, shredded

1 (16-ounce) can tomatoes

½ teaspoon garlic salt

¼ teaspoon ground thyme

¼ teaspoon red pepper flakes

½ teaspoon oregano

1 (8-ounce) can tomato sauce

1. In a large skillet, brown the ground beef over medium-high heat for about 5–6 minutes. Remove the ground beef to a bowl and set aside. In the same skillet, sauté the onions until softened, about 3–5 minutes.

2. In a greased 4- to 6-quart slow cooker, layer the cabbage, onions, tomatoes, garlic salt, thyme, pepper flakes, oregano, and beef. Repeat the layers, ending with beef. Pour the tomato sauce over everything.

3. Cook on low for 8 hours or on high for 4 hours.

Per serving: Calories: 327 | Fat: 15 g | Protein: 33 g | Sodium: 625 mg | Fiber: 5 g | Carbohydrates: 15 g | Sugar: 9 g | GI: Very low

Chicken Pesto Polenta

This recipe uses precooked polenta that is cut and layered in a casserole like lasagna. Most prepared polenta comes in tube form and is naturally gluten-free. Make sure to read the ingredients and call the manufacturer if you have any questions.

INGREDIENTS | SERVES 6

4 boneless, skinless chicken breasts, cut into bite-size pieces

1 cup prepared pesto, divided

1 medium onion, peeled and finely diced

4 cloves garlic, minced

1½ teaspoons dried Italian seasoning

1 (16-ounce) tube prepared polenta, cut into ½" slices

2 cups chopped fresh spinach

1 (14.5-ounce) can diced tomatoes

1 (8-ounce) bag shredded, low-fat Italian cheese blend

1. In a large bowl, combine the chicken pieces with ½ cup pesto, onions, garlic, and Italian seasoning.

2. In a greased 4-quart slow cooker, layer half of the chicken mixture, half of the polenta, half of the spinach, and half of the tomatoes. Continue to layer, ending with tomatoes. Cover and cook on low for 4–6 hours or on high for 2–3 hours.

3. Add the cheese, cover, and continue to cook for 45 minutes to an hour until cheese has melted.

Per serving: Calories: 636 | Fat: 39 g | Protein: 28 g | Sodium: 680 mg | Fiber: 5.5 g | Carbohydrates: 44 g | Sugar: 3.5 g | GI: Low

Make Your Own Pesto

Instead of using prepared pesto, you can easily make your own. In a high-powered blender or food processor, add 2 cups of fresh basil leaves, ½ cup of extra-virgin olive oil, ½ cup of Parmesan, ½ cup of pine nuts, 3 garlic cloves, and salt and pepper to taste. Blend on high for a few minutes until the mixture is creamy. You can use blanched almond flour in place of the Parmesan if you are intolerant to dairy.

Hawaiian Chicken

Pineapple and green peppers give this chicken dish a distinctive and fruity flavor.

INGREDIENTS | SERVES 4

4 boneless, skinless chicken breasts

1 (15-ounce) can sliced pineapple, drained, reserve the juice

½ medium green bell pepper, seeded and sliced

½ medium red bell pepper, seeded and sliced

¼ teaspoon cinnamon

½ teaspoon Chinese five-spice powder

½ teaspoon crushed red pepper

Using Pineapple Juice

When buying canned fruit, try to buy varieties that are canned in natural juices instead of corn syrup. The leftover juice can be saved in the refrigerator to use later as a beverage or even as a natural sweetener for a glass of iced tea or a bowl of warm oatmeal.

1. Place the chicken breasts in a greased 4-quart slow cooker.

2. Place 2 slices of pineapple on top of each piece of chicken. If there are leftover pieces, set them alongside the chicken.

3. Place the red and green pepper slices evenly over all the chicken. Sprinkle the cinnamon, Chinese five-spice powder, and crushed pepper evenly over the chicken.

4. Finally, pour ½ cup of the reserved pineapple juice over the chicken.

5. Cook on high for 2½–3 hours or on low for 5–6 hours.

Per serving: Calories: 336 | Fat: 6 g | Protein: 50 g | Sodium: 275 mg | Fiber: 2 g | Carbohydrates: 17 g | Sugar: 15 g | GI: Low

Peruvian Roast Chicken with Red Potatoes

A traditional Latin American favorite, this chicken dish has become popular in recent years, especially along the East Coast.

INGREDIENTS | SERVES 4

1 (3–4 pound) whole chicken
2½ tablespoons garlic powder
2 tablespoons paprika
1½ tablespoons cumin
2 teaspoons ground black pepper
1 teaspoon salt
½ teaspoon oregano
1 lemon, cut into quarters
2 pounds red potatoes, quartered
4 tablespoons white vinegar
4 tablespoons white wine
2 tablespoons olive oil

Lime Sauce

Peruvian chicken is often served with a dipping sauce. You can make a homemade version by mixing ½ cup of mayonnaise with 2 tablespoons of yellow mustard and 3 tablespoons of lime juice.

1. Wash the chicken with cold water and pat dry. Loosen the skin over the breast meat if possible, being careful not to break the skin.

2. In a small bowl, mix the garlic powder, paprika, cumin, black pepper, salt, and oregano. Rub the chicken generously with the spice mixture. Rub the meat of the chicken under the skin with the spice mixture as well. Place the lemon quarters inside the chicken.

3. Place the potatoes in the bottom of a 6-quart slow cooker. Place the spice-rubbed chicken on top of the potatoes.

4. Drizzle the vinegar, wine, and olive oil over the chicken.

5. Cook on high for 4 hours or on low for 8 hours.

Per serving: Calories: 740 | Fat: 20 g | Protein: 90 g | Sodium: 914 mg | Fiber: 7 g | Carbohydrates: 44 g | Sugar: 3 g | GI: Low

New England Boiled Dinner

Cutting the beef into serving-size pieces before you add it to the slow cooker will produce more tender meat, but you can keep it in one piece if you prefer to carve it at the table.

INGREDIENTS | SERVES 8

1 (3-pound) boneless beef round rump roast

4 cups gluten-free beef broth

2 medium yellow onions, peeled and sliced

1 teaspoon prepared horseradish

1 bay leaf

1 clove of garlic, minced

6 large carrots, peeled and cut into 1" pieces

3 rutabagas, peeled and quartered

4 large potatoes, peeled and quartered

1 small head of cabbage, cut into 8 wedges

2 tablespoons butter

2 tablespoons brown rice flour

1 teaspoon salt, optional

½ teaspoon freshly ground black pepper, optional

Horseradish Gravy

If you prefer a more intense horseradish flavor with cooked beef, increase the amount of horseradish to 1 tablespoon. Taste the pan juices before you thicken them with the butter and brown rice flour mixture, and add more horseradish at that time if you desire. Of course, you can have some horseradish or horseradish mayonnaise available as a condiment for those who want more.

1. Cut the beef into 8 serving-size pieces and add it along with the broth, onions, horseradish, bay leaf, and garlic to a 6-quart slow cooker. Add the carrots, rutabagas, potatoes, and cabbage wedges. Cover and cook on low for 8 hours.

2. Remove the meat and vegetables to a serving platter; cover and keep warm.

3. Increase the slow cooker setting to high; cover and cook until the pan juices begin to bubble around the edges. Mix the butter and flour in a bowl with ½ cup of the pan juices; strain out any lumps and whisk the mixture into the simmering liquid in the slow cooker. Cook and stir for 15 minutes or until the flour flavor is cooked out and the gravy is thickened enough to coat the back of a spoon. Taste for seasoning and add salt and pepper if desired. Serve alongside or over the meat and potatoes.

Per serving: Calories: 543 | Fat: 15 g | Protein: 44 g | Sodium: 875 mg | Fiber: 13 g | Carbohydrates: 57 g | Sugar: 17 g | GI: Moderate

Mexican Pork Roast

This slow cooked pork is an excellent main dish and can serve as a low-glycemic version of tacos. Try serving it topped with chopped tomatoes, shredded lettuce, shredded cheese, salsa, and sour cream!

INGREDIENTS | SERVES 4

1 tablespoon olive oil

1 large sweet onion, peeled and sliced

1 medium carrot, peeled and finely diced

1 jalapeño, seeded and minced

1 clove garlic, peeled and minced

½ teaspoon salt

¼ teaspoon dried Mexican oregano

¼ teaspoon ground coriander

¼ teaspoon freshly ground black pepper

1 (3-pound) pork shoulder or butt roast

1 cup gluten-free chicken broth

Pork and Sweet Potatoes?

Another low-glycemic meal option is to serve this pork over cooked butternut squash or mashed sweet potatoes. Serve with steamed broccoli or asparagus, along with a side of slow cooked black beans.

1. Add the olive oil, onion, carrot, and jalapeño to a 4- to 6-quart slow cooker. Stir to coat the vegetables in the oil. Cover and cook on high for 30 minutes or until the onions are softened. Stir in the garlic.

2. In a small bowl, combine the salt, oregano, coriander, and black pepper. Rub the spice mixture onto the pork roast.

3. Add the rubbed pork roast to the slow cooker. Add the chicken broth. Cover and cook on low for 6 hours or until the pork is tender and pulls apart easily.

4. Use a slotted spoon to remove the pork and vegetables to a serving platter. Cover and let rest for 10 minutes.

5. Increase the temperature of the slow cooker to high. Cook and reduce the pan juices by half.

6. Use 2 forks to shred the pork and mix it in with the cooked onion and jalapeño. Ladle the reduced pan juices over the pork.

Per serving: Calories: 576 | Fat: 28 g | Protein: 67 g | Sodium: 824 mg | Fiber: 1 g | Carbohydrates: 8 g | Sugar: 2 g | GI: Very low

Orange Honey–Glazed Ham

Many people are intimidated by making ham. Using the slow cooker makes it easy and the homemade orange-honey glaze is a breeze to mix up.

INGREDIENTS | SERVES 6

1 (4-pound) bone-in gluten-free ham (discard glaze or seasoning packet)

½ cup seltzer water

½ cup orange juice

¼ cup honey

1–2 tablespoons orange zest

1 teaspoon ground cloves

¼ teaspoon cinnamon

1. Place the ham, seltzer water, and orange juice in a greased 4- to 6-quart slow cooker. Cook on low for 6–8 hours or on high for 3–4 hours.

2. In a small bowl, mix the honey, orange zest, ground cloves, and cinnamon. Spread over the ham. Cook for an additional 45 minutes to an hour, venting the slow cooker lid with a chopstick or spoon handle. The ham should become golden brown and glazed. If necessary, finish the ham off in 350°F oven for 15–20 minutes to get a shiny glaze.

Per serving: Calories: 479 | Fat: 22 g | Protein: 47 g | Sodium: 2,345 mg | Fiber: 0.5 g | Carbohydrates: 20 g | Sugar: 14 g | GI: Low

Spiced–Apple Cider Turkey

This recipe makes candied sweet potatoes while it cooks the turkey in the brown sugar–cider sauce.

INGREDIENTS | SERVES 8

1 (3-pound) boneless turkey breast

½ teaspoon salt

½ teaspoon freshly ground black pepper

2 Gala, Fuji, or Honeycrisp apples, peeled, cored, and sliced

4 large sweet potatoes, peeled and cut in half

½ cup apple cider or apple juice

½ teaspoon ground cinnamon

¼ teaspoon ground cloves

¼ teaspoon ground allspice

2 tablespoons brown sugar

1. Grease a 4- to 6-quart slow cooker with nonstick spray. Add the turkey breast and season it with salt and pepper.

2. Arrange the apple slices over and around the turkey.

3. Add the sweet potato halves to the slow cooker.

4. In a small bowl, combine the cider or juice, cinnamon, cloves, allspice, and brown sugar. Pour the mixture over the ingredients in the slow cooker.

5. Cover and cook on low for 5–6 hours or until the internal temperature of the turkey is 170°F.

Per serving: Calories: 282 | Fat: 1 g | Protein: 42 g | Sodium: 267 mg | Fiber: 3 g | Carbohydrates: 23 g | Sugar: 11 g | GI: Low

Slow-Cooker Cheeseburgers

This meal is reminiscent of "sloppy joes" but with a cheesy twist! Feel free to serve this cheesy ground beef on gluten-free buns with lettuce, tomatoes, and any other hamburger toppings you desire. Try it over cooked rice, pasta, or even cooked spaghetti squash.

INGREDIENTS | SERVES 4

1 pound lean ground beef
¼ cup gluten-free ketchup
2 tablespoons yellow mustard
1 teaspoon dried basil
2 cups mild Cheddar cheese

1. Brown the ground beef in a large skillet over medium heat. Pour off the grease, and add the cooked ground beef to a greased 2.5-quart slow cooker.

2. Add the ketchup, mustard, and basil to the slow cooker. Cook on high for 2–3 hours or on low for 4–5 hours.

3. Thirty minutes before serving, add the shredded Cheddar cheese to the ground beef mixture. When the cheese is melted, spoon 3–4 tablespoons of cheeseburger mixture into each hamburger bun.

Per serving: Calories: 480 | Fat: 20 g | Protein: 41 g | Sodium: 824 mg | Fiber: 3 g | Carbohydrates: 18 g | Sugar: 4 g | GI: Low

Vanilla Poached Pears

Slow poaching makes these pears meltingly tender and infuses them with a rich vanilla flavor.

INGREDIENTS | SERVES 4

4 Bosc pears, peeled
1 vanilla bean, split
2 tablespoons vanilla extract
2 cups water or apple juice

1. Stand the pears up in a 4-quart slow cooker. Add the remaining ingredients.

2. Cook on low for 2 hours or until the pears are tender. Discard all cooking liquid prior to serving.

Per serving: Calories: 115 | Fat: 0 g | Protein: 1 g | Sodium: 6 mg | Fiber: 5 g | Carbohydrates: 26 g | Sugar: 17 g | GI: Low

In a Pinch . . .

If you need an easy dessert, but don't have fresh fruit, use a large can of sliced or halved pears. Drain and rinse them thoroughly. Make the recipe as written, except use only ½ cup of water or apple juice.

Blueberry Cobbler

An old-fashioned cobbler with sweetened fruit on the bottom and a crunchy, biscuit topping, this dessert can be served plain or with ice cream.

INGREDIENTS | SERVES 6

¾ cup water

⅔ cup plus 2 tablespoons sugar

2 tablespoons cornstarch

3 cups fresh or frozen blueberries

½ cup brown rice flour

½ cup arrowroot starch

1 teaspoon baking powder

¼ teaspoon xanthan gum

⅓ cup 2% milk

1 tablespoon melted butter

½ teaspoon cinnamon mixed with 2 teaspoons sugar

2 tablespoons cold butter, cut into small pieces

Make It Easier

If you don't want to make your own fruit filling, use a can of cherry pie filling, apple pie filling, or even a can of whole cranberry jelly. Make the cobbler even easier by replacing the brown rice flour, arrowroot starch, baking powder and xanthan gum with 1 cup of Gluten-Free Bisquick.

1. Grease a 4-quart slow cooker.

2. In a small saucepan, whisk the water, ⅔ cup of sugar, and cornstarch. Cook over high heat, stirring constantly until boiling. Allow to boil for 1 minute. The mixture will turn translucent and thicken. Remove from heat and add the blueberries. Pour blueberry filling into the greased slow cooker.

3. In a small bowl, whisk the flour, arrowroot starch, baking powder, 2 tablespoons sugar, and xanthan gum. Make a well in the center of the dry ingredients and add the milk and melted butter. Mix until you have a thick batter.

4. Drop the batter 1 tablespoon at a time on top of the blueberry filling and use a fork to spread it evenly over the casserole.

5. Sprinkle the cinnamon and sugar mixture over the top of the casserole. Dot with butter.

6. Cover and vent the slow cooker lid with a chopstick or the end of a wooden spoon. Cook on high for 2½–3 hours or until the fruit filling is bubbling on the sides of the topping and the biscuit topping is cooked through.

Per serving: Calories: 307 | Fat: 7 g | Protein: 2 g | Sodium: 91 mg | Fiber: 3 g | Carbohydrates: 62 g | Sugar: 36 g | GI: Moderate

Crustless Lemon Cheesecake

Cheesecake bakes perfectly in the slow cooker. In this recipe, the slow cooker is lined with parchment paper, which makes for very easy cleaning!

INGREDIENTS | SERVES 8

16 ounces cream cheese, softened

⅔ cup sugar

2 large eggs

1 tablespoon cornstarch

1 teaspoon fresh lemon zest

2 tablespoons fresh lemon juice

1. In a large bowl, beat the cream cheese and sugar until smooth.

2. Beat in the eggs and continue beating on the medium speed of a hand-held electric mixer for about 3 minutes.

3. Beat in the remaining ingredients and continue beating for about 1 minute.

4. Line a 4-quart slow cooker with parchment paper. Pour the batter onto the parchment paper.

5. Cover and cook on high for 2½–3 hours or until the cheesecake is set. Remove slow cooker insert and place it in the refrigerator to chill for 2–6 hours. Slice to serve.

Per serving: Calories: 279 | Fat: 20 g | Protein: 5 g | Sodium: 198 mg | Fiber: 0 g | Carbohydrates: 20 g | Sugar: 18 g | GI: Moderate

CHAPTER 13

Desserts and Sweet Treats

Grain-Free Chocolate Chunk Cookies

Even when you follow a low-glycemic diet, you should allow yourself treats occasionally. These high protein, low-carb cookies are a great alternative to the sugar-filled and wheat-laden chocolate chip cookies you used to eat. Plus, they are very easy to make!

INGREDIENTS | MAKES 12 COOKIES

2 cups blanched almond flour

½ cup coconut palm sugar

3 tablespoons arrowroot starch or tapioca starch

½ teaspoon baking soda

2 heaping tablespoons ground flaxseeds (optional)

¼ teaspoon sea salt

3 tablespoons Spectrum Organic Shortening or butter

1 tablespoon vanilla extract

1 teaspoon almond extract

3–4 tablespoons almond milk or water, as needed

1 (3½-ounce) 70% dark chocolate bar, chopped into chunks

A Few Tips

Do not try to make these cookies with leftover almond pulp from homemade almond milk. It doesn't work—the pulp is too wet and doesn't set up while baking. Instead of coconut palm sugar, you can use regular sugar, brown sugar, or honey in these cookies.

1. Preheat the oven to 350°F. Line a large cookie sheet with parchment paper.

2. In a large bowl, whisk the almond flour, coconut palm sugar, arrowroot starch, baking soda, flaxseeds, and salt. Cut the shortening or butter into the dry ingredients with a pastry blender or a knife and fork until the shortening resembles very small peas evenly throughout the dry ingredients.

3. Make a well in the center of the dry ingredients and add the vanilla extract, almond extract, and 3 tablespoons of almond milk. Using a little elbow grease, stir the wet ingredients into the dry ingredients until you have a very thick batter (it might be a bit crumbly).

4. This may take several minutes to incorporate well. If necessary, use an additional tablespoon of almond milk, but don't add too much milk or the cookies will not turn out right. Fold in the chopped chocolate chunks and evenly mix them throughout the dough. Scoop the dough into golf ball–size mounds and place on cookie sheet about 2" apart. Flatten lightly and shape with your hands into round cookies.

5. Bake for 12–15 minutes depending on how crispy you want your cookies. The edges should be golden brown when done. Store leftovers in an airtight container on the counter or in the refrigerator for 2–3 days. These cookies are best the day they are made.

Per serving (1 cookie): Calories: 191 | Fat: 13 g | Protein: 4 g | Sodium: 102 mg | Fiber: 2 g | Carbohydrates: 16 g | Sugar: 11 g | GI: Low

Almond Cranberry Biscotti

This lightly sweetened cookie is perfect with a hot cup of coffee or tea. Change the flavors by adding ½ teaspoon each of ground nutmeg and ground cinnamon, and 2 teaspoons pure vanilla extract in place of the almond extract and cranberries.

INGREDIENTS | MAKES 24 COOKIES

3 cups blanched almond flour

½ cup coconut palm sugar

¼ teaspoon sea salt

1 teaspoon baking soda

¾ cup dried cranberries

¾ cup toasted, sliced almonds

¼ cup melted butter, coconut oil, or light-tasting olive oil

2 large eggs

1 teaspoon pure almond extract

3 tablespoons cold water

1. Preheat the oven to 350°F. Line two large baking sheets with parchment paper. Set aside.

2. In a large bowl, whisk the almond flour, coconut palm sugar, sea salt, baking soda, dried cranberries, and sliced almonds.

3. In a smaller bowl, whisk the butter, eggs, almond extract, and cold water. Pour the wet ingredients into the dry ingredients and stir until you have a thick dough.

4. Shape the dough into two (9" × 3") logs and place them on one baking sheet. Bake for 25–30 minutes until the logs are golden brown around the edges. Allow the logs to cool for 1 hour on the baking sheet.

5. Once the logs are completely cool, move them to a cutting board and using a very sharp, serrated knife, slice each log into 12 diagonal cookies. Place the cookies back on the baking sheets and bake for 15–18 minutes until very crisp.

6. Cool the cookies on the baking sheets 30 minutes, and then serve. Cookies can be stored in an airtight container on the counter for up to 1 week. These cookies also freeze well for up to 2 months.

Per serving (2 cookies): Calories: 295 | Fat: 21 g | Protein: 8 g | Sodium: 166 mg | Fiber: 4 g | Carbohydrates: 21 g | Sugar: 14 g | GI: Moderate

Honey Sesame Cookies

These lightly sweetened cookies are made with sesame seeds that toast as they bake, creating a nutty crunch. These cookies are also egg-free and can easily be made vegan by using maple syrup instead of honey.

INGREDIENTS | MAKES 2 DOZEN COOKIES

1¼ cups blanched almond flour

¼ teaspoon sea salt

½ teaspoon baking soda

⅓ cup honey

⅓ cup roasted tahini (sesame seed butter)

1 tablespoon butter or Spectrum Organic Shortening

1 tablespoon vanilla extract

¼ cup toasted sesame seeds

A Sunny Variation

You can also make these cookies with Sun-Butter, a sunflower seed butter that is a great crunchy alternative to sesame seed–based tahini. For the outer coating instead of using sesame seeds, roughly chop ½ cup of sunflower seeds and roll the cookies in them before baking.

1. Preheat the oven to 350°F. Line a large cookie sheet with parchment paper.

2. In a medium mixing bowl, whisk the almond flour, sea salt, and baking soda.

3. In a smaller bowl, mix the honey, tahini, shortening, and vanilla extract. Stir the wet ingredients into the dry ingredients. Roll the dough into 1" balls. Roll the balls in sesame seeds and place them 1" apart on the cookie sheet.

4. Using the palm of your hand, gently flatten the cookies. Bake for 8–10 minutes until they are golden brown and have the scent of toasted sesame seeds. Cool for 5 minutes on the pan and then transfer to a wire rack to cool completely. Store leftover cookies in an airtight container for up to 5 days.

Per serving (2 cookies): Calories: 163 | Fat: 11 g | Protein: 4 g | Sodium: 110 mg | Fiber: 2 g | Carbohydrates: 12 g | Sugar: 8 g | GI: Low

Low-Sugar Cocoa Nib Cookies

Cocoa nibs are a healthy low-sugar, dairy-free replacement for chocolate chips. They are basically hulled, roasted, and chopped pure cocoa beans. As the primary ingredient in chocolate, these chopped cocoa beans add delicious flavor and crunch to these low-sugar cookies. They can usually be purchased at a natural foods store or a high-end grocery store such as Whole Foods. You can also buy them online from stores such as Amazon.com.

INGREDIENTS | MAKES 2 DOZEN COOKIES

1½ cups blanched almond flour

¼ cup arrowroot starch

½ teaspoon baking soda

¼ teaspoon sea salt

1 egg

⅓ cup honey or maple syrup

2 tablespoons coconut oil or softened butter

1 teaspoon pure vanilla extract

¼ cup raw cocoa nibs

1. Preheat the oven to 350°F. Line a cookie sheet with parchment paper.

2. In a large bowl, whisk the almond flour, arrowroot starch, baking soda, and sea salt thoroughly. Make a well in the center of the dry ingredients.

3. Add the egg, honey, coconut oil, and vanilla extract into the center of the dry ingredients. Stir the wet ingredients into the dry ingredients to create a sticky cookie dough. Fold in the raw cocoa nibs.

4. Drop the cookie dough 1 tablespoon at a time 2" apart onto the lined cookie sheet. Bake for 8–9 minutes until the cookies are golden brown. The cookies will be soft and almost cakelike in texture. Allow the cookies to cool on the pan for 10–15 minutes and then store them in an airtight container on the counter for up to 5 days.

Per serving (2 cookies): Calories: 146 | Fat: 9 g | Protein: 4 g | Sodium: 108 mg | Fiber: 2 g | Carbohydrates: 14 g | Sugar: 8 g | GI: Low

Cinnamon Peach Crisp

A fruit crisp is such an easy dessert to make, and using almond flour makes it even easier because you don't need several flours to create the texture and flavor you want.

INGREDIENTS | SERVES 8

1½ cups blanched almond flour

¼ cup coconut palm sugar or brown sugar

1 teaspoon ground cinnamon

½ teaspoon freshly grated nutmeg

¼ teaspoon sea salt

3 tablespoons butter or coconut oil

7–8 medium peaches, peeled, seeded, and sliced (or a 28-ounce can sliced peaches, drained)

3 tablespoons orange juice or apple juice (unnecessary if using canned peaches)

1. Preheat the oven to 350°F. Grease a 2- or 3-quart casserole dish or an 8" pie plate with nonstick cooking spray or light-tasting olive oil.

2. In a small bowl, mix the flour, sugar, cinnamon, nutmeg, and salt. Cut in the butter or coconut oil with a pastry blender or with a knife and fork until the mixture is crumbly.

3. Place the peaches in the greased casserole dish. Stir in the juice. Sprinkle the flour mixture over the peaches.

4. Bake for 30–40 minutes until the top is golden brown and the peaches are starting to bubble around the edges of the dish.

Per serving: Calories: 247 | Fat: 15 g | Protein: 6 g | Sodium: 76 mg | Fiber: 4.5 g | Carbohydrates: 26 g | Sugar: 20 g | GI: Moderate

Grain-Free Apple Spice Cupcakes

These down-to-earth cupcakes are perfect for an on-the-go breakfast or a 3 P.M. pick-me-up.

INGREDIENTS | SERVES 12

3 cups blanched almond flour

¾ cup coconut palm sugar

1 teaspoon baking soda

1 teaspoon ground cinnamon

1 teaspoon freshly grated nutmeg

½ teaspoon ground ginger

¼ teaspoon ground cardamom (optional)

¼ teaspoon ground cloves

3 large eggs

¾ cup unsweetened applesauce

3 tablespoons light-tasting olive oil or melted coconut oil

2 tablespoons honey

½ teaspoon apple cider vinegar

1 tablespoon vanilla extract

1. Preheat the oven to 350°F. Line a muffin pan with paper liners and grease with nonstick cooking spray or light-tasting olive oil; set aside.

2. Whisk the almond flour, coconut palm sugar, baking soda, and spices in a large bowl and set aside. In another bowl, mix the eggs, applesauce, oil, honey, vinegar, and vanilla. Mix the wet ingredients into the dry ingredients and stir until you have a thick batter. Do not overmix.

3. Spoon the batter into the muffin pans until they are at least three-quarters full.

4. Bake for 18–25 minutes until a toothpick inserted in the middle comes out clean. Let cupcakes cool on a wire rack. Frost with homemade grain-free vanilla icing such as the Creamy Vanilla Frosting in this chapter, if desired. Store in airtight container in refrigerator as these cupcakes are quite moist.

Per serving: Calories: 278 | Fat: 18 g | Protein: 8 g | Sodium: 123 mg | Fiber: 3 g | Carbohydrates: 23 g | Sugar: 18 g | GI: Moderate

Almond-Flour Devil's Food Cake

This rich chocolate cake is perfect for birthday parties. The recipe also makes 12 regular cupcakes; bake for 18–25 minutes until a toothpick inserted in the middle comes out clean.

INGREDIENTS | SERVES 10

Cake

2 cups blanched almond flour

½ cup dark cocoa powder

1¼ cups coconut palm sugar

1 teaspoon baking soda

¼ teaspoon sea salt

3 large eggs

¾ cup unsweetened applesauce or plain pumpkin purée

½ cup water

¼ cup light-tasting olive oil or melted coconut oil

½ teaspoon apple cider vinegar

1 tablespoon vanilla extract

¼ teaspoon pure almond extract

½ cup mini chocolate chips (optional)

Cream Filling

¼ cup chocolate chips

¾ cup heavy whipping cream or coconut cream

1 teaspoon vanilla

Ganache Glaze

4 tablespoons butter or coconut oil

4 ounces unsweetened chocolate

¼ cup chocolate chips

1 tablespoon honey

1. Preheat the oven to 350°F. Line an 8" or 9" cake pan with parchment paper and then grease with a nonstick cooking spray or light-tasting olive oil.

2. In a large bowl, whisk the almond flour, cocoa powder, sugar, baking soda, and salt.

3. In a smaller bowl, whisk the eggs, applesauce, water, oil, vinegar, vanilla, and almond extract. Mix the wet ingredients into the dry ingredients until you have a thick batter. If desired, fold in ½ cup mini chocolate chips.

4. Pour the batter into the cake pan. Bake for 25–35 minutes until a toothpick inserted in the middle comes out clean and the cake is a deep chocolate brown. Allow the cake to cool in the pan for 10 minutes. Turn the cake out onto a wire rack and continue to cool for an additional 40 minutes to 1 hour.

5. Make the cream filling: Melt the chocolate chips in a double boiler or the microwave. In another bowl, whip the heavy whipping cream or coconut cream until it is light and airy. Fold in the vanilla and the melted chocolate.

6. Make the chocolate ganache: Melt the butter or coconut oil with the unsweetened chocolate, chocolate chips, and honey. Stir until thoroughly melted.

7. To the assemble cake, slice the cake in half and spread the filling in the center. Place the other half of cake on top of the filling and slowly pour the chocolate ganache over the cake. Place the cake in the refrigerator until ready to serve.

Per serving: Calories: 528 | Fat: 36 g | Protein: 9 g | Sodium: 216 mg | Fiber: 5 g | Carbohydrates: 51 g | Sugar: 41 g | GI: Moderate

Coconut-Flour Yellow Cake
with Creamy White Frosting

This light, fluffy cake is made primarily with coconut flour, a good option for people who need to be grain-free, but cannot tolerate almonds.

INGREDIENTS | SERVES 10

Cake

¾ cup sifted coconut flour

¾ teaspoon baking soda

⅛ teaspoon sea salt

½ cup coconut palm sugar

6 tablespoons melted butter or coconut oil

3 large eggs

1 cup almond milk or 1 cup coconut milk or hemp milk

1 tablespoon vanilla extract

½ teaspoon apple cider vinegar

Frosting

1 cup unsalted "SunButter" (sunflower seed butter)

1 cup Spectrum Organic Shortening

⅓ cup maple syrup or coconut palm sugar

1. Preheat the oven to 350°F. Line an 8" or 9" cake pan with parchment paper and then grease with nonstick cooking spray or light-tasting olive oil.

2. In a large bowl, whisk the coconut flour, baking soda, salt, and coconut palm sugar. In a smaller bowl, mix the butter, eggs, almond milk, vanilla extract, and vinegar. Pour the wet ingredients into the dry ingredients and mix until you have a thick batter.

3. Pour the batter into the cake pan. To get a rounded cake top, spread the batter evenly in the pan with a rubber spatula that's been dipped in water or spritzed with nonstick cooking spray.

4. Bake for 25–35 minutes until the cake is golden brown and a toothpick inserted in the middle comes out clean. Be careful not to overbake; coconut flour can dry out quickly.

5. Mix the frosting ingredients. Blend on high for 1–2 minutes until thick and creamy. Refrigerate for 10 minutes before using to frost the cake.

6. Frost the top and sides of the cake. You can make this a two-layer cake by slicing the cake through the middle to create two smaller layers.

Per serving: Calories: 499 | Fat: 39 g | Protein: 10 g | Sodium: 277 mg | Fiber: 7 g | Carbohydrates: 29 g | Sugar: 19 g | GI: Moderate

Peanut Butter–Chocolate Chip Cupcakes

These cupcakes will quickly becomes one of the family favorites!

INGREDIENTS | SERVES 18

⅔ cup coconut palm sugar
1 teaspoon baking soda
1¼ cups creamy natural peanut butter
4 large eggs
¼ cup water
½ teaspoon apple cider vinegar
1 tablespoon vanilla extract
¼ cup mini chocolate chips

1. Preheat the oven to 350°F. Line cupcake pans with paper liners and then grease them with nonstick cooking spray or light-tasting olive oil.

2. In a medium bowl, mix the sugar and baking soda. Add the peanut butter and cream them together.

3. In another medium bowl, whisk the eggs, water, vinegar, and vanilla. Pour the egg mixture into the peanut butter mixture and mix with a fork until it's very creamy and light.

4. Spoon the batter into paper liners until they are no more than a half to three-quarters full. The cupcakes need room to rise.

5. Sprinkle a few mini chocolate chips on top of the cupcakes and place in the preheated oven. Bake for 15–18 minutes until golden brown and a toothpick inserted in the middle of a cupcake comes out clean.

6. Allow the cupcakes to cool for about 20 minutes on a wire rack before serving. Cupcakes may deflate slightly as they cool. Store leftovers in an airtight container in the refrigerator for up to 5 days.

Per serving: Calories: 168 | Fat: 10 g | Protein: 6 g | Sodium: 168 mg | Fiber: 1 g | Carbohydrates: 13 g | Sugar: 10 g | GI: Low

Honey Pumpkin Pie

This is a low-maintenance, simple, comforting pumpkin pie for the holidays. You'll never miss the gluten, grains, dairy, or sugar.

INGREDIENTS | SERVES 8

Crust

1½ cups blanched almond flour or finely crushed pecans

¼ teaspoon sea salt

4 tablespoons Spectrum Organic Shortening

Pumpkin Filling

1 (15-ounce) can pumpkin purée

2 teaspoons ground cinnamon

½ teaspoon ground ginger

¼ teaspoon ground cloves

2 large eggs

½ cup honey

½ cup full-fat coconut milk

1. Preheat the oven to 350°F. Grease a 9" deep-dish pie pan.

2. In a small bowl, mix the crust ingredients until the mixture is crumbly.

3. Pour the crust mixture into the pie pan and place a sheet of plastic wrap on top. Use your fingers to press the mixture across the bottom and up the sides of the pie pan to form an easy crust. Remove the plastic wrap and prebake the crust for 10 minutes. Remove it from the oven and set it aside while you make the filling.

4. In a large bowl, whisk the pumpkin, spices, eggs, honey, and coconut milk until thick and creamy. Pour the mixture into the crust. Bake for 45 minutes until the center is set and a knife inserted in the middle comes out clean. The pie will be slightly jiggly when it's finished. If the pie begins to brown too much or burn, gently place a sheet of aluminum foil over the pie while it's cooking.

5. Allow the pie to cool on a wire rack for at least 1 hour. Refrigerate for at least 4–6 hours or overnight before serving.

Per serving: Calories: 307 | Fat: 21 g | Protein: 7 g | Sodium: 96 mg | Fiber: 4 g | Carbohydrates: 27 g | Sugar: 19 g | GI: Moderate

Heavenly Cookie Bars

These cookie bars are amazing! Keep in mind that these bars contain dried fruit, which is not for those following a strict Paleolithic diet regime.

INGREDIENTS | SERVES 48

2 cups raw honey

4 cups almond flour

½ teaspoon nutmeg

½ teaspoon ginger

½ cup chopped dried dates

2 cups ground walnuts

½ cup raisins

1. Preheat the oven to 350°F.

2. Line two cookie sheets with parchment paper.

3. Warm the honey in a medium saucepan over low heat and let cool slightly.

4. Sift together the flour and spices in a medium bowl.

5. Add the honey to flour mixture and stir until well blended.

6. Stir in the dates, walnuts, and raisins.

7. Roll the dough to ¼" thick and cut into squares.

8. Place the squares on the prepared cookie sheets and bake for 10 minutes.

Per serving: Calories: 121 | Fat: 3.5 g | Protein: 2.5 g | Sodium: 1.5 g | Fiber: 2 g | Carbohydrate: 23 g | Sugar: 19 g | GI: Moderate

Whoopie Pies

These sweet treats are exquisite. You will be shocked at how amazing they really are. But beware, they have quite a few calories.

INGREDIENTS | SERVES 12

2 cups almond flour

½ cup coconut flour

½ teaspoon baking soda

1 tablespoon cinnamon

1 teaspoon dried ginger

½ teaspoon allspice

½ teaspoon nutmeg

¼ teaspoon cloves

1 cup raw honey

2 large eggs

1 tablespoon vanilla extract

¼ cup hazelnut flour

Baking Soda

Strict Paleo followers would debate that baking soda is not allowed in the Paleolithic lifestyle. If you are choosing to be a less-strict follower, then baking soda is allowed, but this is not following the true Paleolithic diet.

1. Preheat the oven to 350°F. Cover two cookie sheets with parchment paper.

2. Mix the almond flour, coconut flour, baking soda, cinnamon, ginger, allspice, nutmeg, and cloves in a large bowl.

3. Add the honey, eggs, and vanilla to the flour mixture.

4. Add the hazelnut flour and mix to form a stiff dough.

5. Place ¼-cup scoops of the dough onto the cookie sheets, spacing cookies 2" apart.

6. Bake for 15 minutes. Cool on a wire rack.

7. If desired, sandwich two cookies with the Creamy Vanilla Frosting (see the recipe later in this chapter).

Per serving: Calories: 188 | Fat: 1.5 g | Protein: 4.5 g | Sodium: 65 mg | Fiber: 3 g | Carbohydrate: 43 g | Sugar: 23 g | GI: Moderate

Creamy Vanilla Frosting

This frosting can be used for Whoopie Pies (see recipe in this chapter), but it can also be used to frost any dessert.

INGREDIENTS | SERVES 12

4 tablespoons coconut butter

2 tablespoons raw honey

½ cup cacao nibs

½ teaspoon vanilla extract

½ teaspoon cinnamon

Blend all ingredients in a medium bowl and whisk thoroughly.

Per serving: Calories: 73 | Fat: 4 g | Protein: 1 g | Sodium: 3.8 mg | Fiber: 1 g | Carbohydrate: 9 g | Sugar: 8 g | GI: Low

Almond Butter Cookies

Almond cookies are a great snack. They contain the essential fatty acids omega-6 and omega-3. Almonds are also a source of vitamin E.

INGREDIENTS | SERVES 12

1 cup almond butter

1 large egg white

2 tablespoons unsweetened applesauce

2 tablespoons unsweetened coconut flakes

1 tablespoon cacao powder

1. Preheat the oven to 375°F.

2. Beat all the ingredients together to form a thick batter.

3. Place tablespoon-size scoops of dough onto an ungreased cookie sheet. Bake 10–12 minutes or until lightly brown on top.

Per serving: Calories: 151 | Fat: 14 g | Protein: 3.8 g | Sodium: 8.6 mg | Fiber: 1.5 g | Carbohydrate: 5.5 g | Sugar: 3 g | GI: Low

Chocolate-Coconut Milk Balls

These coconut milk balls are not as creamy as ice cream, but they are a nice alternative. You can change the flavor by changing the fruit purée that you add to the recipe.

INGREDIENTS | SERVES 10

12 tablespoons raw cacao powder

6 tablespoons fresh fruit purée of your choice

6 tablespoons coconut oil

6 tablespoons coconut milk

3 tablespoons unsweetened shredded coconut

2 tablespoons cacao nibs

1 ripe banana

1. Combine all the ingredients in a food processor and pulse until very smooth.

2. Add water if the consistency is not fluid.

3. Pour into ice-cube trays or molds and freeze.

Per serving: Calories: 149 | Fat: 13 g | Protein: 2 g | Sodium: 4 mg | Fiber: 3.5 g | Carbohydrate: 11 g | Sugar: 6 g | GI: Low

Coconut

Coconut has many great properties. This recipe uses all the edible parts of the coconut—the meat, oil, and milk. Coconut provides high amounts of fiber, vitamins, and minerals as well as being good for your skin.

Baked Bananas

This healthy dessert is sure to be a favorite. Make it in bulk and spread it on Paleo pancakes or Paleo banana bread.

INGREDIENTS | SERVES 4

4 small bananas, peeled
½ teaspoon grated orange rind
½ tablespoon fruit purée
1 tablespoon lemon juice
⅛ teaspoon cinnamon
⅛ teaspoon nutmeg
1 tablespoon melted coconut oil
1 tablespoon cacao nibs

1. Preheat the oven to 350°F.

2. Cut each banana lengthwise and across into eight pieces.

3. Arrange the banana slices in a small baking pan.

4. Sprinkle them evenly with the orange rind, fruit purée, lemon juice, cinnamon, nutmeg, and coconut oil.

5. Bake uncovered 35–40 minutes, basting after 15 minutes with the liquid in the dish.

6. Sprinkle the bananas with cacao nibs before serving.

Per serving: Calories: 200 | Fat: 5 g | Protein: 1.5 g | Sodium: 1.5 mg | Fiber: 5 g | Carbohydrate: 41 g | Sugar: 15 g | GI: Moderate

Chocolate-Almond Sliver Cookies

These cookies are a nice treat without the guilt.

INGREDIENTS | SERVES 12

5 large egg whites
3 cups slivered almonds
½ cup cacao nibs
¼ cup raw honey

Nut Alternatives

Feel free to switch it up in recipes where nuts are included. This recipe would work well for pecans, hazelnuts, walnuts, or sunflower or pumpkin seeds. The great thing about these recipes is that you can alter them to fit your needs and tastes.

1. Preheat the oven to 350°F. Spray a cookie sheet with cooking spray.

2. Whisk the egg whites for 30 seconds.

3. Add the almonds, cacao nibs, and honey to the egg whites and mix well.

4. Form 1" balls and place them on the prepared cookie sheet.

5. Bake until lightly brown on top, approximately 10 minutes.

Per serving (1 cookie): Calories: 197 | Fat: 14 g | Protein: 7 g | Sodium: 27 mg | Fiber: 3 g | Carbohydrate: 15 g | Sugar: 9 g | GI: Low

Mango Creamsicle Sorbet

When the weather is hot and you're looking for a cold, refreshing treat, try this homemade sorbet recipe.

INGREDIENTS | SERVES 6

3 cups chopped peeled mangoes or fresh peaches

½ cup cold water

1 cup shredded coconut

2 tablespoons lemon juice

Sorbet

Try this recipe with other favorite fruits. If the sorbet does not seem sweet enough, add honey to the mixture next time. No honey is added here because mango has a high sugar content on its own.

1. In a food processor or blender, combine the mangoes and water; cover and process until smooth.

2. Add the coconut and lemon juice; cover and process until smooth.

3. Transfer to a container and freeze until solid, about 2 hours.

Per serving: Calories: 80 | Fat: 4.5 g | Protein: 1.5 g | Sodium: 2.5 mg | Fiber: 3 g | Carbohydrate: 11 g | Sugar: 8 g | GI: Low

Blueberry Cookie Balls

These antioxidant-packed cookie balls are a great alternative to commercial cookies. They taste great, are all-natural, and will give you energy from all macronutrient categories.

INGREDIENTS | SERVES 12

2 egg whites
5 cups blueberries
4 teaspoons cinnamon
1½ teaspoons ginger
¼ cup raw honey
1 teaspoon vanilla extract

Glycemic Load and Kids

It is particularly important to limit children's sugar intake, because they are more sensitive to mood changes than adults and lack the ability to control their emotions. Recipes that contain fat, protein, and carbohydrates together minimize blood sugar spikes and pitfalls.

1. Preheat the oven to 350°F.

2. Whisk the egg whites in a bowl until frothy.

3. Add all the other ingredients and mix well. Place a sheet of parchment paper on the cookie sheet to prevent cookie balls from sticking to the pan.

4. Scoop out tablespoons of dough and form into balls. Place the balls on a cookie sheet.

5. Bake for 12–15 minutes. Allow to cook for 15 minutes.

6. Place on a pan and chill in the refrigerator for 1 hour.

Per serving (1 ball): Calories: 60 | Fat: 0.5 g | Protein: 1.5 g | Sodium: 12 mg | Fiber: 1.5 g | Carbohydrate: 14 g | Sugar: 10 g | GI: Low

Paleo Chocolate Bars

Your kids will be thrilled when they see these chocolate bars in their lunchboxes. These bars are quick to whip up and quick to eat. The amount of honey can be varied depending on your desired level of sweetness.

INGREDIENTS | SERVES 8

1 tablespoon raw honey

4 tablespoons coconut oil

¼ cup ground almonds

¼ cup ground hazelnuts

¼ cup sunflower seeds

¼ cup cacao powder

¾ cups shredded unsweetened coconut flakes

Natural Sugars

Although natural honey is an acceptable Paleolithic diet food, eat it in moderation. It does cause an increase in blood sugar levels, thus a spike in insulin.

1. Melt the honey and coconut oil in medium saucepan over medium heat.

2. In a large mixing bowl, combine the almonds, hazelnuts, sunflower seeds, cacao powder, and coconut. Mix thoroughly.

3. Add the honey mixture to the bowl and mix well.

4. Pour the dough into an 8" × 8" baking pan and store in the refrigerator or freezer until firm, about 10 minutes.

5. Cut into squares and enjoy.

Per serving (1 square): Calories: 154 | Fat: 15 g | Protein: 2 g | Sodium: 2 mg | Fiber: 2 g | Carbohydrate: 5 g | Sugar: 4 g | GI: Low

APPENDIX A

Additional Information

The Diabetes Network

This website is useful for looking up information about the GI, as well as for determining the GI value of specific foods.
www.diabetesnet.com

The Gluten-Free Mall

This is a fine source for all kinds of rice and a variety of flours. Whether you are worried about gluten or not, it's a resource for many products that may be hard to find in your local stores.
www.celiac.com/glutenfreemall

The Glycemic Index Diet on Web MD

This article explains the glycemic index and offers tips for following a low-glycemic diet. *www.webmd.com/diet/features/glycemic-index-diet*

Irish Oatmeal

Irish oatmeal is cut more coarsely than quick oats for maximum advantage to low GI diets. McCann's and Flavahans' are two brands available nationally in all major food chains.

National Diabetes Information Clearinghouse (NDIC)

NDIC is a service of the National Institute of Diabetes and Digestive and Kidney Diseases, a part of the National Institutes of Health. The mission of NDIC is to increase knowledge and understanding about diabetes among patients, health-care providers, and the public.
http://diabetes.niddk.nih.gov

The Paleo Diet

The original site for the Paleo Diet, created by bestselling author Loren Cordain, PhD.

http://thepaleodiet.com

Trader Joe's

A national chain, Trader Joe's has some of the most interesting foods available. Their frozen foods and other private-label products are excellent, and their nuts are a bargain.

www.traderjoes.com

APPENDIX B

Glycemic Index Reference Books

Brand-Miller, Jennie, Joanna McMillan-Price, and Kaye Foster-Powell. *The Low GI Diet Revolution.* New York: Marlowe & Co., 2005.

Brand-Miller, Jennie, and Kaye Foster-Powell. *The New Glucose Revolution Shopper's Guide to GI Values 2010: The Authoritative Source of Glycemic Index Values for More Than 1,300 Foods.* Cambridge, MA: Da Capo Press, 2010.

Brand-Miller, Jennie, Kaye Foster-Powell, Stephen Colagiuri, and Alan Barclay. *The New Glucose Revolution for Diabetes: The Definitive Guide to Managing Diabetes and Prediabetes Using the Glycemic Index.* New York: Marlowe & Co., 2007.

Brand-Miller, Jennie, Kaye Foster-Powell, Stephen Colagiuri, and Thomas M.S. Wolever. *The Glucose Revolution Pocket Guide to Diabetes.* New York: Marlowe & Co., 2001.

Brand-Miller, Jennie, Kaye Foster-Powell, Stephen Colagiuri, and Thomas M.S. Wolever. *The Glucose Revolution Pocket Guide to Sports Nutrition.* New York: Marlowe & Co., 2001.

Brand-Miller, Jennie, Kaye Foster-Powell, Stephen Colagiuri, and Thomas M.S. Wolever. *The Glucose Revolution Pocket Guide to Your Heart.* New York: Marlowe & Co., 2001.

Brand-Miller, Jennie, Kaye Foster-Powell, Stephen Colagiuri, and Thomas M.S. Wolever. *The New Glucose Revolution.* New York: Marlowe & Co., 1996, 2003, 2005.

Cunningham, Marion. *The Fannie Farmer Cookbook,* 13th ed. New York: Alfred Knopf, 1996.

Gallop, Rick. *The G.I. Diet.* New York: Workman Publishing, 2010.

Woodruff, Sandra. *The Good Carb Cookbook.* New York: Avery Press, 2001.

Standard U.S./Metric Measurement Conversions

VOLUME CONVERSIONS

U.S. Volume Measure	Metric Equivalent
⅛ teaspoon	0.5 milliliter
¼ teaspoon	1 milliliter
½ teaspoon	2 milliliters
1 teaspoon	5 milliliters
½ tablespoon	7 milliliters
1 tablespoon (3 teaspoons)	15 milliliters
2 tablespoons (1 fluid ounce)	30 milliliters
¼ cup (4 tablespoons)	60 milliliters
⅓ cup	90 milliliters
½ cup (4 fluid ounces)	125 milliliters
⅔ cup	160 milliliters
¾ cup (6 fluid ounces)	180 milliliters
1 cup (16 tablespoons)	250 milliliters
1 pint (2 cups)	500 milliliters
1 quart (4 cups)	1 liter (about)

WEIGHT CONVERSIONS

U.S. Weight Measure	Metric Equivalent
½ ounce	15 grams
1 ounce	30 grams
2 ounces	60 grams
3 ounces	85 grams
¼ pound (4 ounces)	115 grams
½ pound (8 ounces)	225 grams
¾ pound (12 ounces)	340 grams
1 pound (16 ounces)	454 grams

OVEN TEMPERATURE CONVERSIONS

Degrees Fahrenheit	Degrees Celsius
200 degrees F	95 degrees C
250 degrees F	120 degrees C
275 degrees F	135 degrees C
300 degrees F	150 degrees C
325 degrees F	160 degrees C
350 degrees F	180 degrees C
375 degrees F	190 degrees C
400 degrees F	205 degrees C
425 degrees F	220 degrees C
450 degrees F	230 degrees C

BAKING PAN SIZES

U.S.	Metric
8 × 1½ inch round baking pan	20 × 4 cm cake tin
9 × 1½ inch round baking pan	23 × 3.5 cm cake tin
11 × 7 × 1½ inch baking pan	28 × 18 × 4 cm baking tin
13 × 9 × 2 inch baking pan	30 × 20 × 5 cm baking tin
2 quart rectangular baking dish	30 × 20 × 3 cm baking tin
15 × 10 × 2 inch baking pan	30 × 25 × 2 cm baking tin (Swiss roll tin)
9 inch pie plate	22 × 4 or 23 × 4 cm pie plate
7 or 8 inch springform pan	18 or 20 cm springform or loose bottom cake tin
9 × 5 × 3 inch loaf pan	23 × 13 × 7 cm or 2 lb narrow loaf or pâté tin
1½ quart casserole	1.5 liter casserole
2 quart casserole	2 liter casserole

Index

Note: Page numbers in **bold** indicate recipe category lists.